9968

DANIEL WEBSTER

DANIEL WEBSTER

By Henry Cabot Lodge
With an introduction by
Prof. Charles M. Wiltse

American Statesmen Series
General Editor, Arthur M. Schlesinger, Jr.
Albert Schweitzer Professor of the Humanities
The City University of New York

CHELSEA HOUSE
NEW YORK 1983

9968

This edition is an edited reprint of the
1899 edition published by Houghton Mifflin,
Boston.

ISBN: 0-87754-184-1

General Introduction

BLAZING THE WAY
Arthur M. Schlesinger, jr.

THE ORIGINAL AMERICAN STATESMEN SERIES consisted of thirty-four titles published between 1882 and 1916. Handsomely printed and widely read, the Series made a notable contribution to the popular appreciation of American history. Its creator was John Torrey Morse, Jr., born in Boston in 1840, graduated from Harvard in 1860 and for nearly twenty restless years thereafter a Boston lawyer. In his thirties he had begun to dabble in writing and editing; and about 1880, reading a volume in John Morley's English Men of Letters Series, he was seized by the idea of a comparable set of compact, lucid and authoritative lives of American statesmen.

It was an unfashionable thought. The celebrated New York publisher Henry Holt turned the project down, telling Morse, "Who ever wants to read American history?" Houghton, Mifflin in Boston proved more receptive, and Morse plunged ahead. His intention was that the American Statesmen Series, when complete, "should present such a picture of the development of the country that the reader who had faithfully read all the volumes would have a full and fair view of the history of the United States told through the medium of the efforts of the men who had shaped our national career. The actors were to develop the drama."

In choosing his authors, Morse relied heavily on the counsel of his cousin Henry Cabot Lodge. Between them, they enlisted an impressive array of talent. Henry Adams, William Graham Sumner, Moses Coit Tyler, Hermann von

Holst, Moorfield Storey and Albert Bushnell Hart were all in their early forties when their volumes were published; Lodge, E. M. Shepard and Andrew C. McLaughlin in their thirties; Theodore Roosevelt in his twenties. Lodge took on Washington, Hamilton and Webster, and Morse himself wrote five volumes. He offered the authors a choice of $500 flat or a royalty of 12.5¢ on each volume sold. Most, luckily for themselves, chose the royalties.

Like many editors, Morse found the experience exasperating. "How I waded among the fragments of broken engagements, shattered pledges! I never really knew when I could count upon getting anything from anybody." Carl Schurz infuriated him by sending in a two-volume life of Henry Clay on a take-it-or-leave-it basis. Morse, who had confined Jefferson, John Adams, Webster and Calhoun to single volumes, was tempted to leave it. But Schurz threatened to publish his work simultaneously if Morse commissioned another life of Clay for the Series; so Morse reluctantly surrendered.

When a former Confederate colonel, Allan B. Magruder, offered to do John Marshall, Morse, hoping for "a good Virginia atmosphere," gave him a chance. The volume turned out to have been borrowed in embarrassing measure from Henry Flanders's *Lives and Times of the Chief Justices.* For this reason, Magruder's *Marshall* is not included in the Chelsea House reissue of the Series; Albert J. Beveridge's famous biography appears in its stead. Other classic biographies will replace occasional Series volumes: John Marshall's *Life of George Washington* in place of Morse's biography; essays on John Adams by John Quincy Adams and Charles Francis Adams, also substituting for a Morse volume; and Henry Adams's *Life of Albert Gallatin* instead of the Series volume by John Austin Stevens.

"I think that only one real blunder was made," Morse recalled in 1931, "and that was in allotting [John] Randolph to Henry Adams." Half a century earlier, however, Morse had professed himself pleased with Adams's *Randolph*. Adams, responding with characteristic self-deprecation, thought the "acidity" of his account "much too decided" but blamed the "excess of acid" on the acidulous subject. The book was indeed hostile but nonetheless stylish. Adams also wrote a life of Aaron Burr, presumably for the Series. But Morse thought Burr no statesman, and on his advice, to Adams's extreme irritation, Henry Houghton of Houghton, Mifflin rejected the manuscript. "Not bad that for a damned bookseller!" said Adams. "He should live for a while at Washington and know our *real* statesmen." Adams eventually destroyed the work, and a fascinating book was lost to history.

The definition of who was or was not a "statesman" caused recurrent problems. Lodge told Morse one day that their young friend Theodore Roosevelt wanted to do Gouverneur Morris. "But, Cabot," Morse said, "you surely don't expect Morris to be in the Series! He doesn't belong there." Lodge replied, "Theodore . . . *needs the money*," and Morse relented. No one objected to Thomas Hart Benton, Roosevelt's other contribution to the Series. Roosevelt turned out the biography in an astonishing four months while punching cows and chasing horse thieves in the Badlands. Begging Lodge to send more material from Boston, he wrote that he had been "mainly evolving [Benton] from my inner consciousness; but when he leaves the Senate in 1850 I have nothing whatever to go by. . . . I hesitate to give him a wholly fictitious date of death and to invent all the work of his later years." In fact, T.R. had done more research than he pretended; and for all its defects, his *Benton* has valuable qualities of vitality and sympathy.

Morse, who would chat to Lodge about "the aristocratic upper crust in which you & I are imbedded," had a fastidious sense of language. Many years later, in the age of Warren G. Harding, he recommended to Lodge that the new President find someone "who can clothe for him his 'ideas' in the language customarily used by educated men." At dinner in a Boston club, a guest commented on the dilemma of the French ambassador who could not speak English. "Neither can Mr. Harding," Morse said. But if patrician prejudice improved Morse's literary taste, it also impaired his political understanding. He was not altogether kidding when he wrote Lodge as the Series was getting under way, "Let the Jeffersonians & the Jacksonians beware! I will poison the popular mind!!"

Still, for all its fidelity to establishment values, the American Statesmen Series had distinct virtues. The authors were mostly from outside the academy, and they wrote with the confidence of men of affairs. Their books are generally crisp, intelligent, spirited and readable. The Series has long been in demand in secondhand bookstores. Most of its volumes are eminently worth republication today, on their merits as well as for the vigorous expression they give to an influential view of the American past.

Born during the Presidency of Martin Van Buren, John Torrey Morse, Jr., died shortly after the second inauguration of Franklin D. Roosevelt in 1937. A few years before his death he could claim with considerable justice that his Series had done "a little something in blazing the way" for the revival of American historical writing in the years to come.

New York
May, 1980

INTRODUCTION

Charles M. Wiltse

The bitterness of the abolitionist crusade that marked the decades preceding the Civil War still lingered into the 1880s, coloring the thinking and the scholarship of what should have been a new beginning. Henry Cabot Lodge, born on May 12, 1850, while the great compromise debates were still ringing through the halls of Congress, shared the heritage of those turbulent times. He was otherwise a convincing choice to write the life of Daniel Webster for the American Statesmen Series.

Lodge had already achieved a solid literary reputation with his work on the *North American Review,* to which he added scholarly acclaim with a life of his great-grandfather, George Cabot, in 1877. His own involvement with Massachusetts politics gave him added insight into the complexities of a political career. He had just completed a life of Alexander

Hamilton in the same Series when he undertook the Webster. With Federalist party politics fresh in his mind, it was inevitable that he should emphasize the Federalist origins of his own Republican party, duly modified by an injection of Whig and Free Soil elements. He had read widely, and from earliest childhood had known those who wrote and were written about: the historians Bancroft, Parkman, Motley, and Prescott; Charles Sumner, who had been Webster's successor in the Senate; and Rufus Choate, whose legal exploits were second only to Webster's own. At Harvard he studied under Henry Adams, whose father, Charles Francis Adams, had read law in Webster's office. At one time or another, both Cabots and Lodges had made use of Webster's legal skill. Add to this background a pleasing literary style, a keen mind trained in historical research, and great industry, and it would be hard to find one better qualified to present Webster to a new generation.

The resulting essay is for the most part balanced, sympathetic, and fair. Lodge departs from objectivity only in his discussion of Webster's role in the Compromise of 1850. In the Seventh of March speech he saw no more than the New England abolitionists had seen at the time of its delivery: a weak and craven capitulation to the slaveholding interest in return for Southern support in the presidential election of 1852. Aside from personal reminiscences, only Edward Everett's *Memoir,* which first appeared by way of introduction to the 1851 edition of Webster's *Works,* and George Ticknor Curtis, whose two-volume *Life* of Webster was published in 1870, took a contrary view. It was not until the twentieth century that historians began to see in Webster's greatest speech an honest effort to save the Union from imminent dissolution. It was easy for Lodge, with the assured judgment of the young, to brush aside the views of Everett and Curtis. They were among Webster's literary executors, presumably prejudiced by personal friendship.

"Nothing can now be said or written," Lodge declares, "which will alter the fact that the people of this country have passed judgment upon Mr. Webster and condemned what he said on the 7th of March, 1850, as wrong in principle and mistaken in policy." The Series editor, John T. Morse, Jr., who was old enough to remember a little of the furor, was harsher still. His brief preface to Lodge's volume begins: "If Daniel Webster had had the good fortune to die on March 6, 1850, the story of his career would have been the despair of biographers. .... It was cruel that the end, which was so near at hand, should yet have suffered this little postponement." Both men conceded that Webster's position was legally correct, but his support of the Fugitive Slave Law was a moral abomination in their eyes, as it had been in the eyes of Garrison and Parker.

With the exception of this stern judgment upon Webster's last major effort in the Senate, Lodge used impartially and skillfully the materials available to him, which were considerable. There are few citations, but he explains in an initial note that he has "carefully examined all the literature contemporary and posthumous" relating to his subject and has found it more than adequate. He did not, by his own admission, use either manuscript or newspaper sources. He acknowledges his major indebtedness to Curtis, whose work was based on a large collection of manuscripts assembled for that purpose immediately after Webster's death. Daniel Fletcher Webster's two volumes of his father's *Private Correspondence,* published in 1856, reproduced many of those manuscripts, and a liberal selection appears in Curtis. Lodge used also the six volumes of Webster's *Works,* edited by Everett in 1851 when Webster himself could still be—and was—consulted. Of the numerous reminiscences of Webster in print by the time Lodge wrote, he clearly made some use of those by Charles W. March (1850), Charles Lanman (1851), Samuel P. Lyman (1853), and Peter Harvey (1877). On the other side he must have considered Theodore Parker's bitterly hostile obituary sermon, as well as Wendell Phillips's contemporary critique of the Seventh of March speech. There is internal evidence that he was familiar with the *Diary of John Quincy Adams,* published in 1877, and of course he knew the congressional debates of Webster's time.

Lodge's treatment of Webster as lawyer is confined to a single chapter devoted too largely to the Dartmouth College case. John M. Shirley's *The Dartmouth College Causes and the Supreme Court of the United States* had appeared in 1879, just in time to be useful, but Lodge, although trained in the law, was not well enough versed in the points at issue to use Shirley's book with adequate cautions. For other Webster cases, Lodge relies upon the handful of legal arguments reproduced in the *Works,* and upon Curtis, who was himself a constitutional lawyer of considerable note. There are brief analyses of such leading constitutional cases as *Gibbons* v. *Ogden, Ogden* v. *Saunders, Bank of the United States* v. *Primrose,* the passenger tax cases, and *Luther* v.

Borden. But the very important Charles River
Bridge case, protracted over nine years in the
Supreme Court of Massachusetts and the Supreme Court of the United States, gets no more
than a mention, while the profitable Spanish
Claims cases that absorbed much of Webster's
professional efforts for three years get half a
sentence. The Girard Will case, on the other
hand, is treated at length although Webster's argument was little more than an appeal to popular prejudice, without bearing on the outcome.
The Salem murder case, a *cause célèbre* in its
time, is ignored.

It is clear that in discussing Webster's legal
career Lodge cares less for the niceties of constitutional reasoning than he does for the skill
of argument. Webster as Lodge sees him was
first and foremost an advocate—the pleader
who could make the most appealing case for
whichever side of a cause had retained him.
The ultimate tribute to Webster the lawyer he
pays not in this book but in his earlier life of
Hamilton, where he quotes Judge Ambrose
Spencer: Hamilton "argued cases before me
while I sat as judge on the bench. Webster has
done the same. In power of reasoning Hamilton
was the equal of Webster; and more than this
can be said of no man."

Webster's first term as Secretary of State was

highlighted by the Ashburton Treaty of 1842, which Lodge summarizes admirably. The Whig attack on Tyler marred the negotiations but showed Webster at his best, coping at once with Ashburton, with the Maine commissioners, with the Whigs, and with the South on the *Creole* issue. However, Lodge tends to pass over the solid accomplishments of Webster's second tour in the State Department, under Fillmore, giving full discussion only to the Hülseman letter.

Lodge is at his best when analysing Webster's oratory. The Plymouth oration, the speeches in the Massachusetts constitutional convention of 1820, on the Greek revolution, on the tariff, all lead up to the Reply to Hayne. Here Lodge becomes lyrical in his praise and extravagant in his judgment. "This great speech," he declares, "marks the highest point attained by Mr. Webster as a public man. He never surpassed it, he never equalled it afterwards. It was his zenith intellectually, politically, and as an orator." After explaining the background and summarizing the content of the speech itself, Lodge turns to the niceties of oratory—phrasing, expression, gesture, tone of voice, personal presence—then compares his subject with the great orators, classical and modern, to Webster's greater honor and glory. It is tribute indeed that one of another generation, who could know Webster only through the printed text and the eyewitness reports handed down by those who both saw and heard, should arrive at so high an estimate. But Lodge was finding what he wished to find. Webster himself, despite the often hostile reaction, came in time to regard the Seventh of March speech as greater even than the Reply to Hayne. There is in fact no basis for comparison. Each was right for its time and place; each served its purpose admirably.

The Republican party of Lodge's day was perhaps still too close to its Federalist, Whig, and Free Soil antecedents to be sure of its own ideology. Lodge does not try to make a post-Civil War Republican out of Daniel Webster, but in his discussion of the earlier parties he injects himself to suggest to the reader what Webster should have done—what responses he might have made to the events of his time that would have placed him, had he lived so long, where Henry Cabot Lodge then stood. He should, Lodge argues, have remained aloof from Clay and Calhoun when the Whig party was being forged out of the fragments of the Jacksonian opposition; he should have waited until the others came to him, to form a new party on the principles of the Reply to Hayne.

He should have joined forces with the Free Soil movement, becoming thereby the political and moral leader of the antislavery forces. And of course he should have denounced the Compromise of 1850.

Had he done these things he might have been, as Lodge implies, the greatest man in the nation's history; but he might as easily have been damned as one who could have saved his country in her hour of trial but chose to turn his back.

Hanover, New Hampshire
August, 1980

BIBLIOGRAPHICAL NOTE

In broad outline our understanding of Webster's career has changed little since Lodge's book was first published in 1883, despite masses of new material. Only the fleshing out of the portrait, the emphasis and the interpretation have altered with time and perspective. The second edition, in 1899 (the one reprinted here), remained unchanged, but a reinterpretation of the American past was beginning. In 1902 Claude H. Van Tyne published a volume of Webster's correspon-

CHARLES M. WILTSE

dence, drawn from the collection given in 1876 to the
New Hampshire Historical Society by Peter Harvey,
perhaps the closest friend of Webster's last few years.
In the same year John Bach McMaster published a
Webster biography that treated the Seventh of March
speech with some objectivity. The following year
Scribner issued an eighteen-volume set of Webster's
Writings and Speeches. Much of this material had been
available to Lodge—the first twelve volumes duplicated
the six-volume *Works* of 1851, and the last two were a
reprinting with minor changes of Fletcher Webster's
Private Correspondence—but the four volumes in between included much new matter.

Thereafter Webster books were frequent. Biographies by Sydney George Fisher (1911), Frederic Austin
Ogg (1914), and Elijah Robinson Kennedy (1924) defended the Seventh of March speech, while Herbert
Darling Foster, writing in the *American Historical Review* of January 1922, undertook to show how real the
threat of disunion had been in 1850. In 1930 Claude
Moore Fuess published a two-volume life of Webster
that remains standard, though obsolescent, to this day.
Later but less complete biographical volumes are those
of Walker Lewis (1969), which is documentary, telling
the story in Webster's words; and Irving Bartlett
(1978), which emphasizes—perhaps overemphasizes—
the dichotomy in Webster between good and evil.

More important than the biographies are several excellent monographs on phases or aspects of Webster's
career, which cannot fail to influence the next attempt
at a "definitive" life. The most significant of these are:

INTRODUCTION

Richard N. Current, *Daniel Webster and the Rise of National Conservatism* (1955); Howard A. Bradley and James A. Winans, *Daniel Webster and the Salem Murder* (1956); Maurice G. Baxter, *Daniel Webster and the Supreme Court* (1966); Norman D. Brown, *Daniel Webster and the Politics of Availability* (1969); Judge Henry J. Friendly, *The Dartmouth College Case and the Public-Private Penumbra* (1969); Stanley L. Kutler, *Privilege and Creative Destruction: The Charles River Bridge Case* (1971); Robert F. Dalzell, Jr., *Daniel Webster and the Trial of American Nationalism, 1843–1852* (1973); Sydney Nathans, *Daniel Webster and Jacksonian Democracy* (1973); Francis N. Stites, *Private Interest and Public Gain: The Dartmouth College Case, 1819* (1973); and Howard Jones, *To the Webster-Ashburton Treaty* (1977).

For future scholars interested in Webster or his times the fourteen-volume set of *The Papers of Daniel Webster* currently being published by Dartmouth College under the editorship of Charles M. Wiltse will be indispensable. Divided into Correspondence (7 vols.), Legal Papers (3 vols.), Diplomatic Papers (2 vols.), and Speeches and Formal Writings (2 vols.), the edition is selective but is reinforced by a microfilm as complete as the surviving documents permit.

DANIEL WEBSTER

CHAPTER I

CHILDHOOD AND YOUTH

No sooner was the stout Puritan Commonwealth of Massachusetts firmly planted than it began rapidly to throw out branches in all directions. With every succeeding year the long, thin, sinuous line of settlements stretched farther and farther away

NOTE. — In preparing this volume I have carefully examined all the literature contemporary and posthumous relating to Mr. Webster. I have not gone beyond the printed material, of which there is a vast mass, much of it of no value, but which contains all and more than is needed to obtain a correct understanding of the man and of his public and private life. No one can pretend to write a life of Webster without following in large measure the narrative of events as given in the elaborate, careful, and scholarly biography which we owe to Mr. George T. Curtis. In many of my conclusions I have differed widely from those of Mr. Curtis, but I desire at the outset to acknowledge fully my obligations to him. I have sought information in all directions, and have obtained some fresh material, and, as I believe, have thrown a new light upon certain points, but this does not in the least diminish the debt which I owe to the ample biography of Mr. Curtis in regard to the details as well as the general outline of Mr. Webster's public and private life.

to the northeast, fringing the wild shores of the
Atlantic with houses and farms gathered together
at the mouths or on the banks of the rivers, and
with the homes of hardy fishermen which clustered
in little groups beneath the shelter of the rocky
headlands. The extension of these plantations was
chiefly along the coast, but there was also a movement up the river courses toward the west and into
the interior. The line of northeastern settlements
began first to broaden in this way very slowly but
still steadily from the plantations at Portsmouth
and Dover, which were nearly coeval with the
flourishing towns of the Bay. These settlements
beyond the Massachusetts line all had one common
and marked characteristic, in their constant exposure to Indian attack from the earliest days
down even to the period of the Revolution. Long
after the dangers of Indian raids had become little
more than a tradition to the populous and flourishing communities of Massachusetts Bay, the towns
and villages of Maine and New Hampshire continued to be the outposts of a dark and bloody border-
land. French and Indian warfare with all its
attendant horrors was the normal condition during
the latter part of the seventeenth and the first
quarter of the eighteenth century. Even after the
destruction of the Jesuit missions, every war in Europe was the signal for the appearance of Frenchmen and savages in northeastern New England,
where their course was marked by rapine and
slaughter, and lighted by the flames of burning

villages. The people thus assailed were not slow in taking frequent and thorough vengeance, and so the conflict, with rare intermissions, went on until the power of France was destroyed, and the awful danger from the north, which had hung over the land for nearly a century, was finally extinguished.

The people who waged this fierce war and managed to make headway in despite of it were engaged at the same time in a conflict with nature which was hardly less desperate. The soil, even in the most favored places, was none of the best, and the predominant characteristic of New Hampshire was the great rock formation which has given it the name of the Granite State. Slowly and painfully the settlers made their way back into the country, seizing on every fertile spot, and wringing subsistence and even a certain prosperity from a niggardly soil and a harsh climate. Their little hamlets crept onward toward the base of those beautiful hills which have now become one of the favorite playgrounds of America, but which then, dark with trackless forests, frowned grimly even in summer, and for the larger part of the year were sheeted with the glittering, untrampled snow from which they derived their name. Stern and strong with the force of an unbroken wilderness, they formed at all times a forbidding background to the sparse settlements in the valleys and on the seashore.

This life of constant battle with nature and with the savages, this work of wresting a subsistence from the unwilling earth while the hand was always armed against a subtle and cruel foe, had, of course, a marked effect upon the people who endured it. That, under such circumstances, men should have succeeded not only in gaining a livelihood, but should have attained also to a certain measure of prosperity, established a free government, founded schools and churches, and built up a small but vigorous and thriving commonwealth, is little short of marvelous. A race which could do this had an enduring strength of character which was sure to make itself felt through many generations, not only on their ancestral soil, but in every region where they wandered in search of a fortune denied to them at home. The people of New Hampshire were of the English Puritan stock. They were the borderers of New England, and were among the hardiest and boldest of their race. Their fierce battle for existence during nearly a century and a half left a deep impress upon them; and although it did not add new traits to their character, it strengthened and developed many of the qualities which chiefly distinguished the Puritan Englishman. These borderers, from lack of opportunity, were ruder than their more favored brethren to the south, but they were also more persistent, more tenacious, and more adventurous. They were a vigorous, bold, unforgiving, fighting race, hard and stern even beyond the ordinary standard of Puritanism.

Among the Puritans who settled in New Hamp-

shire about the year 1636, during the great emigration which preceded the Long Parliament, was
one bearing the name of Thomas Webster. He
was said to be of Scotch extraction, but was, if
this be true, undoubtedly of the Lowland or Saxon
Scotch as distinguished from the Gaels of the
Highlands. He was, at all events, a Puritan of
English race, and his name indicates that his pro-
genitors were sturdy mechanics or handicraftsmen.
This Thomas Webster had numerous descendants,
who scattered through New Hampshire to earn a
precarious living, found settlements, and fight Indians. In Kingston, in the year 1739, was born
one of this family named Ebenezer Webster. The
struggle for existence was so hard for this particular scion of the Webster stock, that he was obliged
in boyhood to battle for a living and pick up learning as he best might by the sole aid of a naturally
vigorous mind. He came of age during the great
French war, and about 1760 enlisted in the then
famous corps known as "Rogers's Rangers." In
the dangers and the successes of desperate frontier
fighting, the "Rangers" had no equal; and of
their hård and perilous experience in the wilderness, in conflict with Indians and Frenchmen,
Ebenezer Webster, strong in body and daring in
temperament, had his full share.

When the war closed, the young soldier and
Indian fighter had time to look about him for a
home. As might have been expected, he clung to
the frontier to which he was accustomed, and in

the year 1763 settled in the northernmost part of
the town of Salisbury. Here he built a log-house,
to which, in the following year, he brought his
first wife, and here he began his career as a
farmer. At that time there was nothing civilized
between him and the French settlements of Canada. The wilderness stretched away from his door
an ocean of forest unbroken by any white man's
habitation; and in these primeval woods, although
the war was ended and the French power overthrown, there still lurked roving bands of savages,
suggesting the constant possibilities of a midnight
foray or a noonday ambush, with their accompani-
ments of murder and pillage. It was a fit home,
however, for such a man as Ebenezer Webster.
He was a borderer in the fullest sense in a commonwealth of borderers. He was, too, a splendid
specimen of the New England race; a true de-
scendant of ancestors who had been for generations
yeomen and pioneers. Tall, large, dark of hair
and eyes, in the rough world in which he found
himself he had been thrown at once upon his own
resources without a day's schooling, and compelled
to depend on his own innate force of sense and
character for success. He had had a full experience of desperate fighting with Frenchmen and
Indians, and, the war over, he had returned to his
native town with his hard-won rank of captain.
Then he had married, and had established his
home upon the frontier, where he remained battling against the grim desolation of the wilderness

and of the winter, and against all the obstacles of soil and climate, with the same hardy bravery with which he had faced the Indians. After ten years of this life, in 1774, his wife died, and within a twelvemonth he married again.

Soon after this second marriage the alarm of war with England sounded, and among the first to respond was the old ranger and Indian fighter, Ebenezer Webster. In the town which had grown up near his once solitary dwelling he raised a company of two hundred men, and marched at their head, a splendid looking leader, dark, massive, and tall, to join the forces at Boston. We get occasional glimpses of this vigorous figure during the war. At Dorchester, Washington consulted him about the state of feeling in New Hampshire. At Bennington, we catch sight of him among the first who scaled the breastworks, and again coming out of the battle, his swarthy skin so blackened with dust and gunpowder that he could scarcely be recognized. We hear of him once more at West Point, just after Arnold's treason, on guard before the general's tent, and learn that in that hour of doubt and suspicion Washington said to him, "Captain Webster, I believe I can trust you." That was what everybody seems to have felt about this strong, silent, uneducated man. His neighbors, like his general, trusted him. They gave him every office in their gift, and finally he was made judge of the local court. In the intervals of his toilsome and adventurous life he had

picked up a little book-learning, but the lack of
more barred the way to the higher honors which
would otherwise have been easily his. There were
splendid sources of strength in this man, the outcome of such a race, from which his children could
draw. He possessed, to begin with, a powerful
physique and a rugged constitution, and he had
an imposing bodily presence and appearance. He
had courage, energy, and tenacity, all in high
degree. He was business-like, a man of few
words, determined, and efficient. He had a great
capacity for affection and self-sacrifice, noble aspirations, a vigorous mind, and, above all, a strong,
pure character which invited trust. Force of will,
force of mind, force of character; these were the
three predominant qualities in Ebenezer Webster.
His life forms the necessary introduction to that
of his celebrated son, and it is well worth study,
because we can learn from it how much that son
got from a father so finely endowed, and how far
he profited by such a rich inheritance.

By his first wife Ebenezer Webster had five
children. By his second wife, Abigail Eastman,
a woman of good sturdy New Hampshire stock, he
had likewise five. Of these, the second son and
fourth child was born on the eighteenth of January, 1782, and was christened Daniel. The infant was a delicate and rather sickly little being.
Some cheerful neighbors predicted after inspection
that it would not live long, and the poor mother,
overhearing them, caught the child to her bosom

and wept over it. She little dreamed of the iron constitution hidden somewhere in the small frail body, and still less of all the glory and sorrow to which her baby was destined.

For many years, although the boy disappointed the village Cassandras by living, he continued weak and delicate. Manual labor, which began very early with the children of New Hampshire farmers, was out of the question in his case, and so Daniel was allowed to devote much of his time to play, for which he showed a decided aptitude. It was play of the best sort, in the woods and fields, where he learned to love nature and natural objects, to wonder at floods, to watch the habits of fish and birds, and to acquire a keen taste for field sports. His companion was an old British sailor, who carried the child on his back, rowed with him on the river, taught him the angler's art, and, best of all, poured into his delighted ear endless stories of an adventurous life, of Admiral Byng and Lord George Germaine, of Minden and Gibraltar, of Prince Ferdinand and General Gage, of Bunker Hill, and finally of the American armies, to which the soldier-sailor had deserted. The boy repaid this devoted friend by reading the newspapers to him; and he tells us in his autobiography that he could not remember a time when he did not read, so early was he taught by his mother and sisters, in true New England fashion. At a very early age he began to go to school; sometimes in his native town, sometimes in another, as the district school moved from place to place. The masters who taught in these schools knew nothing but the barest rudiments, and even some of those imperfectly. One of them who lived to a great age, enlightened perhaps by subsequent events, said that Webster had great rapidity of acquisition and was the quickest boy in school. He certainly proved himself the possessor of a very retentive memory, for when this pedagogue offered a jackknife as a reward to the boy who should be able to recite the greatest number of verses from the Bible, Webster, on the following day, when his turn came, arose and reeled off verses until the master cried "enough," and handed him the coveted prize. Another of his instructors kept a small store, and from him the boy bought a handkerchief on which was printed the Constitution of the United States just then adopted, and, as he read everything and remembered much, he read that famous instrument to which he was destined to give so much of his time and thought. When Mr. Webster said that he read better than any of his masters, he was probably right. The power of expression and of speech and readiness in reply were his greatest natural gifts, and, however much improved by cultivation, were born in him. His talents were known in the neighborhood, and the passing teamsters, while they watered their horses, delighted to get "Webster's boy," with his delicate look and great dark eyes, to come out beneath the shade of the trees and read the

Bible to them with all the force of his childish eloquence. He describes his own existence at that time with perfect accuracy. "I read what I could get to read, went to school when I could, and when not at school, was a farmer's youngest boy, not good for much for want of health and strength, but expected to do something." That something consisted generally in tending the saw-mill, but the reading went on even there. He would set a log, and while it was going through would devour a book. There was a small circulating library in the village, and Webster read everything it contained, committing most of the contents of the precious volumes to memory, for books were so scarce that he believed this to be their chief purpose.

In the year 1791 the brave old soldier, Ebenezer Webster, was made a judge of the local court, and thus got a salary of three or four hundred dollars a year. This accession of wealth turned his thoughts at once toward that education which he had missed, and he determined that he would give to his children what he had irretrievably lost himself. Two years later he disclosed his purpose to his son, one hot day in the hay-field, with a manly regret for his own deficiencies and a touching pathos which the boy never forgot. The next spring his father took Daniel to Exeter Academy. This was the boy's first contact with the world, and there was the usual sting which invariably accompanies that meeting. His schoolmates laughed at his rustic dress and manners, and the poor little farm lad felt it bitterly. The natural and unconscious power by which he had delighted the teamsters was stifled, and the greatest orator of modern times never could summon sufficient courage to stand up and recite verses before these Exeter schoolboys. Intelligent masters, however, perceived something of what was in the lad, and gave him a kindly encouragement. He rose rapidly in the classes, and at the end of nine months his father took him away in order to place him as a pupil with a neighboring clergyman. As they drove over, about a month later, to Boscawen, where Dr. Wood, the future preceptor, lived, Ebenezer Webster imparted to his son the full extent of his plan, which was to end in a college education. The joy at the accomplishment of his dearest and most fervent wish, mingled with a full sense of the magnitude of the sacrifice and of the generosity of his father, overwhelmed the boy. Always affectionate and susceptible of strong emotion, these tidings overcame him. He laid his head upon his father's shoulder and wept.

With Dr. Wood Webster remained only six months. He went home on one occasion, but haying was not to his tastes. He found it "dull and lonesome," and preferred rambling in the woods with his sister in search of berries, so that his indulgent father sent him back to his studies. With the help of Dr. Wood in Latin, and another tutor in Greek, he contrived to enter Dartmouth

College in August, 1797. He was, of course, hastily and poorly prepared. He knew something of Latin, very little of Greek, and next to nothing of mathematics, geography, or history. He had devoured everything in the little libraries of Salisbury and Boscawen, and thus had acquired a desultory knowledge of a limited amount of English literature, including Addison, Pope, Watts, and a translation of "Don Quixote." But however little he knew, the gates of learning were open, and he had entered the precincts of her temple, feeling dimly but surely the first pulsations of the mighty intellect with which he was endowed.

"In those boyish days," he wrote many years afterwards, "there were two things which I did dearly love, reading and playing, — passions which did not cease to struggle when boyhood was over, (have they yet altogether?) and in regard to which neither *cita mors* nor the *victoria læta* could be said of either." In truth they did not cease, these two strong passions. One was of the head, the other of the heart; one typified the intellectual, the other the animal strength of the boy's nature; and the two contending forces went with him to the end. The childhood of Webster has an interest which is by no means usual. Great men in their earliest years are generally much like other boys, despite the efforts of their biographers to prove the contrary. If they are not, they are very apt to be little prigs like the second Pitt, full of "wise saws and modern instances." Webster was

neither the one nor the other. He was simple,
natural, affectionate, and free from pertness or
precocity. At the same time there was an innate
power which impressed all those who approached
him without their knowing exactly why, and there
was abundant evidence of uncommon talents.
Webster's boyish days are pleasant to look upon,
but they gain a peculiar lustre from the noble
character of his father, the deep solicitude of his
mother, and the generous devotion and self-sacrifice of both parents. There was in this something
prophetic. Every one about the boy was laboring
and sacrificing for him from the beginning, and
this was not without its effect upon his character.
A little anecdote which was current in Boston
many years ago condenses the whole situation.
The story may be true or false, — it is very probably unfounded, — but it contains an essential truth
and illustrates the character of the boy and the
atmosphere in which he grew up. Ezekiel, the
oldest son, and Daniel were allowed on one occasion to go to a fair in a neighboring town, and
each was furnished with a little money from the
slender store at home. When they returned in
the evening, Daniel was radiant with enjoyment;
Ezekiel rather silent. Their mother inquired as
to their adventures, and finally asked Daniel what
he did with his money. "Spent it," was the reply. "And what did you do with yours, Ezekiel?"
"Lent it to Daniel." That answer sums up the
story of Webster's home life in childhood, of

much of the larger life of later days. All his friends were giving or lending to Daniel of their money, their time, their activity, their love and affection. This petting was partly due to Webster's delicate health as a boy, but it was also in great measure owing to his nature. He was one of those rare and fortunate beings who without exertion draw to themselves the devotion of other people, and are always surrounded by men and women eager to do and to suffer for them. The boy accepted all that was showered upon him, not without an obvious sense that it was his due. He took it in the royal spirit which is characteristic of such natures; but in those childish days when laughter and tears came readily, he repaid the generous and sacrificing love with the warm and affectionate gratitude of an earnest nature and a naturally loving heart. He was never cold, or selfish, or designing. Others loved him and sacrificed to him, but he loved them in return and appreciated their sacrifices. These conditions of his early days must, however, have had an effect upon his disposition and increased his belief in the fitness of having the devotion of other people as one of his regal rights and privileges, while, at the same time, it must have helped to expand his affections and give warmth to every generous feeling.

The passions for reading and play went with him to Dartmouth, the little New Hampshire college of which he was always so proud and so fond.

The instruction there was of good quality enough, but it was meagre in quantity and of limited range, compared to what is offered by most good high schools of the present day. In the reminiscences of his fellow students there is abundant material for a picture of Webster at that time. He was recognized by all as the foremost man in the college, as easily first, with no second. Yet at the same time Mr. Webster was neither a student nor a scholar in the truest sense of the words. He read voraciously all the English literature he could lay his hands on, and remembered everything he read. He achieved familiarity with Latin and with Latin authors, and absorbed a great deal of history. He was the best general scholar in the college. He was not only not deficient but he showed excellence at recitation in every branch of study. He could learn anything if he tried. But with all this he never gained more than a smattering of Greek and still less of mathematics, because those studies require, for anything more than a fair proficiency, a love of knowledge for its own sake, a zeal for learning incompatible with indolence, and a close, steady, and disinterested attention. These were not the characteristics of Mr. Webster's mind. He had a marvelous power of rapid acquisition, but he learned nothing unless he liked the subject and took pleasure in it or else was compelled to the task. This is not the stuff from which the real student, with an original or inquiring mind, is made; but it is only fair to say that this estimate, drawn from the opinions of his fellow students, coincided with his own, for he was too large-minded and too clear-headed to have any small vanity or conceit in judging himself. He said soon after he left college, and with perfect truth, that his scholarship was not remarkable, nor equal to what he was credited with. He explained his reputation after making this confession by saying that he read carefully, meditated on what he had read, and retained it so that on any subject he was able to tell all he knew to the best advantage, and was careful never to go beyond his depth. There is no better analysis of Mr. Webster's strongest qualities of mind than this, made by himself in reference to his college standing. Rapid acquisition, quick assimilation of ideas, an iron memory, and a remarkable power of stating and displaying all he knew characterized him then as in later life. The extent of his knowledge and the range of his mind, not the depth or soundness of his scholarship, were the traits which his companions remembered. One of them says that they often felt that he had a more extended understanding than the tutors to whom he recited, and this was probably true. The Faculty of the college recognized in Webster the most remarkable man who had ever come among them, but they could not find good grounds to award him the prizes, which, by his standing among his fellows, ought by every rule to have been at his feet. He had all the promise of a great man, but he was not a fine scholar.

He was studious, punctual, and regular in all his habits, and so dignified that his friends would as soon have thought of seeing President Wheelock indulge in boyish disorders as of seeing him do so. Yet with all his dignity and seriousness of talk and manner, he was a thoroughly genial companion, full of humor and fun and agreeable conversation. He had few intimates, but many friends. He was generally liked as well as universally admired, was a leader in the college societies, active and successful in sports, simple, hearty, unaffected, without a touch of priggishness and with a wealth of wholesome animal spirits.

But in these college days, besides the vague feeling of students and professors that they had among them a very remarkable man, there is a clear indication that the qualities which afterwards raised Webster to fame and power were already apparent, and affected the little world about him. All his contemporaries of that time speak of his eloquence. The gift of speech, the unequaled power of statement, which were born in him, just like the musical tones of his voice, could not be repressed. There was no recurrence of the diffidence of Exeter. His native genius led him irresistibly along the inevitable path, and he loved to speak, to hold the attention of a listening audience. He practiced off-hand speaking, but he more commonly prepared himself by meditating on his subject and making notes, which, however, he never used after he had once taken the floor.

He would enter the class-room or debating society, and begin in a low voice and almost sleepy manner, and would then gradually rouse himself like a lion, and pour forth his words until he had his hearers completely under his control, and glowing with enthusiasm.

We see, too, at this time, the first evidence of that other great gift of bountiful nature in his commanding presence. He was tall and in those days of youth quite thin, with high cheek bones and dark skin, but he was even then impressive. The boys about him never forgot the look of his deep-set eyes, or the sound of the solemn tones of his voice, his dignity of mien, and his absorption in his subject. Above all, they were conscious of something indefinable which conveyed a sense of greatness. It is not usual to dwell so much upon mere physical attributes and appearance, but we must recur to them again and again, for Mr. Webster's personal presence was one of the great elements of his success; it was the fit companion and even a part of his genius, and was the cause of his influence, and of the wonder and admiration which followed him, as much almost as anything he ever said or did.

To Mr. Webster's college career belong the first fruits of his intellect. He edited, during one year, a small weekly journal, and thus eked out his slender means. Besides his strictly editorial labors, he printed some short pieces of his own, which have vanished, and he also indulged in

poetical effusions, which he was fond of sending
to absent friends. His rhymes are without any
especial character, neither much better nor much
worse than most college verses, and they have no
intrinsic value beyond showing that their author,
whatever else he might be, was no poet. But in
his own field something of this time, having a real
importance, has come down to us. The fame of
his youthful eloquence, so far beyond anything
ever known in the college, was noised abroad, and
in the year 1800 the citizens of Hanover, the college town, asked him to deliver the Fourth of July
oration. In this production, which was thought
of sufficient merit to deserve printing, Mr. Webster sketched rapidly and exultingly the course of
the Revolution, threw in a little Federal politics,
and eulogized the happy system of the new Constitution. Of this and his other early orations he
always spoke with a good deal of contempt, as
examples of bad taste, which he wished to have
buried and forgotten. Accordingly his wholesale
admirers and supporters who have done most of
the writing about him, and who always sneezed
when Mr. Webster took snuff, have echoed his
opinions about these youthful productions, and
beyond allowing to them the value which everything Websterian has for the ardent worshiper,
have been disposed to hurry them over as of no
moment. Compared to the reply to Hayne or
the Plymouth oration, the Hanover speech is, of
course, a poor and trivial thing. Considered, as

it ought to be, by itself and in itself, it is not only
of great interest as Mr. Webster's first utterance
on public questions, but it is something of which
he had no cause to feel ashamed. The sentiments
are honest, elevated, and manly, and the political
doctrine is sound. Mr. Webster was then a boy
of eighteen, and he therefore took his politics
from his father and his father's friends. For
the same reason he was imitative in style and
mode of thought. All boys of that age, whether
geniuses or not, are imitative, and Mr. Webster,
who was never profoundly original in thought, was
no exception to the rule. He used the style of
the eighteenth century, then in its decadence, and
very florid, inflated, and heavy it was. Yet his
work was far better and his style simpler and more
direct than that which was in fashion. He indulged, too, in a good deal of patriotic glorification.
One is disposed to smile at his boyish Federalism
describing Napoleon as "the gasconading pilgrim
of Egypt," and Columbia as "seated in the forum
of nations, and the empires of the world amazed
at the bright effulgence of her glory." These sentences are the acme of fine writing, very boyish
and very poor; but they are not fair examples of
the whole, which is much plainer and more vigorous than might have been expected. Moreover,
the thought is the really important thing. We see
plainly that the speaker belongs to the new era
and the new generation of national measures and
nationally minded men. There is no colonialism

about him. He is in full sympathy with the Washingtonian policy of independence in our foreign relations and of complete separation from the affairs of Europe. But the main theme and the moving spirit of this oration are most important of all. The boy Webster preached love of country, the grandeur of American nationality, fidelity to the Constitution as the bulwark of nationality, and the necessity and the nobility of the union of the States; and that was the message which the man Webster delivered to his fellow men. The enduring work which Mr. Webster did in the world, and his meaning and influence in American history, are all summed up in the principles enunciated in that boyish speech at Hanover. The statement of the great principles was improved and developed until it towered above this first expression as Mont Blanc does above the village nestled at its foot, but the essential substance never altered in the least.

Two other college orations have been preserved. One is a eulogy on a classmate who died before finishing his course, the other is a discourse on "Opinion," delivered before the society of the "United Fraternity." There is nothing of especial moment in the thought of either, and the improvement in style over the Hanover speech, though noticeable, is not very marked. In the letters of that period, however, amid the jokes and fun, we see that Mr. Webster was already following his natural bent, and turning his attention to politics.

He manifests the same spirit in his correspondence as in his oration, and shows occasionally an unusual maturity of judgment. His criticism of Hamilton's famous letter to Adams, to take the most striking instance, is both keen and sound.

After taking his degree in due course in 1801, Mr. Webster returned to his native village, and entered the office of a lawyer next door to his father's house, where he began the study of the law in compliance with his father's wish, but without any very strong inclination of his own. Here he read some law and more English literature, and passed a good deal of time in fishing and shooting. Before the year was out, however, he was obliged to drop his legal studies and accept the post of schoolmaster in the little town of Fryeburg, Maine.

This change was due to an important event in the Webster family which had occurred some time before. The affection existing between Daniel and his elder brother Ezekiel was peculiarly strong and deep. The younger and more fortunate son, once started in his education, and knowing the desire of his elder brother for the same advantages, longed to obtain them for him. One night in vacation, after Daniel had been two years at Dartmouth, the brothers discussed at length the all-important question. The next day Daniel broached the matter to his father. The judge was taken by surprise. He was laboring already under heavy pecuniary burdens caused by the expenses of Daniel's education. The farm was heavily mortgaged, and Ebenezer Webster knew that he was old before his time and not destined to many more years of life. With the perfect and self-sacrificing courage which he always showed, he did not shrink from this new demand, although Ezekiel was the prop and mainstay of the house. He did not think for a moment of himself, yet, while he gave his consent, he made it conditional on that of the mother and daughters whom he felt he was soon to leave. But Mrs. Webster had the same spirit as her husband. She was ready to sell the farm, to give up everything for the boys, provided they would promise to care in the future for her and their sisters. More utter self-abnegation and more cheerful and devoted self-sacrifice have rarely been exhibited, and it was all done with a simplicity which commands our reverence. It was more than should have been asked, and a boy less accustomed than Daniel Webster to the devotion of others, even with the incentive of brotherly love, might have shrunk from making the request. The promise of future support was easily made, but the hard pinch of immediate sacrifice had to be borne at once. The devoted family gave themselves up to the struggle to secure an education for both boys, instead of one, and for years they did battle with debt and the pressure of poverty. Ezekiel began his studies and entered college the year Daniel graduated; but the resources were running low, — so low that the law had to be abandoned and money earned without delay; and hence the schoolmastership.

At no time in his life does Mr. Webster's character appear in a fairer or more lovable light than during this winter at Fryeburg. He took his own share in the sacrifices he had done so much to entail, and he carried it cheerfully. Out of school hours he copied endless deeds, an occupation which he loathed above all others, in order that he might give all his salary to his brother. The burden and heat of the day in this struggle for education fell chiefly on the elder brother in the years which followed; but here Daniel did his full part, and deserves the credit for it.

He was a successful teacher. His perfect dignity, his even temper and imperturbable equanimity made his pupils like and respect him. The survivors, in their old age, recalled the impression he made upon them, and especially remembered the solemn tones of his voice at morning and evening prayer, extemporaneous exercises which he scrupulously maintained. His letters at this time are like those of his college days, full of fun and good humor and kind feeling. He had his early love affairs, but was saved from matrimony by the liberality of his affections, which were not confined to a single object. He laughs pleasantly and good-naturedly over his fortunes with the fair sex, and talks a good deal about them, but his first loves do not seem to have been very deep or lasting. Wherever he went he produced an impression on all who saw him. In Fryeburg it was his eyes which people seem to have remembered best. He was still very thin in face and figure, and he tells us himself that he was known in the village as "All-eyes;" and one of the boys, a friend of later years, refers to Mr. Webster's "full, steady, large, and searching eyes." There never was a time in his life when those who saw him did not afterwards speak of his looks, generally either of the wonderful eyes or the imposing presence.

There was a circulating library in Fryeburg, and this he read through in his usual rapacious and retentive fashion. Here, too, he was called on for a Fourth of July oration. This speech, which has been recently printed, dwells much on the Constitution and the need of adhering to it in its entirety. There is a distinct improvement in his style in the direction of simplicity, but there is no marked advance in thought or power of expression over the Hanover oration. Two months after delivering this address he returned to Salisbury and resumed the study of the law in Mr. Thompson's office. He now plunged more deeply into law books, and began to work at his profession with real zeal, while at the same time he read much and thoroughly in the best Latin authors. In the months which ensued his mind expanded, and ambition began to rise within him. His horizon was a limited one; the practice of his profession, as he saw it carried on about him, was small and petty; but his mind could not be shackled. He saw the lions in the path plainly, but he also perceived the great opportunities which the law

was to offer in the United States, and he prophesied that we, too, should soon have our Mansfields
and Kenyons. The hand of poverty was heavy
upon him, and he was chafing and beating his
wings against the iron bars with which circumstances had imprisoned him. He longed for a
wider field, and eagerly desired to finish his studies in Boston, but saw no way to get there, except
by a "miracle."

This miracle came through Ezekiel, who had
been doing more for himself and his family than
any one else, but who, after three years in college,
was at the end of his resources, and had taken, in
his turn, to keeping school. Daniel went to Boston, and there obtained a good private school for
his brother. The salary thus earned by Ezekiel
was not only sufficient for himself, but enabled
Daniel to gratify the cherished wish of his heart,
and come to the New England capital to conclude
his professional studies.

The first thing to be done was to gain admit-
tance to some good office. Mr. Webster was lucky
enough to obtain an introduction to Mr. Gore,
with whom, as with the rest of the world, that
wonderful look and manner, apparent even then,
through boyishness and rusticity, stood him in
good stead. Mr. Gore questioned him, trusted
him, and told him to hang up his hat, begin work
as clerk at once, and write to New Hampshire for
his credentials. The position thus obtained was
one of fortune's best gifts to Mr. Webster. It

not only gave him an opportunity for a wide study
of the law under wise supervision, but it brought
him into daily contact with a trained barrister and
an experienced public man.   Christopher Gore,
one of the most eminent members of the Boston
bar and a distinguished statesman, had just returned from England, whither he had been sent
as one of the commissioners appointed under the
Jay treaty.   He was a fine type of the aristocratic
Federalist leader, one of the most prominent of
that little group which from the "headquarters of
good principles" in Boston so long controlled the
politics of Massachusetts.   He was a scholar, gentleman, and man of the world, and his portrait
shows us a refined, high-bred face, suggesting a
French marquis of the eighteenth century rather
than the son of a New England sea-captain.   A
few years later, Mr. Gore was chosen governor of
Massachusetts, and defeated when a candidate for
reëlection, largely, it is supposed, because he rode
in a coach and four (to which rumor added out-
riders) whenever he went to his estate at Wal-
tham.   This mode of travel offended the sensibilities of his democratic constituents, but did not
prevent his being subsequently chosen to the Senate of the United States, where he served a term
with much distinction.   The society of such a
man was invaluable to Mr. Webster at this time.
It taught him many things which he could have
learned in no other way, and appealed to that
strong taste for everything dignified and refined

which was so marked a trait of his disposition and habits. He saw now the real possibilities which he had dreamed of in his native village; and while he studied law deeply and helped his brother with his school, he also studied men still more thoroughly and curiously. The professional associates and friends of Mr. Gore were the leaders of the Boston bar when it had many distinguished men whose names hold high places in the history of American law. Among them were Theophilus Parsons, chief justice of Massachusetts; Samuel Dexter, the ablest of them all, fresh from service in Congress and the Senate and as secretary of the treasury; Harrison Gray Otis, fluent and graceful as an orator; James Sullivan, afterwards governor, and Daniel Davis, the solicitor-general. All these and many more Mr. Webster saw and watched, and he has left in his diary discriminating sketches of Parsons and Dexter, whom he greatly admired, and of Sullivan, of whom he had a poor opinion professionally.

Towards the end of the year 1804, while Mr. Webster was thus pleasantly engaged in studying his profession, getting a glimpse of the world, and now and then earning a little money, an opening came to him which seemed to promise immediate and assured prosperity. The judges of his father's court of common pleas offered him the vacant clerk-ship, worth about fifteen hundred dollars annually. This was wealth to Mr. Webster. With this income he could relieve the family from debt, make his father's last years comfortable, and smooth

Ezekiel's path to the bar. When, however, he announced his good luck to Mr. Gore, and his intention of immediately going home to accept the position, that gentleman, to Mr. Webster's great surprise, strongly urged a contrary course. He pointed out the possible reduction of the salary, the fact that the office depended on the favor of the judges, and, above all, that it led to nothing, and destroyed the chances of any really great career. This wise mentor said: "Go on and finish your studies. You are poor enough, but there are greater evils than poverty; live on no man's favor; what bread you do eat, let it be the bread of independence; pursue your profession, make yourself useful to your friends and a little formidable to your enemies, and you have nothing to fear." Mr. Webster, always susceptible to outside influences, saw the wisdom of this advice, and accepted it. It would have been well if he had never swerved even by a hair's breadth from the high and sound principles which it inculcated; but he acted then at least without delay. Going at once to Salisbury, he broke the news of his unlooked-for determination to his father, who was utterly amazed. Pride in his son's high spirit mingled somewhat with disappointment at the prospect of continued hardships; but the brave old man accepted the decision with the Puritan stoicism which was so marked a trait in his character, and the matter ended there.

Returning to Boston, Mr. Webster was admitted to the bar in March, 1805. Mr. Gore moved his admission, and, in the customary speech, prophesied his student's future eminence with a sure knowledge of the latent powers which had dictated his own advice in the matter of the clerkship. Soon after this, Mr. Webster returned to New Hampshire and opened his office in the little town of Boscawen, in order that he might be near his father. Here he devoted himself assiduously to business and study for more than two years, working at his profession, and occasionally writing articles for the "Boston Anthology." During this time he made his first appearance in court, his father being on the bench. He gathered together a practice worth five or six hundred dollars a year, a very creditable sum for a young country practitioner, and won a reputation which made him known in the State.

In April, 1806, after a noble, toiling, unselfish life of sixty-seven years, Ebenezer Webster died. Daniel assumed his father's debts, waited until Ezekiel was admitted to the bar, and then, transferring his business to his brother, moved, in the autumn of 1807, to Portsmouth. This was the principal town of the State, and offered, therefore, the larger field which he felt he needed to give his talents sufficient scope. Thus the first period in his life closed, and he started out on the extended and distinguished career which lay before him. These early years had been years of hardship, but they were among the best of his life. Through great difficulties and by the self-sacrifice of his family, he had made his way to the threshold of the career for which he was so richly endowed. He had passed an unblemished youth; he had led a clean, honest, hard-working life; he was simple, manly, affectionate. Poverty had been a misfortune, not because it had warped or soured him, for he smiled at it with cheerful philosophy, nor because it had made him avaricious, for he never either then or at any time cared for money for its own sake, and nothing could chill the natural lavishness of his disposition. But poverty accustomed him to borrowing and to debt, and this was a misfortune to a man of Mr. Webster's temperament. In those early days he was anxious to pay his debts; but they did not lie heavy upon him or carry a proper sense of responsibility, as they did to Ezekiel and to his father. He was deeply in debt; his books, even, were bought with borrowed money, all which was natural and inevitable; but the trouble was that it never seems to have weighed upon him or been felt by him as of much importance. He was thus early brought into the habit of debt, and was led unconsciously to regard debts and borrowing as he did the sacrifices of others, as the normal modes of existence. Such a condition was to be deplored, because it fostered an unfortunate tendency in his moral nature. With this exception, Mr. Webster's early years present a bright picture, and one which any man had a right to regard with pride and affection.

CHAPTER II

THE occasion of Mr. Webster's first appearance
in court has been the subject of varying tradition.
It is certain, however, that in the counties where
he practiced during his residence at Boscawen, he
made an unusual and very profound impression.
The effect then produced is described in homely
phrase by one who knew him well. The reference
is to a murder trial, in which Mr. Webster gained
his first celebrity.

" There was a man tried for his life, and the judges
chose Webster to plead for him ; and, from what I can
learn, he never has spoken better than he did there
where he first began. He was a black, raven-haired
fellow, with an eye as black as Death's, and as heavy as
a lion's, — that same heavy look, not sleepy, but as if
he did n't care about anything that was going on about
him or anything anywhere else. He did n't look as if
he was thinking about anything, but as if he *would* think
like a hurricane if he once got waked up to it. They
say the lion looks so when he is quiet. . . . Webster
would sometimes be engaged to argue a case just as it
was coming to trial. That would set him to thinking.
It would n't wrinkle his forehead, but made him rest-

less. He would shift his feet about, and run his hand
up over his forehead, through his Indian-black hair, and
lift his upper lip and show his teeth, which were as
white as a hound's."

Of course the speech so admired then was infinitely below what was done afterwards. The very
next was probably better, for Mr. Webster grew
steadily. This observer, however, tells us not
what Mr. Webster said, but how he looked. It
was the personal presence which dwelt with every
one at this time.

Thus with his wonderful leonine look and large,
dark eyes, and with the growing fame which he
had won, Mr. Webster betook himself to Portsmouth. He had met some of the leading lawyers
already, but now he was to be brought into direct
and almost daily competition with them. At that
period in New England there was a great rush of
men of talent to the bar, then casting off its colonial fetters and emerging to an independent life.
The pulpit had ceased to attract, as of old; medi-
cine was in its infancy; there were none of the
other manifold pursuits of to-day, and politics did
not offer a career apart. Outside of mercantile
affairs, therefore, the intellectual forces of the old
Puritan commonwealths, overflowing with life, and
feeling the thrill of youthful independence and the
confidence of rapid growth in business, wealth, and
population, were concentrated in the law. Even
in a small State like New Hampshire, presenting
very limited opportunities, there was, relatively

speaking, an extraordinary amount of ability among the members of the bar, notwithstanding the fact that they had but just escaped from the condition of colonists. Common sense was the divinity of both the courts and the profession. The learning was neither extensive nor profound, but practical knowledge, sound principles, and shrewd management were conspicuous. Jeremiah Smith, the chief justice, a man of humor and cultivation, was a well read and able judge; George Sullivan was ready of speech and fertile in expedients; and Parsons and Dexter of Massachusetts, both men of national reputation, appeared from time to time in the New Hampshire courts. Among the most eminent was William Plumer, then senator and afterwards governor of the State, a well-trained, clear-headed, judicious man. He was one of Mr. Webster's early antagonists, and defeated him in their first encounter. Yet at the same time, although a leader of the bar and a United States senator, he seems to have been oppressed with a sense of responsibility and even of inequality by this thin, black-eyed young lawyer from the back country. Mr. Plumer was a man of cool and excellent judgment, and he thought that Mr. Webster on this occasion was too excursive and declamatory. He also deemed him better fitted by mind and temperament for politics than for the law, an opinion fully justified in the future, despite Mr. Webster's eminence at the bar. In another case, where they were opposed, Mr. Plumer quoted a

passage from Peake's "Law of Evidence." Mr.
Webster criticised the citation as bad law, pronounced the book a miserable two-penny compila-
tion, and then, throwing it down with a fine dis-
dain, said, "So much for Mr. Thomas Peake's
compendium of the ' Law of Evidence.' " Such
was his manner that every one present appeared to
think the point settled, and felt rather ashamed of
ever having heard of Mr. Peake or his unfortunate
book. Thereupon Mr. Plumer produced a volume
of reports by which it appeared that the despised
passage was taken word for word from one of Lord
Mansfield's decisions. The wretched Peake's character was rehabilitated, and Mr. Webster silenced.
This was an illustration of a failing of Mr. Webster at that time. He was rough and unceremo-
nious, and even overbearing, both to court and
bar, the natural result of a new sense of power in
an inexperienced man. This harshness of manner,
however, soon disappeared. He learned rapidly
to practice the stately and solemn courtesy which
distinguished him through life.

There was one lawyer, however, at the head of
his profession in New Hampshire, who had more
effect upon Mr. Webster than any other whom he
ever met there or elsewhere. This was the man
to whom the Shaker said: "By thy size and thy
language [1] I judge that thou art Jeremiah Mason."

[1] Mr. Mason, as is well known, was six feet seven inches in
height, and his language, always very forcible and direct, was,
when he was irritated, if we may trust tradition, at times somewhat profane.

Mr. Mason was one of the greatest common-law-yers this country has ever produced. Keen and penetrating in intellect, he was master of a relent-less logic and of a style which, though simple and homely, was clear and correct to the last point. Slow and deliberate in his movements, and senten-tious in his utterances, he dealt so powerfully with evidence and so lucidly with principles of law that he rarely failed to carry conviction to his hearers. He was particularly renowned for his success in getting verdicts. Many years afterwards Mr. Webster gave it as his deliberate opinion that he had never met with a stronger intellect, a mind of more native resources or quicker and deeper vision than were possessed by Mr. Mason, whom in men-tal reach and grasp and in closeness of reasoning he would not allow to be second even to Chief Justice Marshall. Mr. Mason, on his side, with his usual sagacity, at once detected the great tal-ents of Mr. Webster. In the first case where they were opposed, a murder trial, Mr. Webster took the place of the attorney-general for the prosecu-tion. Mr. Mason, speaking of the impression made by his youthful and then unknown opponent, said : —

" He broke upon me like a thunder shower in July, sudden, portentous, sweeping all before it. It was the first case in which he appeared at our bar ; a criminal prosecution in which I had arranged a very pretty de-fense, as against the attorney-general, Atkinson, who was able enough in his way, but whom I knew very well

how to take. Atkinson being absent, Webster conducted the case for him, and turned, in the most masterly manner, the line of my defenses, carrying with him
all but one of the jurors, so that I barely saved my client
by my best exertions. I was never more surprised than
by this remarkable exhibition of unexpected power. It
surpassed, in some respects, anything which I have ever
since seen even in him."

With all his admiration for his young antagonist, however, one cannot help noticing that the
generous and modest but astute counsel for the
defense ended by getting a disagreement which
was equivalent to winning his case.

Fortune showered many favors upon Mr. Webster, but none more valuable than that of having
Jeremiah Mason as his chief opponent at the New
Hampshire bar. Mr. Mason had no spark of
envy in his composition. He not only regarded
with pleasure the great abilities of Mr. Webster,
but he watched with kindly interest the rapid rise
which soon made this stranger from the country
his principal competitor and the champion commonly chosen to meet him in the courts. He gave
Mr. Webster his friendship, stanch, and unvarying, until his death; he gave freely also of his
wisdom and experience in advice and counsel.
Best of all was the opportunity for instruction and
discipline which Mr. Webster gained by repeated
contests with such a man. The strong qualities
of Mr. Webster's mind rapidly developed by constant practice and under such influences. He

showed more and more in every case his wonderful instinct for seizing on the very heart of a question, and for extricating the essential points from the midst of confused details and clashing arguments. He displayed, too, more strongly every day his capacity for close, logical reasoning and for telling retort, backed by a passion and energy none the less effective from being but slowly called into activity. In a word, the unequaled power of stating facts or principles, which was the predominant quality of Mr. Webster's genius, grew steadily with a vigorous vitality, while his eloquence developed in a similar striking fashion. Much of this growth and improvement was due to the sharp competition and bright example of Mr. Mason. But the best lesson that Mr. Webster learned from his wary yet daring antagonist was in regard to style. When he saw Mr. Mason go close to the jury box, and in a plain style and conversational manner, force conviction upon his hearers, and carry off verdict after verdict, Mr. Webster felt as he had never done before the defects of his own modes of expression. His florid phrases looked rather mean, insincere, and tasteless, besides being weak and ineffective. From that time he began to study simplicity and directness, which ended in the perfection of a style unsurpassed in modern oratory. The years of Mr. Webster's professional life in Portsmouth under the tuition of Mr. Mason were of inestimable service to him.

Early in this period, also, Mr. Webster gave

up his bachelor existence, and made for himself a
home.   When he first appeared at church in Portsmouth the minister's daughter noted and remembered his striking features and look, and regarded
him as one with great capacities for good or evil.
But the interesting stranger was not destined to
fall a victim to any of the young ladies of Portsmouth.   In the spring of 1808 he slipped away
from his new friends and returned to Salisbury,
where, in May, he was married.   The bride he
brought back to Portsmouth was Grace Fletcher,
daughter of the minister of Hopkinton.   Mr.
Webster is said to have seen her first at church
in Salisbury, whither she came on horseback in a
tight-fitting black velvet dress, and looking, as he
said, "like an angel."   She was certainly a very
lovely and charming woman, of delicate and refined
sensibilities and bright and sympathetic mind.   She
was a devoted wife, the object of her husband's
first and strongest love, and the mother of his children.   It is very pleasant to look at Mr. Webster
in his home during these early years of his married
life.   It was a happy, innocent, untroubled time.
He was advancing in his profession, winning fame
and respect, earning a sufficient income, blessed in
his domestic relations, and with his children growing up about him.   He was social by nature, and
very popular everywhere.   Genial and affectionate
in disposition, he attached everybody to him, and
his hearty humor, love of mimicry, and fund of
anecdote made him a delightful companion, and led

Mr. Mason to say that the stage had lost a great actor in Webster.

But while he was thus enjoying professional success and the contented happiness of his fireside, he was slowly but surely drifting into the current of politics, whither his genius led him, and which had for him an irresistible attraction. Mr. Webster took both his politics and his religion from his father, and does not appear to have questioned either. He had a peculiarly conservative cast of mind. In an age of revolution and skepticism he showed no trace of the questioning spirit which then prevailed. Even in his earliest years he was a firm believer in existing institutions, in what was fixed and established. He had a little of the disposition of Lord Thurlow, who, when asked by a dissenter why, being a notorious free-thinker, he so ardently supported the Established Church, replied: "I support the Church of England because it is established. Establish your religion, and I'll support that." But if Mr. Webster took his religion and politics from his father in an unquestioning spirit, he accepted them in a mild form. He was a liberal Federalist because he had a wide mental vision, and by nature took broad views of everything. His father, on the other hand, was a rigid, intolerant Federalist of a thorough-going Puritan type. Being taken ill once in a town of Democratic proclivities, he begged to be carried home. "I was born a Federalist," he said, "I have lived a Federalist, and I won't die in a

Democratic town." In the same way Ezekiel
Webster's uncompromising Federalism shut him
out from political preferment, and he would never
modify his principles one jot in order to gain the
seat in Congress which he might easily have obtained by slight concessions. The broad and liberal spirit of Daniel Webster rose superior to the
rigid and even narrow opinions of his father and
brother, but perhaps it would have been better for
him if he had had in addition to his splendid mind
the stern, unbending force of character which made
his father and brother stand by their principles
with immovable Puritan determination. Liberal
as he was, however, in his political opinions, the
same conservative spirit which led him to adopt
his creed made him sustain it faithfully and constantly when he had once accepted it. He was a
steady and trusted party man, although neither
then nor at any time a blind, unreasoning partisan.

Mr. Webster came forward gradually as a political leader by occasional addresses and speeches,
at first with long intervals between them, and then
becoming more frequent, until at last he found
himself fairly engaged in a public career. In
1804, at the request of some of his father's friends,
he published a pamphlet, entitled, "An Appeal to
Old Whigs," in the interest of Gilman, the Federal candidate for governor. He seems to have
had a very poor opinion of this performance, and
his interest in the success of the party at that juncture was very slight. In 1805 he delivered a

Fourth of July oration at Salisbury, which has not been preserved; and in the following year he gave another before the "Federal gentlemen" of Concord, which was published. The tone of this speech is not very partisan, nor does it exhibit the bitter spirit of the Federalists, although he attacked the administration, was violent in urging the protection of commerce, and was extremely savage in his remarks about France. At times the style is forcible, and even rich, but, as a rule, it is still strained and artificial. The oration begins eagerly with an appeal for the Constitution and the Republic, the ideas always uppermost in Mr. Webster's mind. As a whole, it shows a distinct improvement in form, but there are no marks of genius to raise it above the ordinary level of Fourth of July speeches. His next production was a little pamphlet, published in 1808, on the embargo, which was then paralyzing New England, and crushing out her prosperity. This essay is important because it is the first clear instance of the remarkable faculty which Mr. Webster had of seizing on the vital point of a subject, and bringing it out in such a way that everybody could see and understand it. In this case the point was the distinction between a temporary embargo and one of unlimited duration. Mr. Webster contended that the latter was unconstitutional. The great mischief of the embargo was in Jefferson's concealed intention that it should be unlimited in point of time, a piece of recklessness and deceit

never fully appreciated until it had all passed into
history. This Mr. Webster detected and brought
out as the most illegal and dangerous feature of
the measure, while he also discussed the general
policy in its fullest extent. In 1809 he spoke before the Phi Beta Kappa Society, upon "The State
of our Literature," an address without especial
interest except as showing a very marked improvement in style, due, no doubt, to the influence of
Mr. Mason.

During the next three years Mr. Webster was
completely absorbed in the practice of his profession, and not until the declaration of war with
England had stirred and agitated the whole country did he again come before the public. The
occasion of his reappearance was the Fourth of
July celebration in 1812, when he addressed the
Washington Benevolent Society at Portsmouth.
The speech was a strong, calm statement of the
grounds of opposition to the war. He showed
that "maritime defense, commercial regulations,
and national revenue" were the very cornerstones
of the Constitution, and that these great interests
had been crippled and abused by the departure
from Washington's policy. He developed, with
great force, the principal and the most unanswerable argument of his party, that the navy had
been neglected and decried because it was a Federalist scheme, when a navy was what we wanted
above all things, and especially when we were
drifting into a maritime conflict. He argued

strongly in favor of a naval war, and measures of
naval defense, instead of wasting our resources by
an invasion of Canada. So far he went strictly
with his party, merely invigorating and enforcing
their well-known principles. But when he came
to defining the proper limits of opposition to the
war he modified very essentially the course pre-
scribed by advanced Federalist opinions. The
majority of that party in New England were prepared to go to the very edge of the narrow legal
line which divides constitutional opposition from
treasonable resistance. They were violent, bitter,
and uncompromising in their language and purposes. From this Mr. Webster was saved by his
breadth of view, his clear perceptions, and his intense national feeling. He says on this point: —

"With respect to the war in which we are now involved, the course which our principles require us to
pursue cannot be doubtful. It is now the law of the
land, and as such we are bound to regard it. Resistance and insurrection form no part of our creed. The
disciples of Washington are neither tyrants in power nor
rebels out. If we are taxed to carry on this war we
shall disregard certain distinguished examples and shall
pay. If our personal services are required we shall
yield them to the precise extent of our constitutional
liability. At the same time the world may be assured
that we know our rights and shall exercise them. We
shall express our opinions on this, as on every measure
of the government, — I trust without passion, I am certain without fear. By the exercise of our constitutional

right of suffrage, by the peaceable remedy of election,
we shall seek to restore wisdom to our councils, and
peace to our country."

This was a sensible and patriotic opposition.
It represented the views of the moderate Federalists, and traced the lines which Mr. Webster
consistently followed during the first years of his
public life.   The address concluded by pointing
out the French trickery which had provoked the
war, and by denouncing an alliance with French
despotism and ambition.

This oration was printed, and ran at once through
two editions.   It led to the selection of Mr. Webster as a delegate to an assembly of the people of
the county of Rockingham, a sort of mass convention, held in August, 1812.   There he was placed
on the committee to prepare the address, and was
chosen to write their report, which was adopted
and published.   This important document, widely
known at the time as the "Rockingham Memorial,"
was a careful argument against the war, and a
vigorous and able presentation of the Federalist
views.   It was addressed to the President, whom
it treated with respectful severity.   With much
skill it turned Mr. Madison's own arguments
against himself, and appealed to public opinion by
its clear and convincing reasoning.   In one point
the memorial differed curiously from the oration
of a month before.   The latter pointed to the suffrage as the mode of redress; the former distinctly
hinted at and almost threatened secession even

while it deplored a dissolution of the Union as a possible result of the administration's policy. In the one case Mr. Webster was expressing his own views, in the other he was giving utterance to the opinions of the members of his party among whom he stood. This little incident shows the susceptibility to outside influences which formed such an odd trait in the character of a man so imperious by nature. When acting alone he spoke his own opinions. When in a situation where public opinion was concentrated against him, he submitted to modifications of his views with a curious and indolent indifference.

The immediate result to Mr. Webster of the ability and tact which he displayed at the Rockingham convention was his election to the thirteenth Congress, where he took his seat in May, 1813. There were then many able men in the House. Mr. Clay was speaker, and on the floor were John C. Calhoun, Langdon Cheves, and William Lowndes of South Carolina, Forsyth and Troup of Georgia, Ingersoll of Pennsylvania, Grundy of Tennessee, and McLean of Ohio, all conspicuous in the young nationalist war party. Macon and Eppes were representatives of the old Jeffersonian Republicans, while the Federalists were strong in the possession of such leaders as Pickering of Massachusetts, Pitkin of Connecticut, Grosvenor and Benson of New York, Hanson of Maryland, and William Gaston of North Carolina. It was a House in which any one might have been glad to win dis-

tinction. That Mr. Webster was considered, at
the outset, to be a man of great promise is shown
by the fact that he was placed on the Committee
on Foreign Relations, of which Mr. Calhoun was
the head, and which, in the war time, was the
most important committee of the House.

Mr. Webster's first act was a characteristic one.
Early in June he introduced a set of resolutions
calling upon the President for information as to
the time and mode in which the repeal of the
French decrees had been communicated to our
government. His unerring sagacity, in singling
out the weak point in his enemy's armor and in
choosing his own keenest weapon, was never better
illustrated than on this occasion. We know now
that in the negotiations for the repeal of the decrees, the French government tricked us into war
with England by most profligate lying. It was
apparent then that there was something wrong,
and that either our government had been deceived,
or had withheld the publication of the repealing
decree until war was declared, so that England
might not have a pretext for rescinding the obnoxious orders. Either horn of the dilemma, therefore, was disagreeable to the administration, and
a disclosure could hardly fail to benefit the Federalists. Mr. Webster supported his resolutions
with a terse and simple speech of explanation, so
far as we can judge from the meagre abstract
which has come down to us. The resolutions,
however, were a firebrand, and lighted up an

angry and protracted debate, but the ruling party,
as Mr. Webster probably foresaw, did not dare
to vote them down, and they passed by large majorities. Mr. Webster spoke but once, and then
very briefly, during the progress of the debate,
and soon after returned to New Hampshire. With
the exception of these resolutions, he took no active part whatever in the business of the House
beyond voting steadily with his party, a fact of
which we may be sure because he was always on
the same side as that stanch old partisan, Timothy
Pickering.

After a summer passed in the performance of
his professional duties, Mr. Webster returned to
Washington. He was late in his coming, Congress having been in session nearly three weeks
when he arrived to find that he had been dropped
from the Committee on Foreign Relations. The
dominant party probably discovered that he was
a young man of rather too much promise and too
formidable an opponent for such an important
post. His resolutions had been answered at the
previous session, after his departure, and the report, which consisted of a lame explanation of the
main point, and an elaborate defense of the war,
had been quietly laid aside. Mr. Webster desired
debate on this subject, and succeeded in carrying
a reference of the report to a committee of the
whole, but his opponents prevented its ever coming
to discussion. In the long session which ensued,
Mr. Webster again took comparatively little part

in general business, but he spoke oftener than before.   He seems to have been reserving his strength
and making sure of his ground.   He defended the
Federalists as the true friends of the navy and he
resisted with great power the extravagant attempt
to extend martial law to all citizens suspected of
treason.   On January 14, 1814, he made a long
and well reported speech against a bill to encourage enlistments.   This is the first example of the
eloquence which Mr. Webster afterwards carried
to such high perfection.   Some of his subsequent
speeches far surpass this one, but they differ from
it in degree, not in kind.   He was now master of
the style at which he aimed.   The vehicle was
perfected and his natural talent gave that vehicle
abundance of thought to be conveyed.   The whole
speech is simple in form, direct and forcible.   It
has the elasticity and vigor of great strength, and
glows with eloquence in some passages.   Here, too,
we see for the first time that power of deliberate
and measured sarcasm which was destined to become in his hands such a formidable weapon.   The
florid rhetoric of the early days is utterly gone,
and the thought comes to us in those short and
pregnant sentences and in the well chosen and
effective words which were afterwards so typical
of the speaker.   The speech itself was a party
speech and a presentation of party arguments.   It
offered nothing new, but the familiar principles
had hardly ever been stated in such a striking and
impressive fashion.   Mr. Webster attacked the

war policy and the conduct of the war, and advocated defensive warfare, a navy, and the abandon-
ment of the restrictive laws that were ruining our
commerce, which had been the main cause of the
adoption of the Constitution. The conclusion of
this speech is not far from the level of Mr. Webster's best work. It is too long for quotation, but
a few sentences will show its quality: —

" Give up your futile projects of invasion. Extinguish
the fires that blaze on your inland frontier. Establish
perfect safety and defense there by adequate force. Let
every man that sleeps on your soil sleep in security. Stop
the blood that flows from the veins of unarmed yeo-
manry and women and children. Give to the living time
to bury and lament their dead in the quietness of private
sorrow. Having performed this work of beneficence
and mercy on your inland border, turn, and look with
the eye of justice and compassion on your vast population along the coast. Unclench the iron grasp of your
embargo. Take measures for that end before another
sun sets. . . . Let it no longer be said that not one
ship of force, built by your hands, yet floats upon the
ocean. . . . If then the war must be continued, go to
the ocean. If you are seriously contending for maritime rights, go to the theatre where alone those rights
can be defended. Thither every indication of your fortune points you. There the united wishes and exertions
of the nation will go with you. Even our party divisions, acrimonious as they are, cease at the water's
edge."

Events soon forced the policy urged by Mr.
Webster upon the administration, whose friends

carried first a modification of the embargo, and before the close of the session introduced a bill for its total repeal. The difficult task of advocating this measure devolved upon Mr. Calhoun, who sustained his cause more ingeniously than ingenuously. He frankly admitted that restriction was a failure as a war measure, but he defended the repeal on the ground that the condition of affairs in Europe had changed since the restrictive policy was adopted. It had indeed changed since the embargo of 1807, but not since the imposition of that of 1813, which was the one under discussion.

Mr. Calhoun laid himself open to most unmerciful retorts, which was his misfortune, not his fault, for the embargo had been utterly and hopelessly wrong from the beginning. Mr. Webster, however, took full advantage of the opportunity thus presented. His opening congratulations are in his best vein of stately sarcasm, and are admirably put. He followed this up by a new argument of great force, showing the colonial spirit of the restrictive policy. He also dwelt with fresh vigor on the identification with France necessitated by the restrictive laws, a reproach which stung Mr. Calhoun and his followers more than anything else. He then took up the embargo policy and tore it to pieces, — no very difficult undertaking, but well performed. The shifty and shifting policy of the government was especially distasteful to Mr. Webster, with his lofty conception of con-

sistent and steady statesmanship, a point which is
well brought out in the following passage: —

"In a commercial country, nothing can be more objectionable than frequent and violent changes. The
concerns of private business do not endure such rude
shocks but with extreme inconvenience and great loss.
It would seem, however, that there is a class of politicians to whose taste all change is suited, to whom whatever is unnatural seems wise, and all that is violent
appears great. . . . The Embargo Act, the Non-Im-
portation Act, and all the crowd of additions and sup-
plements, together with all their garniture of messages,
reports, and resolutions, are tumbling undistinguished
into one common grave. But yesterday this policy had
a thousand friends and supporters; to-day it is fallen
and prostrate, and few 'so poor as to do it reverence.'
Sir, a government which cannot administer the affairs of
a nation without so frequent and such violent alterations
in the ordinary occupations and pursuits of private life,
has, in my opinion, little claim to the regard of the community."

All this is very characteristic of Mr. Webster's
temperament in dealing with public affairs, and
is a very good example of his power of dignified
reproach and condemnation.

Mr. Calhoun had said at the close of his speech,
that the repeal of the restrictive measures should
not be allowed to affect the double duties which
protected manufactures. Mr. Webster discussed
this point at length, defining his own position,
which was that of the New England Federalists,
who believed in free trade as an abstract principle,

and considered protection only as an expedient of which they wanted as little as possible. Mr. Webster set forth these views in his usual effective and lucid manner, but they can be considered more fitly at the period when he dealt with the tariff as a leading issue of the day and of his own public life.

Mr. Webster took no further action of importance at this session, not even participating in the great debate on the loan bill; but, by the manner in which these two speeches were referred to and quoted in Congress for many days after they were delivered, we can perceive the depth of their first impression. I have dwelt upon them at length because they are not in the collected edition of his speeches, where they well deserve a place, and, still more, because they are the first examples of his parliamentary eloquence which show his characteristic qualities and the action of his mind. Mr. Webster was a man of slow growth, not reaching his highest point until he was nearly fifty years of age, but these two speeches mark an advanced stage in his progress. The only fresh point that he made was when he declared that the embargo was colonial in spirit; and this thought proceeded from the vital principle of Mr. Webster's public life, his intense love for nationality and union, which grew with his growth and strengthened with his strength. In other respects, these speeches presented simply the arguments and opinions of his party. They fell upon the ear of Congress and the country with a new and ringing sound because they were stated so finely and with such simplicity. Certainly one of them, and probably both, were delivered without any immediate preparation, but they really had the preparation of years, and were the utterance of thoughts which had been garnered up by long meditation. He wisely confined himself at this time to a subject which had been long before his mind, and upon which he had gathered all the essential points by observation and by a study of the multitude of speeches and essays with which the country had been deluged. These early speeches, like some of the best of his prime, although nominally unprepared, were poured forth from the overflowing resources which had been the fruit of months of reflection, and which had been stored up by an unyielding memory. They had really been in preparation ever since the embargo pamphlet of 1808, and that was one reason for their ripeness and terseness, for their easy flow and condensed force. I have examined with care the debates in that Congress. There were many able and experienced speakers on the floor. Mr. Clay, it is true, took no part, and early in the session went to Europe. But Mr. Calhoun led in debate, and there were many others second only to him. Among all the speeches, however, those delivered by Mr. Webster stand out in sharp relief. His utterances were as clear and direct as those of Mr. Calhoun, but they had none of the South Carolinian's dryness. We can best judge of their merit and their effect by comparing them with those of his associates. They were not only forcible, but they were vivid also and full of life, and his words when he was roused fell like the blows of a hammer on an anvil. They lacked the polish and richness of his later efforts, but the force and power of statement and the purity of diction were all there, and men began to realize that one destined to great achievements had entered the field of American politics.

This was very apparent when Mr. Webster came back to Washington for the extra session called in September, 1814. Although he had made previously but two set speeches, and had taken comparatively little part in every-day debate, he was now acknowledged, after his few months of service, to be one of the foremost men in the House, and the strongest leader in his party. He differed somewhat at this time from the prevailing sentiment of the Federalists in New England, for the guiding principle of his life, his love of nationality, overrode all other influences. He discountenanced the measures which led to the Hartford Convention, and he helped to keep New Hampshire out of that movement; but it is an entire mistake to represent him as an independent Federalist at this period. The days of Mr. Webster's independent politics came later, when the Federalists had ceased to exist as a party and when no new ties had been formed. In the winter of

1814 and 1815, although, like many of the moderate Federalists, he disapproved of the separatist movement in New England, on all other party questions he acted consistently with the straitest of the sect. Sensibly enough, he did not consider the convention at Hartford, although he had nothing to do with it, either treasonable or seditious; and yet, much as he disliked its supposed purposes, he did not hesitate, in a speech on the Enlistment Bill, to use them as a threat to deter the administration from war measures. This was a favorite Federalist practice, gloomily to point out at this time the gathering clouds of domestic strife, in order to turn the administration back from war, that poor frightened administration of Mr. Madison, which had for months been clutching frantically at every straw which seemed to promise a chance of peace.

But although Mr. Webster went as steadily and even more strongly with his party in this session, he did more and better service than ever before, partly, perhaps, because on the questions which arose, his party was, in the main, entirely right. The strength of his party feeling is shown by his attitude in regard to the war taxes, upon which he made a quiet but effective speech. He took the ground that, as a member of the minority, he could not prevent the taxes nor stop hostilities, but he could protest against the war, its conduct, and its authors, by voting against the taxes. There is a nice question of political ethics here as

to how far an opposition ought to go in time of
national war and distress, but it is certainly impossible to give a more extreme expression to parliamentary opposition than to refuse the supplies
at a most critical moment in a severe conflict.
To this last extreme of party opposition to the
administration, Mr. Webster went. It was as
far as he could go and remain loyal to the Union.
But there he stopped absolutely. With the next
step, which went outside the Union, and which his
friends at home were considering, he would have
nothing to do, and he would not countenance any
separatist schemes. In the national Congress,
however, he was prepared to advance as far as the
boldest and bitterest in opposition, and he either
voted against the war taxes or abstained from voting on them, in company with the strictest partisans of the Pickering type.

There is no need to suppose from this that Mr.
Webster had lost in the least the liberality or
breadth of view which always characterized him.
He was no narrower then than when he entered
Congress, or than when he left it. He went with
his party because he believed it to be right, — as
at that moment it undoubtedly was. The party,
however, was still extreme and bitter, as it had
been for ten years, but Mr. Webster was neither.
He went all lengths with his friends in Congress,
but he did not share their intensity of feeling or
their fierce hostility to individuals. The Federalists, for instance, as a rule had ceased to call upon

Mr. Madison, but in such intolerance Mr. Webster declined to indulge. He was always on good
terms with the President and with all the hostile
leaders. His opposition was extreme in principle,
but not in manner; it was vigorous and uncompromising, but also stately and dignified. It was
part of his large and indolent nature to accept
much and question little; to take the ideas most
easy and natural to him, those of his friends and
associates, and of his native New England, without
needless inquiry and investigation. It was part
of the same nature, also, to hold liberal views
after he had fairly taken sides, and never, by con-
founding individuals with principles and purposes,
to import into politics the fiery, biting element of
personal hatred and malice.

His position in the House once assured, we find
Mr. Webster taking a much more active part in
the daily debates than before. On these occasions
we hear of his "deliberate, conversational" manner, another of the lessons learned from Mr.
Mason when that gentleman, standing so close to
the jury box that he could have "laid his finger
on the foreman's nose," as Mr. Webster said,
chatted easily with each juryman, and won a succession of verdicts. But besides the daily debate,
Mr. Webster spoke at length on several important
occasions. This was the case with the Enlistment
Bill, which involved a forced draft, including
minors, and was deemed unconstitutional by the
Federalists. Mr. Webster had "a hand," as he

puts it, — a strong one, we may be sure, — in kill-
ing "Mr. Monroe's conscription."

The most important measure, however, with
which Mr. Webster was called to deal, and to
which he gave his best efforts, was the attempt to
establish a national bank. There were three parties in the House on this question. The first represented the "old Republican" doctrines, and was
opposed to any bank. The second represented
the theories of Hamilton and the Federalists, and
favored a bank with a reasonable capital, specie-
paying, and free to decide about making loans to
the government. The third body was composed
of members of the national war party, who were
eager for a bank merely to help the government
out of its appalling difficulties. They, therefore,
favored an institution of large capital, non-specie-
paying, and obliged to make heavy loans to the
government, which involved, of course, an irredeemable paper currency. In a word, there was
the party of no bank, the party of a specie bank,
and the party of a huge paper-money bank. The
second of these parties, with which of course
Mr. Webster acted, held the key of the situation. No bank could be established unless it
was based on their principles. The first bill,
proposing a paper-money bank, originated in the
House, and was killed there by a strong majority,
Mr. Webster making a long speech against it
which has not been preserved. The next bill came
from the Senate, and was also for a paper-money

bank. Against this scheme Mr. Webster made a second elaborate speech, which is reprinted in his works. His genius for arranging and stating facts held its full strength in questions of finance, and he now established his reputation as a master in that difficult department of statesmanship. His recent studies of economical questions in late English works and in English history gave freshness to what he said, and in clearness of argument, in range of view, and wisdom of judgment, he showed himself a worthy disciple of the school of Hamilton. His argument proceeded on the truest economical and commercial principles, and was, indeed, unanswerable. He then took his stand as the foe of irredeemable paper, whether in war or peace, and of wild, unrestrained banking, a position from which he never wavered, and in support of which he rendered to the country some of his best service as a public man. The bill was defeated by the casting vote of the speaker. When the result was announced, Mr. Calhoun was utterly overwhelmed. He cared little for the bank but deeply for the government, which, as it was not known that peace had been made, seemed to be on the verge of ruin. He came over to Mr. Webster, and, bursting into tears, begged the latter to aid in establishing a proper bank, a request which was freely granted.

The vote was then reconsidered, the bill recommitted and brought back, with a reduced capital, and freed from the government power to force loans and suspend specie payments. This measure was passed by a large majority, composed of the Federalists and the friends of the government, but it was the plan of the former which had prevailed. The President vetoed the bill for a variety of reasons, duly stated, but really, as Mr. Webster said, because a sound bank of this sort was not in favor with the administration. Another paper-money scheme was introduced, and the conflict began again, but was abruptly terminated by the news of peace, and on March 4 the thirteenth Congress came to an end.

The fourteenth Congress, to which he had been reëlected, Mr. Webster said many years afterward, was the most remarkable for talents of any he had ever seen. To the leaders of marked ability in the previous Congress, most of whom had been reëlected, several others were added. Mr. Clay returned from Europe to take again an active part. Mr. Pinkney, the most eminent practicing lawyer in the country, recently attorney-general and minister to England, whom John Randolph, with characteristic insolence, "believed to be from Maryland," was there until his appointment to the Russian mission. Last, but not least, there was John Randolph himself, wildly eccentric and venomously eloquent, — sometimes witty, always odd and amusing, talking incessantly on everything, so that the reporters gave him up in despair, and with whom Mr. Webster came to a definite understanding before the close of the session.

Mr. Webster did not take his seat until February, being detained at the North by the illness of his daughter Grace. When he arrived he found Congress at work upon a bank bill possessing the same objectionable features of paper money and large capital as the former schemes which he had helped to overthrow. He began his attack upon this dangerous plan by considering the evil condition of the currency. He showed that the currency of the United States was sound because it was gold and silver, in his opinion the only constitutional medium, but that the country was flooded by the irredeemable paper of the state banks. Congress could not regulate the state banks, but they could force them to specie payments by refusing to receive any notes which were not paid in specie by the bank which issued them. Passing to the proposed national bank, he reiterated the able arguments which he had made in the previous Congress against the large capital, the power to suspend specie payments, and the stock feature of the bank, which he thought would lead to speculation and control by the state banks. This last point is the first instance of that financial foresight for which Mr. Webster was so remarkable, and which shows so plainly the soundness of his knowledge in regard to economical matters. A violent speculation in bank stock did ensue, and the first years of the new institution were troubled, disorderly, and anything but creditable. The opposition of Mr. Webster and those who thought with

him, resulted in the reduction of the capital and
the removal of the power to suspend specie payments.   But although shorn of its most obnoxious
features, Mr. Webster voted against the bill on
its final passage on account of the participation
permitted to the government in its management.
He was quite right, but, after the bank was well
established, he supported it as Lord Thurlow
promised to do in regard to the dissenter's religion.   Indeed, Mr. Webster ultimately so far
lost his original dislike to this bank that he became one of its warmest adherents.   The plan
was defective, but the scheme, on the whole, worked
better than had been expected.

Immediately after the passage of the bank bill,
Mr. Calhoun introduced a bill requiring the revenue to be collected in lawful money of the United
States.   A sharp debate ensued, and the bill was
lost.   Mr. Webster at once offered resolutions
requiring all government dues to be paid in coin,
in treasury notes, or in notes of the Bank of the
United States.   He supported these resolutions,
thus daringly put forward just after the principle
they involved had been voted down, in a speech
of singular power, clear, convincing, and full of
information and illustration.   He elaborated the
ideas contained in his previous remarks on the
currency, displaying with great force the evils of
irredeemable paper, and the absolute necessity of
a sound currency based on specie payments.   He
won a signal victory by the passage of his resolu-

tions, which brought about resumption, and, after the bank was firmly established, gave us a sound currency and a safe medium of exchange. This was one of the most conspicuous services ever rendered by Mr. Webster to the business interests and good government of the country, and he deserves the full credit, for he triumphed where Mr. Calhoun had just been defeated.

Mr. Webster took more or less part in all the questions which afterwards arose in the House, especially on the tariff, but his great efforts were those devoted to the bank and the currency. The only other incident of the session was an invitation to fight a duel sent him by John Randolph. This was the only challenge ever received by Mr. Webster. He never could have seemed a very happy subject for such missives, and, moreover, he never indulged in language calculated to provoke them. Randolph, however, would have challenged anybody or anything, from Henry Clay to a field-mouse, if the fancy happened to strike him. Mr. Webster's reply is a model of dignity and veiled contempt. He refused to admit Randolph's right to an explanation, alluded to that gentleman's lack of courtesy in the House, denied his right to call him out, and wound up by saying that he did not feel bound to risk his life at any one's bidding, but should "always be prepared to repel, in a suitable manner, the aggression of any man who may presume on this refusal." One cannot help smiling over this last clause, with its sugges-

tion of personal violence, as the two men rise before the fancy, — the big, swarthy black-haired
son of the northern hills, with his robust common
sense, and the sallow, lean, sickly Virginia planter,
not many degrees removed mentally from the pa-
tients in Bedlam.

In the affairs of the next session of the fourteenth Congress Mr. Webster took scarcely any
part. He voted for Mr. Calhoun's internal improvement bill, although without entering the debate, and he also voted to pass the bill over Mr.
Madison's veto. This was sound Hamiltonian
Federalism, and in entire consonance with the national sentiments of Mr. Webster. On the constitutional point, which he is said to have examined
with some care, he decided in accordance with the
opinions of his party, and with the doctrine of
liberal construction, to which he always adhered.

On March 4, 1817, the fourteenth Congress
expired, and with it the term of Mr. Webster's
service. Five years were to intervene before he
again appeared in the arena of national politics.
This retirement from active public life was due to
professional reasons. In nine years Mr. Webster
had attained to the very summit of his profession
in New Hampshire. He was earning two thousand dollars a year, and in that hardy and poor
community he could not hope to earn more. To
a man with such great and productive talents, and
with a growing family, a larger field had become
an absolute necessity. In June, 1816, therefore,

Mr. Webster removed from Portsmouth to Boston. That he gained by the change is apparent from the fact that the first year after his removal his professional income did not fall short of twenty thousand dollars. The first suggestion of the possibilities of wealth offered to his abilities in a suitable field came from his going to Washington. There, in the winter of 1813 and 1814, he was admitted to the bar of the Supreme Court of the United States, before which he tried two or three cases, and this opened the vista of a professional career, which he felt would give him verge and room enough, as well as fit remuneration. From this beginning the Supreme Court practice, which soon led to the removal ·to Boston, rapidly increased, until, in the last session of his term, it occupied most of his time. This withdrawal from the duties of Congress, however, was not due to a sacrifice of his time to his professional engagements, but to the depression caused by his first great grief, which must have rendered the noise and dust of debate most distasteful to him. Mr. and Mrs. Webster had arrived in Washington for this last session, in December, 1816, and were recalled to Boston by the illness of their little daughter Grace, who was their oldest child, singularly bright and precocious, with much of her father's look and talent, and of her mother's sensibility. She was a favorite with her father, and tenderly beloved by him. After her parents' return she sank rapidly, the victim of consumption.

When the last hour was at hand, the child, rousing from sleep, asked for her father. He came, raised her upon his arm, and, as he did so, she smiled upon him and died. It is a little incident in the life of a great man, but a child's instinct does not err at such a moment, and her dying smile sheds a flood of soft light upon the deep and warm affections of Mr. Webster's solemn and reserved nature. It was the first great grief. Mr. Webster wept convulsively as he stood beside the dead, and those who saw him so wrung by anguish of the heart never forgot the sight.

Thus the period which began at Portsmouth in 1807 closed in Boston, in 1817, with the death of the eldest born. In that decade Mr. Webster had advanced with great strides from the position of a raw and youthful lawyer in a back country town of New Hampshire. He had reached the highest professional eminence in his own State, and had removed to a wider sphere, where he at once took rank with the best lawyers. He was a leading practitioner in the highest national court. During his two terms in Congress he had become a leader of his party, and had won a solid national reputation. In those years he had rendered conspicuous service to the business interests of the nation, and had established himself as one of the ablest statesmen of the country in matters of finance. He had defined his position on the tariff as a free-trader in theory and a very moderate protectionist when protection was unavoidable, a true representative of the doctrine of the New England Federalists. He had taken up his ground as the champion of specie payments and of the liberal interpretation of the Constitution, which authorized internal improvements. While he had not shrunk from extreme opposition to the administration during the war, he had kept himself entirely clear from the separatist sentiment of New England in the year 1814. He left Congress with a realizing sense of his own growing powers, and, rejoicing in his strength, he turned to his profession and to his new duties in his new home.

CHAPTER III

THERE is a vague tradition that when Mr. Webster took up his residence in Boston, some of the
worthies of that ancient Puritan town were disposed at first to treat him rather cavalierly and
make him understand that because he was great
in New Hampshire it did not follow that he was
also great in Massachusetts. They found very
quickly, however, that it was worse than useless
to attempt anything of this sort with a man who,
by his mere look and presence whenever he entered a room, drew all eyes to himself and hushed
the murmur of conversation. It is certain that
Mr. Webster soon found himself the friend and
associate of all the agreeable and distinguished
men of the town, and that he rapidly acquired
that general popularity which, in those days, went
with him everywhere. It is also certain that he
at once and without effort assumed the highest
position at the bar as the recognized equal of its
most eminent leaders. With an income increased
tenfold and promising still further enlargement,
a practice in which one fee probably surpassed

the earnings of three months in New Hampshire, with an agreeable society about him, popular abroad, happy and beloved at home, nothing could have been more auspicious than these opening years of his life in Boston.

The period upon which he then entered, and during which he withdrew from active public service to devote himself to his profession, was a very important one in his career. It was a period marked by a rapid intellectual growth and by the first exhibition of his talents on a large scale. It embraces, moreover, two events, landmarks in the life of Mr. Webster, which placed him before the country as one of the first and the most eloquent of her constitutional lawyers, and as the great master in the art of occasional oratory. The first of these events was the argument in the Dartmouth College case; the second was the delivery of the Plymouth oration.

I do not propose to enter into or discuss the merits or demerits of the constitutional and legal theories and principles involved in the famous "college causes," or in any other of the great cases subsequently argued by Mr. Webster. In a biography of this kind it is sufficient to examine Mr. Webster's connection with the Dartmouth College case, and endeavor, by a study of his arguments in that and in certain other hardly less important causes, to estimate properly the character and quality of his abilities as a lawyer, both in the ordinary acceptation of the term and in dealing with constitutional questions.

The complete history of the Dartmouth College
case is very curious and deserves more than a passing notice.   Until within three years it is not too
much to say that it was quite unknown, and its
condition is but little better now.   In 1879 Mr.
John M. Shirley published a volume entitled the
"Dartmouth College Causes," which is a monument of careful study and thorough research.
Most persons would conclude that it was a work
of merely legal interest, appealing to a limited
class of professional readers.   Even those into
whose hands it chanced to come have probably
been deterred from examining it as it deserves by
the first chapter, which is very obscure, and by
the confusion of the narrative which follows.   Yet
this monograph, which has so unfortunately suffered from a defective arrangement of material, is
of very great value, not only to our legal and constitutional history, but to the political history of
the time and to a knowledge of the distinguished
actors in a series of events which resulted in the
establishment of one of the most far-reaching of
constitutional doctrines, one that has been a living
question ever since the year 1819, and is at this
moment of vast practical importance.   Mr. Shirley
has drawn forth from the oblivion of manuscript
a collection of documents which, taken in conjunction with those already in print, throws a flood of
light upon a dark place of the past and gives to
a dry constitutional question the vital and human
interest of political and personal history.

In his early days, Eleazer Wheelock, the founder of Dartmouth College, had had much religious controversy with Dr. Bellamy of Connecticut, who was like himself a graduate of Yale. Wheelock was a Presbyterian and a liberal, Bellamy a Congregationalist and strictly orthodox. The charter of Dartmouth was free from any kind of religious discrimination. By his will the elder Wheelock provided in such a way that his son succeeded him in the presidency of the college. In 1793 Judge Niles, a pupil of Bellamy, became a trustee of the college, and he and John Wheelock represented the opposite views which they respectively inherited from tutor and father. They were formed for mutual hostility, and the contest began some twelve years before it reached the public. The trustees and the president were then all Federalists, and there would seem to have been no differences of either a political or a religious nature. The trouble arose from the resistance of a minority of the trustees to what they termed the "family dynasty." Wheelock, however, maintained his ascendency until 1809, when his enemies obtained a majority in the board of trustees, and thereafter admitted no friend of the president to the government, and used every effort to subdue the dominant dynasty.

In New Hampshire, at that period, the Federalists were the ruling party, and the Congregationalists formed the state church. The people were, in practice, taxed to support Congregational churches, and the clergy of that denomination were exempted from taxation. All the Congregational ministers were stanch Federalists and most of their parishioners were of the same party. The college, the only seat of learning in the State, was one of the Federalist and Congregational strongholds.

After several years of fruitless and bitter conflict, the Wheelock party, in 1815, brought their grievances before the public in an elaborate pamphlet. This led to a rejoinder and a war of pamphlets ensued, which was soon transferred to the newspapers, and created a great sensation and a profound interest. Wheelock now contemplated legal proceedings. Mr. Plumer was in ill health, Judge Smith and Mr. Mason were allied with the trustees, and the president therefore went to Mr. Webster, consulted him professionally, paid him, and obtained a promise of his future services. About the time of this consultation, Wheelock sent a memorial to the legislature, charging the trustees with misapplication of the funds, and various breaches of trust, religious intolerance, and a violation of the charter in their attacks upon the presidential office, and prayed for a committee of investigation. The trustees met him boldly and offered a sturdy resistance, denying all the charges, especially that of religious intolerance; but the committee was voted by a large majority. On August 5, Wheelock, as soon as he learned that the committee was to have a hearing, wrote to Mr. Webster, reminding him of their consultation,

inclosing a fee of twenty dollars, and asking him
to appear before the committee. Mr. Webster
did not come, and Wheelock had to go on as best
he could without him. One of Wheelock's friends,
Mr. Dunham, wrote a very indignant letter to
Mr. Webster on his failure to appear; to which
Mr. Webster replied that he had seen Wheelock
and they had contemplated a suit in court, but
that at the time of the hearing he was otherwise
engaged, and moreover that he did not regard a
summons to appear before a legislative committee
as a professional call, adding that he was by no
means sure that the president was wholly in the
right. The truth was, that many of Mr. Webster's strongest personal and political friends, and
most of the leaders with whom he was associated
in the control of the Federalist party, were either
trustees themselves or closely allied with the trustees. In the interval between the consultation
with Wheelock and the committee hearing, these
friends and leaders saw Mr. Webster, and pointed
out to him that he must not desert them, and that
this college controversy was fast developing into
a party question. Mr. Webster was convinced,
and abandoned Wheelock, making, as has been
seen, a very unsatisfactory explanation of his conduct. In this way he finally parted company with
Wheelock, and was thereafter irrevocably engaged
on the side of the trustees.

Events now moved rapidly. The trustees, without heeding the advice of Mr. Mason to delay,

removed Wheelock from the presidency, and appointed in his place the Rev. Francis Brown. This fanned the flame of popular excitement, and such a defiance of the legislative committee threw the whole question into politics. As Mr. Mason had foreseen when he warned the trustees against hasty action, all the Democrats, all members of sects other than the Congregational, and all freethinkers generally, were united against the trustees, and consequently against the Federalists. The election came on. Wheelock, who was a Federalist, went over to the enemy, carrying his friends with him, and Mr. Plumer, the Democratic candidate, was elected governor, together with a Democratic legislature. Mr. Webster perceived at once that the trustees were in a bad position. He advised that every effort should be made to soothe the Democrats, and that the purpose of founding a new college should be noised abroad, in order to create alarm. Strategy, however, was vain. Governor Plumer declared against the trustees in his message, and the legislature, in June, 1816, despite every sort of protest and remonstrance, passed an act to reorganize the college, and virtually to place it within the control of the State. The governor and council at once proceeded to choose trustees and overseers under the new law, and among those thus selected was Joseph Story of Massachusetts.

Both boards of trustees assembled. The old board turned out Judge Woodward, their secretary, who was a friend to Wheelock and secretary also of the new board, and, receiving a thousand dollars from a friend of one of the professors, resolved to fight. President Brown refused to obey the summons of the new trustees, who expelled the old board by resolution. Thereupon the old board brought suit against Woodward for the college seal and other property, and the case came on for trial in May, 1817. Mr. Mason and Judge Smith appeared for the college, George Sullivan and Ichabod Bartlett for Woodward and the state board. The case was argued and then went over to the September term of the same year, at Exeter, when Mason and Smith were joined by Mr. Webster.

The cause was then argued again on both sides and with signal ability. In point of talent the counsel for the college were vastly superior to their opponents, but Sullivan and Bartlett were nevertheless strong men and thoroughly prepared. Sullivan was a good lawyer and a fluent and ready speaker, with great power of illustration. Bartlett was a shrewd, hard-headed man, very keen and incisive, and one whom it was impossible to outwit or deceive. He indulged, in his argument, in some severe reflections upon Mr. Webster's conduct toward Wheelock, which so much incensed Mr. Webster that he referred to Mr. Bartlett's argument in a most contemptuous way, and strenuously opposed the publication of the remarks "personal or injurious to counsel."

The weight of the argument for the college fell upon Mason and Smith, who spoke for two and four hours respectively. Sullivan and Bartlett occupied three hours, and the next day Mr. Webster closed for the plaintiffs in a speech of two hours. Mr. Webster spoke with great force, going evidently beyond the limits of legal argument, and winding up with a splendid sentimental appeal which drew tears from the crowd in the Exeter court-room, and which he afterwards used in an elaborated form and with similar effect before the Supreme Court at Washington.

It now becomes necessary to state briefly the points at issue in this case, which were all fully argued by the counsel on both sides. Mr. Mason's brief, which really covered the whole case, was that the acts of the legislature were not obligatory, 1, because they were not within the general scope of legislative power; 2, because they violated certain provisions of the Constitution of New Hampshire restraining legislative power; 3, because they violated the Constitution of the United States. In Farrar's report of Mason's speech, twenty-three pages are devoted to the first point, eight to the second, and six to the third. In other words, the third point, involving the great constitutional doctrine on which the case was finally decided at Washington, the doctrine that the legislature, by its acts, had impaired the obligation of a contract, was passed over lightly. In so doing Mr. Mason was not alone. Neither he nor Judge Smith nor

Mr. Webster nor the court nor the counsel on the other side, attached much importance to this point. Curiously enough, the theory had been originated many years before, by Wheelock himself, at a time when he expected that the minority of the trustees would invoke the aid of the legislature against him, and his idea had been remembered. It was revived at the time of the newspaper controversy, and was pressed upon the attention of the trustees and upon that of their counsel. But the lawyers attached little weight to the suggestion, although they introduced it and argued it briefly. Mason, Smith, and Webster all relied for success on the ground covered by the first point in Mason's brief. This is called by Mr. Shirley the "Parsons' view," from the fact that it was largely drawn from an argument made by Chief Justice Parsons in regard to visitatorial powers at Harvard College. Briefly stated, the argument was that the college was an institution founded by private persons for particular uses; that the charter was given to perpetuate such uses; that misconduct of the trustees was a question for the courts, and that the legislature, by its interference, transcended its powers. To these general principles, strengthened by particular clauses in the Constitution of New Hampshire, the counsel for the college trusted for victory. The theory of impairing the obligation of contracts they introduced, but they did not insist on it, or hope for much from it. On this point, however, and, of course, on this alone, the case

went up to the Supreme Court. In December,
1817, Mr. Webster wrote to Mr. Mason, regret-
ting that the case went up on "one point only."
He occupied himself at this time in devising cases
which should raise what he considered the really
vital points, and which, coming within the jurisdiction of the United States, could be taken to the
Circuit Court, and thence to the Supreme Court
at Washington. These cases, in accordance with
his suggestion, were begun, but before they came
on in the Circuit Court, Mr. Webster made his
great effort in Washington. Three quarters of
his legal argument were there devoted to the points
in the Circuit Court cases, which were not in any
way before the Supreme Court in the College v.
Woodward. So little, indeed, did Mr. Webster
think of the great constitutional question which
has made the case famous, that he forced the other
points in where he admitted that they had no
proper standing, and argued them at length.
They were touched upon by Marshall, who, however, decided wholly upon the constitutional question, and they were all thrown aside by Judge
Washington, who declared them irrelevant, and
rested his decision solely and properly on the constitutional point. Two months after his Washington argument, Mr. Webster, still urging forward
the Circuit Court cases, wrote to Mr. Mason that
all the questions must be brought properly before
the Supreme Court, and that, on the "general
principle" that the state legislature could not

divest vested rights, strengthened by the constitutional provisions of New Hampshire, he was sure they could defeat their adversaries. Thus this doctrine of "impairing the obligation of contracts," which produced a decision in its effects more far-reaching and of more general interest than perhaps any other ever made in this country, was imported into the case at the suggestion of laymen, was little esteemed by counsel, and was comparatively neglected in every argument.

It is necessary to go back now, for a moment, in the history of the case. The New Hampshire court decided against the plaintiffs on every point, and gave a very strong and elaborate judgment, which Mr. Webster acknowledged was "able, plausible, and ingenious." After much wrangling, the counsel agreed on a special verdict, and took the case up on a writ of error to the Supreme Court. Mason and Smith were unable or unwilling to go to Washington, and the case was intrusted to Mr. Webster, who secured the assistance of Mr. Joseph Hopkinson of Philadelphia. The case for the State, hitherto ably managed, was now confided to Mr. John Holmes of Maine, and Mr. Wirt, the attorney-general, who handled it very badly. Holmes, an active, fluent Democratic politician, made a noisy, rhetorical, political speech, which pleased his opponents and disgusted his clients and their friends. Mr. Wirt, loaded with business cares of every sort, came into court quite unprepared, and endeavored to make up for his deficiencies by declamation. On the other side the case was managed with consummate skill. Hopkinson was a sound lawyer, and, being thoroughly prepared, made a good legal argument. The burden of the conflict was, however, borne by Mr. Webster, who was more interested personally than professionally, and who, having raised money in Boston to defray the expenses of the suit, came into the arena at Washington armed to the teeth, and in the full lustre of his great powers.

The case was heard on March 10, 1818, and was opened by Mr. Webster. He had studied the arguments of his adversaries below, and the vigorous hostile opinion of the New Hampshire judges. He was in possession of the thorough argument emanating from the penetrating mind of Mr. Mason and fortified and extended by the ample learning and judicial wisdom of Judge Smith. To the work of his eminent associates he could add nothing more than one not very important point, and a few cases which his far-ranging and retentive memory supplied. All the notes, minutes, and arguments of Smith and Mason were in his hands. It is only just to say that Mr. Webster tells all this himself, and that he gives all credit to his colleagues, whose arguments he says "he clumsily put together," and of which he adds that he could only be the reciter. The faculty of obtaining and using the valuable work of other men, one of the characteristic qualities of a high and commanding order of mind, was even then strong in Mr.

Webster. But in that bright period of early manhood it was accompanied by a frank and generous
acknowledgment of all and more than all the
intellectual aid he received from others. He truly
and properly awarded to Mason and Smith all
the credit for the law and for the legal points and
theories set forth on their side, and modestly says
that he was merely the arranger and reciter of
other men's thoughts. But how much that arrangement and recitation meant! There were,
perhaps, no lawyers better fitted than Mason and
Smith to examine a case and prepare an argument
enriched with everything that learning and sagacity could suggest. But when Mr. Webster burst
upon the court and the nation with his great appeal, it was certain that there was no man in the
land who could so arrange arguments and facts,
who could state them so powerfully and with such
a grand and fitting eloquence.

The legal part of the argument was printed in
Farrar's report and also in Wheaton's, after it
had been carefully revised by Mr. Webster with
the arguments of his colleagues before him. This
legal and constitutional discussion shows plainly
enough Mr. Webster's easy and firm grasp of
facts and principles, and his power of strong, effective, and lucid statement; but it is in its very
nature dry, cold, and lawyer-like. It gives no
conception of the glowing vehemence of the delivery, or of those omitted portions of the speech
which dealt with matters outside the domain of

law, and which were introduced by Mr. Webster with such telling and important results. He spoke for five hours, but in the printed report his speech occupies only three pages more than that of Mr. Mason in the court below. Both were slow speakers, and thus there is a great difference in time to be accounted for, even after making every allowance for the peroration which we have from another source, and for the wealth of legal and historical illustration with which Mr. Webster amplified his presentation of the question. "Something was left out," Mr. Webster says, and that something which must have occupied in its delivery nearly an hour was the most conspicuous example of the generalship by which Mr. Webster achieved victory, and which was wholly apart from his law. This art of management had already been displayed in the treatment of the cases made up for the Circuit Courts, and in the elaborate and irrelevant legal discussion which Mr. Webster introduced before the Supreme Court. But this management now entered on a much higher stage, where it was destined to win victory, and exhibited in a high degree tact and knowledge of men. Mr. Webster was fully aware that he could rely, in any aspect of the case, upon the sympathy of Marshall and Washington. He was equally certain of the unyielding opposition of Duvall and Todd; the other three judges, Johnson, Livingston, and Story, were known to be adverse to the college, but were possible converts. The first point was to increase the sympathy of the chief justice to an eager and even passionate support. Mr. Webster knew the chord to strike, and he touched it with a master hand. This was the "something left out," of which we know the general drift, and we can easily imagine the effect. In the midst of all the legal and constitutional arguments, relevant and irrelevant, even in the pathetic appeal which he used so well in behalf of his Alma Mater, Mr. Webster boldly and yet skillfully introduced the political view of the case. So delicately did he do it that an attentive listener did not realize that he was straying from the field of "mere reason" into that of political passion. Here no man could equal him or help him, for here his eloquence had full scope, and on this he relied to arouse Marshall, whom he thoroughly understood. In occasional sentences he pictured his beloved college under the wise rule of Federalists and of the Church. He depicted the party assault that was made upon her. He showed the citadel of learning threatened with unholy invasion and falling helplessly into the hands of Jacobins and free-thinkers. As the tide of his resistless and solemn eloquence, mingled with his masterly argument, flowed on, we can imagine how the great chief justice roused like an old war-horse at the sound of the trumpet. The words of the speaker carried him back to the early years of the century, when, in the full flush of manhood, at the head of his court, the last stronghold of Federalism, the last bulwark of sound government, he had faced the power of the triumphant Democrats. Once more it was Marshall against Jefferson, — the judge against the President. Then he had preserved the ark of the Constitution. Then he had seen the angry waves of popular feeling breaking vainly at his feet. Now, in his old age, the conflict was revived. Jacobinism was raising its sacrilegious hand against the temples of learning, against the friends of order and good government. The joy of battle must have glowed once more in the old man's breast as he grasped anew his weapons and prepared with all the force of his indomitable will to raise yet another constitutional barrier across the path of his ancient enemies.

We cannot but feel that Mr. Webster's lost passages, embodying this political appeal, did the work, and that the result was settled when the political passions of the chief justice were fairly aroused. Marshall would probably have brought about the decision by the sole force of his imperious will. But Mr. Webster did a good deal of effective work after the arguments were all finished, and no account of the case would be complete without a glance at the famous peroration with which he concluded his speech and in which he boldly flung aside all vestige of legal reasoning, and spoke directly to the passions and emotions of his hearers.

When he had finished his argument he stood silent for some moments, until every eye was fixed upon him, then, addressing the chief justice, he said: —

"This, sir, is my case. It is the case not merely of that humble institution, it is the case of every college in our land. . . .

"Sir, you may destroy this little institution; it is weak; it is in your hands! I know it is one of the lesser lights in the literary horizon of our country. You may put it out. But if you do so you must carry through your work! You must extinguish, one after another, all those greater lights of science which for more than a century have thrown their radiance over our land. It is, sir, as I have said, a small college. And yet there are those who love it."

Here his feelings mastered him; his eyes filled with tears, his lips quivered, his voice was choked. In broken words of tenderness he spoke of his attachment to the college, and his tones seemed filled with the memories of home and boyhood; of early affections and youthful privations and struggles.

"The court-room," says Mr. Goodrich, to whom we owe this description, "during these two or three minutes presented an extraordinary spectacle. Chief Justice Marshall, with his tall and gaunt figure bent over as if to catch the slightest whisper, the deep furrows of his cheek expanded with emotion and his eyes suffused with tears; Mr. Justice Washington, at his side, with his small and emaciated frame, and countenance more like marble than I ever saw on any other human being, — leaning forward with an eager, troubled look; and

the remainder of the court at the two extremities, pressing, as it were, to a single point, while the audience
below were wrapping themselves round in closer folds
beneath the bench, to catch each look and every movement of the speaker's face. . . .

"Mr. Webster had now recovered his composure, and,
fixing his keen eye on the chief justice, said in that
deep tone with which he sometimes thrilled the heart of
an audience : —

"'Sir, I know not how others may feel' (glancing
at the opponents of the college before him), 'but for
myself, when I see my Alma Mater surrounded, like
Cæsar in the senate-house, by those who are reiterating
stab after stab, I would not, for this right hand, have
her turn to me, and say, *Et tu quoque, mi fili! And
thou too, my son!*'"

This outbreak of feeling was perfectly genuine.
Apart from his personal relations to the college,
he had the true oratorical temperament, and no
man can be an orator in the highest sense unless
he feels intensely, for the moment at least, the
truth and force of every word he utters. To move
others deeply he must be deeply moved himself.
Yet at the same time Mr. Webster's peroration,
and, indeed, his whole speech, was a model of
consummate art. Great lawyer as he undoubtedly
was, he felt on this occasion that he could not rely
on legal argument and pure reason alone. Without appearing to go beyond the line of propriety,
without indulging in a declamation unsuited to the
place, he had to step outside of legal points and in

a freer air, where he could use his keenest and strongest weapons, appeal to the court not as lawyers but as men subject to passion, emotion, and prejudice. This he did boldly, delicately, successfully, and thus he won his case.

The replies of the opposing counsel were poor enough after such a speech. Holmes's declamation sounded rather cheap, and Mr. Wirt, thrown off his balance by Mr. Webster's exposure of his ignorance, did but slight justice to himself or his cause. March 12 the arguments were closed, and the next day, after a conference, the chief justice announced that the court could agree on nothing and that the cause must be continued for a year, until the next term. The fact probably was that Marshall found the judges five to two against the college, and that the task of bringing them into line was not a light one.

In this undertaking, however, he was powerfully aided by the counsel and all the friends of the college. The old board of trustees had already paid much attention to public opinion. The press was largely Federalist, and, under the pressure of what was made a party question, they had espoused warmly the cause of the college. Letters and essays had appeared, and pamphlets had been circulated, together with the arguments of the counsel at Exeter. This work was pushed with increased eagerness after the argument at Washington, and the object now was to create about the three doubtful judges an atmosphere of public opinion which

should imperceptibly bring them over to the college.   Johnson, Livingston, and Story were all
men who would have started at the barest suspicion of outside influence even in the most legiti-
mate form of argument, which was all that was
ever thought of or attempted. This made the
task of the trustees very delicate and difficult in
developing a public sentiment which should sway
the judges without their being aware of it.   The
printed arguments of Mason, Smith, and Webster
were carefully sent to certain of the judges, but
not to all.   All documents of a similar character
found their way to the same quarters.   The leading Federalists were aroused everywhere, so that
the judges might be made to feel their opinion.
With Story, as a New England man, a Democrat
by circumstances, a Federalist by nature, there
was but little difficulty.   A thorough review of
the case, joined with Mr. Webster's argument,
caused him soon to change his first impression.
To reach Livingston and Johnson was not so easy,
for they were out of New England, and it was
necessary to go a long way round to get at them.
The great legal upholder of Federalism in New
York was Chancellor Kent.   His first impression,
like that of Story, was decidedly against the college, but after much effort on the part of the trustees and their able allies, Kent was converted,
partly through his reason, partly through his Federalism, and then his powers of persuasion and
his great influence on opinion came to bear very

directly on Livingston, more remotely on Johnson. The whole business was managed like a quiet, decorous political campaign. The press and the party were everywhere actively interested. At first, and in the early summer of 1818, before Kent was converted, matters looked badly for the trustees. Mr. Webster knew the complexion of the court, and hoped little from the point raised in Trustees *v.* Woodward. Still, no one despaired, and the work was kept up until, in September, President Brown wrote to Mr. Webster in reference to the argument: —

" It has already been, or shortly will be, read by all the *commanding* men of New England and New York ; and so far as it has gone it has united them all, without a single exception within my knowledge, in one broad and impenetrable phalanx for our defense and support. New England and New York *are gained.* Will not this be sufficient for our present purposes ? If not, I should recommend reprinting. And on this point you are the best judge. I prevailingly think, however, that the current of opinion from this part of the country is setting so strongly towards the South that we may safely trust to its force alone to accomplish whatever is necessary."

The worthy clergyman writes of public opinion as if the object was to elect a president. All this effort, however, was well applied, as was found when the court came together at the next term. In the interval the State had become sensible of the defects of their counsel, and had retained Mr. Pinkney, who stood at that time at the head of

the bar of the United States. He had all the
qualifications of a great lawyer, except perhaps
that of robustness. He was keen, strong, and
learned; diligent in preparation, he was ready and
fluent in action, a good debater, and master of a
high order of eloquence. He was a most formidable adversary, and one whom Mr. Webster,
then just at the outset of his career, had probably
no desire to meet in such a doubtful case as this.[1]
Even here, however, misfortune seemed to pursue
the State, for Mr. Pinkney was on bad terms with
Mr. Wirt, and acted alone. He did all that was
possible; prepared himself elaborately in the law
and history of the case, and then went into court

[1] Mr. Peter Harvey, in his *Reminiscences* (p. 122), has an anecdote in regard to Webster and Pinkney, which places the former
in the light of a common and odious bully, an attitude as alien to
Mr. Webster's character as can well be conceived. The story is
undoubtedly either wholly fictitious or so grossly exaggerated as
to be practically false. In a pamphlet by the Right Reverend
William Pinkney published in 1878, of which I did not know
when this note was published, the Harvey story is completely
refuted. On the page preceding the account of this incident,
Mr. Harvey makes Webster say that he never received a challenge from Randolph, whereas in Webster's own letter, published
by Mr. Curtis, there is express reference to a note of challenge
received from Randolph. This is a fair example of these *Reminiscences*. A more untrustworthy book it would be impossible
to imagine. There is not a statement in it which can be safely
accepted, unless supported by other evidence. It puts its subject
throughout in the most unpleasant light, and nothing has ever
been written about Webster so well calculated to injure and
belittle him as these feeble and distorted recollections of his loving and devoted Boswell. It is the reflection of a great man
upon the mirror of a small mind and weak memory.

ready to make the wisest possible move by asking
for a reargument. Marshall, however, was also
quite prepared. Turning his "blind ear," as some
one said, to Pinkney, he announced, as soon as he
took his seat, that the judges had come to a conclusion during the vacation. He then read one
of his great opinions, in which he held that the
college charter was a contract within the meaning
of the Constitution, and that the acts of the New
Hampshire legislature impaired this contract, and
were therefore void. To this decision four judges
assented in silence, although Story and Washington subsequently wrote out opinions. Judge Todd
was absent, through illness, and Judge Duvall
dissented. The immediate effect of the decision
was to leave the college in the hands of the victorious Federalists. In the precedent which it established, however, it had much deeper and more
far-reaching results. It brought within the scope
of the Constitution of the United States every
charter granted by a State, limited the action of
the States in a most important attribute of sover-
eignty, and extended the jurisdiction of the highest federal court more than any other judgment
ever rendered by them. From the day when it
was announced to the present time, the doctrine
of Marshall in the Dartmouth College case has
continued to exert an enormous influence, and has
been constantly sustained and attacked in litiga-
tion of the greatest importance.

The defendant Woodward having died, Mr.

Webster moved that the judgment be entered *nunc pro tunc*. Pinkney and Wirt objected on the ground that the other causes on the docket contained additional facts, and that no final judgment should be entered until these causes had been heard. The court, however, granted Mr. Webster's motion. Mr. Pinkney then tried to avail himself of the stipulation in regard to the special verdict, that any new and material facts might be added or any facts expunged. Mr. Webster peremptorily declined to permit any change, obtained judgment against Woodward, and obliged Mr. Pinkney to consent that the other causes should be remanded, without instructions, to the Circuit Court, where they were heard by Judge Story, who rendered a decree *nisi* for the college. This closed the case, and such were the last displays of Mr. Webster's dexterous and vigorous management of the famous "college causes."

The popular opinion of this case seems to be that Mr. Webster, with the aid of Mr. Mason and Judge Smith, developed a great constitutional argument, which he forced upon the acceptance of the court by the power of his close and logical reasoning, and thus established an interpretation of the Constitution of vast moment. The truth is that the suggestion of the constitutional point, not a very remarkable idea in itself, originated, as has been said, with a layman, was regarded by Mr. Webster as a forlorn hope, and was very briefly discussed by him before the Supreme Court.

He knew, of course, that if the case were to be decided against Woodward, it could only be on the constitutional point, but he evidently thought that the court would not take the view of it which was favorable to the college. The Dartmouth College case was unquestionably one of Mr. Webster's great achievements at the bar, but it has been rightly praised on mistaken grounds. Mr. Webster made a very fine presentation of the arguments mainly prepared by Mason and Smith. He transcended the usual legal limits with a burst of eloquent appeal which stands high among the famous passages of his oratory. In what may be called the strategy of the case he showed the best generalship and the most skillful management. He also proved himself to be possessed of great tact and to be versed in the knowledge of men, qualities not usually attributed to him because their exercise involved an amount of care and painstaking foreign to his indolent and royal temperament, which almost always relied on weight and force for victory.

Mr. Webster no doubt improved in details, and made better arguments at the bar than he did upon this occasion, but the Dartmouth College case, on the whole, shows his legal talents so nearly at their best, and in such unusual variety, that it is a fit point at which to pause in order to consider some of his other great legal arguments and his position and abilities as a lawyer. For this purpose it is quite sufficient to confine ourselves to the cases mentioned by Mr. Curtis, and to the legal arguments preserved in the collection of Mr. Webster's speeches.

Five years after the Dartmouth College decision, Mr. Webster made his famous argument in the case of Gibbons v. Ogden. The case was called suddenly, and Mr. Webster prepared his argument in a single night of intense labor. The facts were all before him, but he showed a readiness in arrangement only equaled by its force. The question was whether the State of New York had a right under the Constitution to grant a monopoly of steam navigation in its waters to Fulton and Livingston. Mr. Webster contended that the acts making such a grant were unconstitutional, because the power of Congress to regulate commerce was, within certain limitations, exclusive. He won his cause, and the decision, from its importance, probably enhanced the contemporary estimate of his effort. The argument was badly reported, but it shows all its author's strongest qualities of close reasoning and effective statement. The point in issue was neither difficult nor obscure, and afforded no opportunity for a display of learning. It was purely a matter of constitutional interpretation, and could be discussed chiefly in a historical manner and from the standpoint of public interests. This was particularly fitted to Mr. Webster's cast of mind, and he did his subject full justice. It was pure argument on general principles. Mr. Webster does not reach that point of intense clearness and condensation which characterized Marshall and Hamilton, in whose writings we are fascinated by the beauty of the intellectual display, and are held fast by each succeeding line, which always comes charged with fresh meaning. Nevertheless, Mr. Webster touches a very high point in this most difficult form of argument, and the impressiveness of his manner and voice carried all that he said to its mark with a direct force in which he stood unrivaled.

In Ogden v. Saunders, heard in 1827, Mr. Webster argued that the clause prohibiting state laws impairing the obligation of contracts covered future as well as past contracts. He defended his difficult position with astonishing ability, but the court very correctly decided against him. The same qualities which appear in these cases are shown in the others of a like nature, which were conspicuous among the multitude with which he was intrusted. We find them also in cases involving purely legal questions, such as the Bank of the United States v. Primrose, and The Providence Railroad Co. v. The City of Boston, accompanied always with that ready command of learning which an extraordinary memory made easy. There seemed to be no diminution of Mr. Webster's great powers in this field as he advanced in years. In the Rhode Island case and in the Passenger Tax cases, argued when he was sixty-six years old, he rose to the same high plane of clear, impressive, effective reasoning as when he defended his Alma Mater.

Two causes, however, demand more than a passing mention, — the Girard will case and the Rhode Island case. The former involved no constitutional points. The suit was brought to break the will of Stephen Girard, and the question was whether the bequest to found a college could be construed to be a charitable devise. On this question Mr. Webster had a weak case in point of law, but he readily detected a method by which he could go boldly outside the law, as he had done to a certain degree in the Dartmouth College case, and substitute for argument an eloquent and impassioned appeal to emotion and prejudice. Girard was a free-thinker, and he provided in his will that no priest or minister of any denomination should be admitted to his college. Assuming that this excluded all religious teaching, Mr. Webster then laid down the proposition that no bequest or gift could be charitable which excluded Christian teaching. In other words, he contended that there was no charity except Christian charity, which, the poet assures us, is so rare. At this day such a theory would hardly be gravely propounded by any one. But Mr. Webster, on the ground that Girard's bequest was derogatory to Christianity, pronounced a very fine discourse defending and eulogizing, with much eloquence, the Christian religion. The speech produced a great effect. One is inclined to think that it was the cause of the court's evading the question raised by Mr. Webster, and sustaining the will, a result they were bound to reach in any event, on other grounds. The speech certainly produced a great sensation, and was much admired, especially by the clergy, who caused it to be printed and widely distributed. It did not impress lawyers quite so favorably, and we find Judge Story writing to Chancellor Kent that "Webster did his best for the other side, but it seems to me altogether an address to the prejudices of the clergy." The subject, in certain ways, had a deep attraction for Mr. Webster. His imagination was excited by the splendid history of the Church, and his conservatism was deeply stirred by a system which, whether in the guise of the Romish hierarchy, or the Church of England, or in the form of powerful dissenting sects, was, as a whole, imposing by its age, its influence, and its moral grandeur. Moreover, it was one of the great established bulwarks of well-ordered and civilized society. All this appealed strongly to Mr. Webster, and he made the most of his opportunity and of his shrewdly-chosen ground. Yet the speech on the Girard will is not one of his best efforts. It has not the subdued but intense fire which glowed so splendidly in his great speeches in the Senate. It lacked the stately pathos which came always when Mr. Webster was deeply moved. It was delivered in 1844, and was slightly tinged with the pompousness which manifested itself in his late years, and especially on religious topics.

No man has a right to question the religious sincerity of another, unless upon evidence so full and clear that, in such cases, it is rarely to be found. There is certainly no cause for doubt in Mr. Webster's case. He was both sincere and honest in religion, and had a real and submissive faith. But he accepted his religion as one of the great facts and proprieties of life. He did not reach his religious convictions after much burning questioning and many bitter experiences. In this he did not differ from most men of this age, and it only amounts to saying that Mr. Webster did not possess a deeply religious temperament. He did not have the ardent proselyting spirit which is the surest indication of a profoundly religious nature; the spirit of the Saracen emir crying, "Forward! Paradise is under the shadow of our swords." When, therefore, he turned his noble powers to a defense of religion, he did not speak with that impassioned fervor which, coming from the depths of a man's heart, savors of inspiration and seems essential to the highest religious eloquence. He believed thoroughly every word he uttered, but he did not feel it, and in things spiritual the heart must be enlisted as well as the head. It was wittily said of a well-known anti-slavery leader, that had he lived in the Middle Ages he would have gone to the stake for a principle, under a misapprehension as to the facts. Mr. Webster not only could never have misapprehended facts, but, if he had flourished in the Middle Ages he would have

been a stanch and honest supporter of the strongest government and of the dominant church. Perhaps this defines his religious character as well as
anything, and explains why the argument in the
Girard will case, fine as it was, did not reach the
elevation and force which he so often displayed
upon other themes.

The Rhode Island case grew out of the troubles
known at that period as Dorr's rebellion. It
involved a discussion not only of the constitutional
provisions for suppressing insurrections and securing to every State a republican form of government, but also of the general history and theory
of the American governments, both state and national. There was thus offered to Mr. Webster
that full scope and large field in which he delighted, and which were always peculiarly favorable to his talents. His argument was purely
constitutional, and although not so closely reasoned, perhaps, as some of his earlier efforts, is,
on the whole, as fine a specimen as we have of his
intellectual power as a constitutional lawyer at the
bar of the highest national tribunal. Mr. Webster did not often transcend the proper limits of
purely legal discussion in the courts, and yet even
when the question was wholly legal, the court-
room would be crowded by women as well as men,
to hear him speak. It was so at the hearing
of the Girard suit; and during the strictly legal
arguments in the Charles River Bridge case, the
court-room, Judge Story says, was filled with a

brilliant audience, including many ladies, and he adds that "Webster's closing reply was in his best manner, but with a little too much *fierté* here and there." The ability to attract such audiences gives an idea of the impressiveness of his manner and of the beauty of his voice and delivery better than anything else, for these qualities alone could have drawn the general public and held their attention to the cold and dry discussion of laws and constitutions.

There is a little anecdote told by Mr. Curtis in connection with this Rhode Island case, which illustrates very well two striking qualities in Mr. Webster as a lawyer. The counsel in the court below had been assisted by a clever young lawyer named Bosworth, who had elaborated a point which he thought very important, but which his seniors rejected. Mr. Bosworth was sent to Washington to instruct Mr. Webster as to the cause, and, after he had gone through the case, Mr. Webster asked if that was all. Mr. Bosworth modestly replied that there was another view of his own which his seniors had rejected, and then stated it briefly. When he concluded, Mr. Webster started up and exclaimed, "Mr. Bosworth, by the blood of all the Bosworths who fell on Bosworth field, that is *the* point of the case. Let it be included in the brief by all means." This is highly characteristic of one of Mr. Webster's strongest attributes. He always saw with an unerring glance "*the* point" of a case or a debate. A great surgeon will detect

the precise spot where the knife should enter when
disease hides it from other eyes, and often with
apparent carelessness will make the necessary in-
cision at the exact place when a deflection of a
hair's breadth or a tremor of the hand would bring
death to the patient.   Mr. Webster had the same
intellectual dexterity, the mingled result of nature
and art.   As the tiger is said to have a sure instinct for the throat of his victim, so Mr. Webster
always seized on the vital point of a question.
Other men would debate and argue for days, perhaps, and then Mr. Webster would take up the
matter, and grasp at once the central and essential
element which had been there all along, pushed
hither and thither, but which had escaped all eyes
but his own.   He had preëminently

> " The calm eye that seeks
> 'Midst all the huddling silver little worth
> The one thin piece that comes, pure gold."

The anecdote further illustrates the use which
Mr. Webster made of the ideas of other people.
He did not say to Mr. Bosworth, here is the true
point of the case, but he saw that something was
wanting, and asked the young lawyer what it was.
The moment the proposition was stated he recognized its value and importance at a glance.   He
might and probably would have discovered it for
himself, but his instinct was to get it from some
one else.

It is one of the familiar attributes of great intellectual power to be able to select subordinates

wisely; to use other people and other people's
labor and thought to the best advantage, and to
have as much as possible done for one by others.
This power of assimilation Mr. Webster had to a
marked degree. There is no depreciation in saying that he took much from others, for it is a
capacity characteristic of the strongest minds, and
so long as the debt is acknowledged, such a faculty
is a subject for praise, not criticism. But when
the recipient becomes unwilling to admit the obligation which is no detraction to himself, and without which the giver is poor indeed, the case is
altered. In his earliest days Mr. Webster used
to draw on one Parker Noyes, a mousing, learned
New Hampshire lawyer, and freely acknowledged
the debt. In the Dartmouth College case, as has
been seen, he over and over again gave simply and
generously all the credit for the learning and the
points of the brief to Mason and Smith, and yet
the glory of the case has rested with Mr. Webster
and always will. He gained by his frank honesty
and did not lose a whit. But in his latter days,
when his sense of justice had grown somewhat
blunted and his nature was perverted by the un-
measured adulation of the little immediate circle
which then hung about him, he ceased to admit
his obligations as in his earlier and better years.
From no one did Mr. Webster receive so much
hearty and generous advice and assistance as from
Judge Story, whose calm judgment and wealth of
learning were always at his disposal. They were

given not only in questions of law, but in regard
to the Crimes Act, the Judiciary Act, and the
Ashburton treaty. After Judge Story's death,
Mr. Webster not only declined to allow the publication by the judge's son and biographer of Story's
letters to himself, but he refused to permit even
the publication of extracts from his own letters,
intended merely to show the nature of the services
rendered to him by Story. A cordial assent would
have enhanced the reputation of both. The refusal is a blot on the intellectual greatness of the
one and a source of bitterness to the descendants
and admirers of the other. It is to be regretted
that the extraordinary ability which Mr. Webster
always showed in grasping and assimilating masses
of theories and facts, and in drawing from them
what was best, should ever have been sullied by
a want of gratitude which, properly and freely
rendered, would have made the lustre of his own
fame shine still more brightly.

A close study of Mr. Webster's legal career, in
the light of contemporary reputation and of the
best examples of his work, leads to certain quite
obvious conclusions. He had not a strongly original or creative legal mind. This was chiefly due
to nature, but in some measure to a dislike to the
slow processes of investigation and inquiry, which
were always distasteful to him, although he was
entirely capable of intense and protracted exertion.
He cannot, therefore, be ranked with the illustri-
ous few, among whom we count Mansfield and

Marshall as the most brilliant examples, who not only declared what the law was, but who made it. Mr. Webster's powers were not of this class, yet, except in these highest and rarest qualities, he stands in the front rank of the lawyers of his country and his age. Without extraordinary profundity of thought or depth of learning, he had a wide, sure, and ready knowledge both of principles and cases. Add to this quick apprehension, unerring sagacity for vital and essential points, a perfect sense of proportion, an almost unequaled power of statement, backed by reasoning at once close and lucid, and we may fairly say that Mr. Webster, who possessed all these qualities, need fear comparison with but very few among the great lawyers of that period either at home or abroad.

CHAPTER IV

THE MASSACHUSETTS CONVENTION AND THE PLYMOUTH ORATION

THE conduct of the Dartmouth College case, and its result, at once raised Mr. Webster to a position at the bar second only to that held by Mr. Pinkney. He was now constantly occupied by most important and lucrative engagements, but in 1820 he was called upon to take a leading part in a great public work which demanded the exertion of all his talents as statesman, lawyer, and debater. The lapse of time and the setting off of the Maine district as a State had made a convention necessary, in order to revise the Constitution of Massachusetts. This involved the direct resort to the people, the source of all power, which is only required to effect a change in the fundamental law of the State. On these rare occasions it has been the honored custom in Massachusetts to lay aside all the qualifications attaching to ordinary legislatures and to choose the best men, without regard to party, public office, or domicile, for the performance of this important work. No better or abler body could have been assembled for this purpose than that which met in convention at

Boston in November, 1820. Among these distinguished men were John Adams, then in his eighty-fifth year, and one of the framers of the original Constitution of 1780, Chief Justice Parker, of the Supreme Bench, the Federal judges, and many of the leaders at the bar and in business. The two most conspicuous men in the convention, however, were Joseph Story and Daniel Webster, who bore the burden in every discussion; and there were three subjects, upon which Mr. Webster spoke at length, that deserve more than a passing allusion.

Questions of party have, as a rule, found but little place in the constitutional assemblies of Massachusetts. This was peculiarly the case in 1820, when the old political divisions were dying out, and new ones had not yet been formed. At the same time widely opposite views found expression in the convention. The movement toward thorough and complete democracy was gathering headway, and directing its force against many of the old colonial traditions and habits of government embodied in the existing Constitution. That portion of the delegates which favored certain radical changes was confronted and stoutly opposed by those who, on the whole, inclined to make as few alterations as possible, and desired to keep things about as they were. Mr. Webster, as was natural, was the leader of the conservative party, and his course in this convention is an excellent illustration of this marked trait in his disposition and character.

One of the important questions concerned the abolition of the profession of Christian faith as a qualification for holding office. On this point the line of argument pursued by Mr. Webster is extremely characteristic. Although an unvarying conservative throughout his life, he was incapable of bigotry, or of narrow and illiberal views. At the same time the process by which he reached his opinion in favor of removing the religious test shows more clearly than even ultra-conservatism could, how free he was from any touch of the reforming or innovating spirit. He did not urge that, on general principles, religious tests were wrong, that they were relics of the past and in hopeless conflict with the fundamental doctrines of American liberty and democracy. On the contrary, he implied that a religious test was far from being of necessity an evil. He laid down the sound doctrine that qualifications for office were purely matters of expediency, and then argued that it was wise to remove the religious test because, while its principle would be practically enforced by a Christian community, it was offensive to some persons to have it engrafted on the Constitution. The speech in which he set forth these views was an able and convincing one, entirely worthy of its author, and the removal of the test was carried by a large majority. It is an interesting example of the combination of steady conservatism and breadth of view which Mr. Webster always displayed. But it also brings into strong relief his aversion to radical general principles as grounds of action, and his inborn hostility to far-reaching change.

His two other important speeches in this convention have been preserved in his works, and are purely and wholly conservative in tone and spirit. The first related to the basis of representation in the Senate, whose members were then apportioned according to the amount of taxable property in the districts. This system, Mr. Webster thought, should be retained, and his speech was a most masterly discussion of the whole system of government by two houses. He urged the necessity of a basis of representation for the upper house different from that of the lower, in order to make the former fully serve its purpose of a check and balance to the popular branch. This important point he handled in the most skillful manner, and there is no escape from his conclusion that a difference of origin in the two legislative branches of the government is essential to the full and perfect operation of the system. This difference of origin, he argued, could be obtained only by the introduction of property as a factor in the basis of representation. The weight of his speech was directed to defending the principle of a suitable representation of property, which was a subject requiring very adroit treatment. The doctrine is one which probably would not be tolerated now in any part of this country, and even in 1820, in Massachusetts, it was a delicate matter to advocate it, for it

was hostile to the general sentiment of the people.
Having established his position that it was all
important to make the upper branch a strong and
effective check, he said that the point in issue was
not whether property offered the best method of
distinguishing between the two houses, but whether
it was not better than no distinction at all. This
being answered affirmatively, the next question to
be considered was whether property, not in the
sense of personal possessions and personal power,
but in a general sense, ought not to have its due
influence in matters of government. He maintained the justice of this proposition by showing
that our constitutions rest largely on the general
equality of property, which, in turn, is due to our
laws of distribution. This led him into a discussion of the principles of the distribution of property. He pointed out the dangers arising in England from the growth of a few large estates, while
on the other hand he predicted that the rapid and
minute subdivision of property in France would
change the character of the government, and, far
from strengthening the crown, as was then generally prophesied, would have a directly opposite
effect, by creating a large and united body of
small proprietors, who would sooner or later control the country. He illustrated, in this way, the
value and importance of a general equality of
property, and of steadiness in legislation affecting
it. These were the reasons, he contended, for
making property the basis of the check and bal-

ance furnished to our system of government by an
upper house. Moreover, all property being subject to taxation for the purpose of educating the
children of both rich and poor, it deserved some
representation for this valuable aid to government.
It is impossible, in a few lines,[1] to do justice to
Mr. Webster's argument. It exhibited a great
deal of tact and ingenuity, especially in the distinction so finely drawn between property as an
element of personal power and property in a general sense, and so distributed as to be a bulwark
of liberty. The speech is, on this account, an
interesting one, for Mr. Webster was rarely ingenious, and hardly ever got over difficulties by fine-
spun distinctions. In this instance adroitness was
very necessary, and he did not hesitate to employ
it. By his skillful treatment, by his illustrations
drawn from England and France, which show the
accuracy and range of his mental vision in matters
of politics and public economy, both at home and
abroad, and with the powerful support of Judge
Story, Mr. Webster carried his point. The element of property representation in the Senate was
retained, but so wholly by the ability of its advocate that it was not long afterwards removed.

Mr. Webster's other important speech related
to the judiciary. The Constitution provided that
the judges, who held office during good behavior,
should be removable by the governor on an address

[1] My brief statement is merely a further condensation of the
excellent abstract of this speech made by Mr. Curtis.

from the legislature.   This was considered to meet cases of incompetency or of personal misconduct, which could not be reached by impeachment.   Mr. Webster desired to amend the clause so as to require a two thirds vote for the passage of the address, and that reasons should be assigned, and a hearing assured to the judge who was the subject of the proceedings.   These changes were all directed to the further protection of the bench, and it was in this connection that Mr. Webster made a most admirable and effective speech on the well-worn but noble theme of judicial independence. He failed to carry conviction, however, and his amendments were all lost.   The perils which he anticipated have never arisen, and the good sense of the people of Massachusetts has prevented the slightest abuse of what Mr. Webster rightly esteemed a dangerous power.

Mr. Webster's continual and active exertion throughout the session of this convention brought him great applause and admiration, and showed his powers in a new light.   Judge Story, with generous enthusiasm, wrote to Mr. Mason, after the convention adjourned: —

"Our friend Webster has gained a noble reputation. He was before known as a lawyer; but he has now secured the title of an eminent and enlightened statesman. It was a glorious field for him, and he has had an ample harvest.   The whole force of his great mind was brought out, and, in several speeches, he commanded universal admiration.   He always led the van, and was most skillful and instantaneous in attack and retreat. He fought, as I have told him, in the 'imminent deadly breach;' and all I could do was to skirmish, in aid of him, upon some of the enemy's outposts. On the whole, I never was more proud of any display than his in my life, and I am much deceived if the well-earned popularity, so justly and so boldly acquired by him on this occasion, does not carry him, if he lives, to the presidency."

While this convention, so memorable in the career of Mr. Webster and so filled with the most absorbing labors, was in session, he achieved a still wider renown in a very different field. On the 22d of December, 1820, he delivered at Plymouth the oration which commemorated the two hundredth anniversary of the landing of the Pilgrims. The theme was a splendid one, both in the intrinsic interest of the event itself, in the character of the Pilgrims, in the vast results which had grown from their humble beginnings, and in the principles of free government, which had spread from the cabins of the exiles over the face of a continent, and had become the common heritage of a great people. We are fortunate in having a description of the orator, written at the time by a careful observer and devoted friend, Mr. George Ticknor, who says: —

"*Friday Evening.* — I have run away from a great levee there is downstairs, thronging in admiration round Mr. Webster, to tell you a little word about his oration. Yet I do not dare to trust myself about it, and I warn you beforehand that I have not the least confidence in my own opinion. His manner carried me away completely ; not, I think, that I could have been so carried away if it had been a poor oration, for of that, I apprehend, there can be no fear. It *must* have been a great, a very great performance, but whether it was so absolutely unrivaled as I imagined when I was under the immediate influence of his presence, of his tones, of his looks, I cannot be sure till I have read it, for it seems to me incredible.

"I was never so excited by public speaking before in my life. Three or four times I thought my temples would burst with the gush of blood ; for, after all, you must know that I am aware it is no connected and compacted whole, but a collection of wonderful fragments of burning eloquence, to which his whole manner gave tenfold force. When I came out I was almost afraid to come near to him. It seemed to me as if he was like the mount that might not be touched and that burned with fire. I was beside myself, and am so still."

"*Saturday*. — Mr. Webster was in admirable spirits. On Thursday evening he was considerably agitated and oppressed, and yesterday morning he had not his natural look at all ; but since his entire success he has been as gay and playful as a kitten. The party came in one after another, and the spirits of all were kindled brighter and brighter, and we fairly sat up till after two o'clock. I think, therefore, we may now safely boast the Plymouth expedition has gone off admirably."

Mr. Ticknor was a man of learning and scholarship, just returned from a prolonged sojourn in Europe, where he had met and conversed with all the most distinguished men of the day, both in

England and on the Continent. He was not, therefore, disposed by training or recent habits to indulge a facile enthusiasm, and such deep emotion as he experienced must have been due to no ordinary cause. He was, in fact, profoundly moved because he had been listening to one of the great masters of eloquence exhibiting, for the first time, his full powers in a branch of the art much more cultivated in America by distinguished men of all professions than is the custom elsewhere. The Plymouth oration belongs to what, for lack of a better name, we must call occasional oratory. This form of address, taking an anniversary, a great historical event or character, a celebration, or occasion of any sort as a starting point, permits either a close adherence to the original text or the widest latitude of treatment. The field is a broad and inviting one. That it promises an easy success is shown by the innumerable productions of this kind which, for many years, have been showered upon the country. That the promise is fallacious is proved by the very small number among the countless host of such addresses which survive the moment of their utterance. The facility of saying something is counterbalanced by the difficulty of saying anything worth hearing. The temptation to stray and to mistake platitude for originality is almost always fatal.

Mr. Webster was better fitted than any man who has ever lived in this country for the perilous task of occasional oratory. The freedom of movement which renders most speeches of this class diluted and commonplace was exactly what he needed. He required abundant intellectual room for a proper display of his powers, and he had the rare quality of being able to range over vast spaces of time and thought without becoming attenuated in what he said. Soaring easily, with a powerful sweep he returned again to earth without jar or shock. He had dignity and grandeur of thought, expression, and manner, and a great subject never became small by his treatment of it. He had, too, a fine historical imagination, and could breathe life and passion into the dead events of the past.

Mr. Ticknor speaks of the Plymouth oration as impressing him as a series of eloquent fragments. The impression was perfectly correct. Mr. Webster touched on the historical event, on the character of the Pilgrims, on the growth and future of the country, on liberty and constitutional principles, on education, and on human slavery. This was entirely proper to such an address. The difficulty lay in doing it well, and Mr. Webster did it as perfectly as it ever has been done. The thoughts were fine, and were expressed in simple and beautiful words. The delivery was grand and impressive, and the presentation of each successive theme glowed with subdued fire. There was no straining after mere rhetorical effect, but an artistic treatment of a succession of great subjects in a general and yet vivid and picturesque fashion. The emotion produced by the Plymouth

oration was akin to that of listening to the strains
of music issuing from a full-toned organ. Those
who heard it did not seek to gratify their reason
or look for conviction to be brought to their understanding. It did not appeal to the logical fac-
ulties or to the passions, which are roused by the
keen contests of parliamentary debate. It was the
divine gift of speech, the greatest instrument given
to man, used with surpassing talent, and the joy
and pleasure which it brought were those which
come from listening to the song of a great singer,
or looking upon the picture of a great artist.

The Plymouth oration, which was at once printed
and published, was received with a universal burst
of applause. It had more literary success than
anything which had at that time appeared, except
from the pen of Washington Irving. The public,
without stopping to analyze their own feelings, or
the oration itself, recognized at once that a new
genius had come before them, a man endowed with
the noble gift of eloquence, and capable by the
exercise of his talents of moving and inspiring
great masses of his fellow men. Mr. Webster was
then of an age to feel fully the glow of a great
success, both at the moment and when the cooler
and more critical approbation came. He was fresh
and young, a strong man rejoicing to run the race.
Mr. Ticknor says, in speaking of the oration: —

"The passage at the end, where, spreading his arms
as if to embrace them, he welcomed future generations
to the great inheritance which we have enjoyed, was

spoken with the most attractive sweetness and that peculiar smile which in him was always so charming.   The
effect of the whole was very great.   As soon as he got
home to our lodgings, all the principal people then in
Plymouth crowded about him.   He was full of anima-
tion, and radiant with happiness.   But there was something about him very grand and imposing at the same
time.   I never saw him at any time when he seemed to
me to be more conscious of his own powers, or to have
a more true and natural enjoyment from their possession."

Amid all the applause and glory, there was one
letter of congratulation and acknowledgment which
must have given Mr. Webster more pleasure than
anything else.   It came from John Adams, who
never did anything by halves.   Whether he praised
or condemned, he did it heartily and ardently, and
such an oration on New England went straight to
the heart of the eager, warm-blooded old patriot.
His commendation, too, was worth having, for he
spoke as one having authority.   John Adams had
been one of the eloquent men and the most forcible
debater of the first Congress.   He had listened to
the great orators of other lands.   He had heard
Pitt and Fox, Burke and Sheridan, and had been
present at the trial of Warren Hastings.   His un-
stinted praise meant and still means a great deal,
and it concludes with one of the finest and most
graceful of compliments.   The oration, he says,

"is the effort of a great mind richly stored with every
species of information.   If there be an American who

can read it without tears, I am not that American. It enters more perfectly into the genuine spirit of New England than any production I ever read. The observations on the Greeks and Romans; on colonization in general; on the West India islands; on the past, present, and future of America, and on the slave trade, are sagacious, profound, and affecting in a high degree."

"Mr. Burke is no longer entitled to the praise — the most consummate orator of modern times."

"What can I say of what regards myself? To my humble name, *Exegisti monumentum œre perennius.*"

Many persons consider the Plymouth oration to be the finest of all Mr. Webster's efforts in this field. It is certainly one of the very best of his productions, but he showed on the next great occasion a distinct improvement, which he long maintained. Five years after the oration at Plymouth, he delivered the address on the laying of the corner-stone of Bunker Hill monument. The superiority to the first oration was not in essentials, but in details, the fruit of a ripening and expanding mind. At Bunker Hill, as at Plymouth, he displayed the massiveness of thought, the dignity and grandeur of expression, and the range of vision which are all so characteristic of his intellect and which were so much enhanced by his wonderful physical attributes. But in the later oration there is a greater finish and smoothness. We appreciate the fact that the Plymouth oration is a succession of eloquent fragments; the same is true of the Bunker Hill address, but we no longer realize

it. The continuity is, in appearance, unbroken,
and the whole work is rounded and polished. The
style, too, is now perfected. It is at once plain,
direct, massive, and vivid. The sentences are
generally short and always clear, but never monotonous. The preference for Anglo-Saxon words
and the exclusion of Latin derivatives are marked,
and we find here in rare perfection that highest
attribute of style, the union of simplicity, pictur-
esqueness, and force.

In the. first Bunker Hill oration Mr. Webster
touched his highest point in the difficult task of
commemorative oratory. In that field he not only
stands unrivaled, but no one has approached him.
The innumerable productions of this class by other
men, many of a high degree of excellence, are forgotten, while those of Webster form part of the
education of every American schoolboy, are widely
read, and have entered into the literature and
thought of the country. The orations of Plymouth
and Bunker Hill are grouped in Webster's works
with a number of other speeches professedly of the
same kind. But only a very few of these are
strictly occasional; the great majority are chiefly,
if not wholly, political speeches, containing merely
passages here and there in the same vein as his
great commemorative addresses. Before finally
leaving the subject, however, it will be well to
glance for a moment at the few orations which
properly belong to the same class as the first two
which we have been considering.

The Bunker Hill oration, after the lapse of only
a year, was followed by the celebrated eulogy upon
Adams and Jefferson. This usually and with justice is ranked in merit with its two immediate predecessors. As a whole it is not, perhaps, quite
so much admired, but it contains the famous imaginary speech of John Adams, which is the best
known and most hackneyed passage in any of these
orations. The opening lines, "Sink or swim, live
or die, survive or perish, I give my hand and my
heart to this vote," since Mr. Webster first pronounced them in Faneuil Hall, have risen even to
the dignity of a familiar quotation. The passage,
indeed, is perhaps the best example we have of
the power of Mr. Webster's historical imagination.
He had some fragmentary sentences, the character
of the man, the nature of the debate, and the circumstances of the time to build upon, and from
these materials he constructed a speech which was
absolutely startling in its life-like force. The
revolutionary Congress, on the verge of the tremendous step which was to separate them from
England, rises before us as we read the burning
words which the imagination of the speaker put
into the mouth of John Adams. They are not
only instinct with life, but with the life of impending revolution, and they glow with the warmth and
strength of feeling so characteristic of their supposed author. It is well known that the general
belief at the time was that the passage was an
extract from a speech actually delivered by John

Adams. Mr. Webster, as well as Mr. Adams's son and grandson, received numerous letters of inquiry on this point, and it is possible that many people still persist in this belief as to the origin of the passage. Such an effect was not produced by mere clever imitation, for there was nothing to imitate, but by the force of a powerful historic imagination and a strong artistic sense in its management.

In 1828 Mr. Webster delivered an address before the Mechanics' Institute in Boston, on "Science in connection with the Mechanic Arts," a subject which was outside of his usual lines of thought, and offered no especial attractions to him. This oration is graceful and strong, and possesses sufficient and appropriate eloquence. It is chiefly interesting, however, from the reserve and self-control, dictated by a nice sense of fitness, which it exhibited. Omniscience was not Mr. Webster's foible. He never was guilty of Lord Brougham's weakness of seeking to prove himself master of universal knowledge. In delivering an address on science and invention, there was a strong temptation to an orator like Mr. Webster to substitute glittering rhetoric for real knowledge; but the address at the Mechanics' Institute is simply the speech of a very eloquent and a liberally educated man upon a subject with which he had only the most general acquaintance.

The other orations of this class were those on "The Character of Washington," the second Bun-

ker Hill address, "The Landing at Plymouth,"
delivered in New York at the dinner of the Pilgrim
Society, the remarks on the death of Judge Story
and of Mr. Mason, and finally the speech on laying the corner-stone for the addition to the Capitol, in 1851. These were all comparatively brief
speeches, with the exception of that at Bunker
Hill, which, although very fine, was perceptibly
inferior to his first effort when the corner-stone of
the monument was laid. The address on the character of Washington, to an American the most
dangerous of great and well-worn topics, is of a
high order of eloquence. The theme appealed to
Mr. Webster strongly and brought out his best
powers, which were peculiarly fitted to do justice
to the noble, massive, and dignified character of
the subject. The last of these addresses, that on
the addition to the Capitol, was in a prophetic
vein, and, while it shows but little diminution of
strength, has a sadness even in its splendid antici-
pations of the future, which makes it one of the
most impressive of its class. All those which have
been mentioned, however, show the hand of the
master and are worthy to be preserved in the volumes which contain the noble series that began in
the early flush of genius with the brilliant oration
in the Plymouth church, and closed with the words
uttered at Washington, under the shadow of the
Capitol, when the light of life was fading and the
end of all things was at hand.

CHAPTER V

THE thorough knowledge of the principles of government and legislation, the practical statesmanship, and the capacity for debate shown in the state convention, combined with the splendid oration at Plymouth to make Mr. Webster the most conspicuous man in New England, with the single exception of John Quincy Adams. There was, therefore, a strong and general desire that he should return to public life. He accepted with some reluctance the nomination to Congress from the Boston district in 1822, and in December, 1823, took his seat.

The six years which had elapsed since Mr. Webster left Washington had been a period of political quiet. The old parties had ceased to represent any distinctive principles, and the Federalists scarcely existed as an organization. Mr. Webster, during this interval, had remained almost wholly quiescent in regard to public affairs. He had urged the visit of Mr. Monroe to the North, which had done so much to hasten the inevitable dissolution of parties. He had received Mr. Calhoun when that gentleman visited Boston, and their friendship and apparent intimacy were such that the South Carolinian was thought to be his host's candidate for the presidency. Except for this and the part which he took in the Boston opposition to the Missouri Compromise and to the tariff, matters to be noticed in connection with later events, Mr. Webster had held aloof from political conflict.

When he returned to Washington in 1823, the situation was much altered from that which he had left in 1817. In reality there were no parties, or only one; but the all-powerful Republicans who had adopted, under the pressure of foreign war, most of the Federalist principles so obnoxious to Jefferson and his school, were split up into as many factions as there were candidates for the presidency. It was a period of transition in which personal politics had taken the place of those founded on opposing principles, and this "era of good feeling" was marked by the intense bitterness of the conflicts produced by these personal rivalries. In addition to the factions which were battling for the control of the Republican party and for the great prize of the presidency, there was still another faction, composed of the old Federalists, who, although without organization, still held to their name and their prejudices, and clung together more as a matter of habit than with any practical object. Mr. Webster had been one of the Federalist leaders in the old days, and when he returned to public life with all the distinction

which he had won in other fields, he was at once
recognized as the chief and head of all that now
remained of the great party of Washington and
Hamilton.   No Federalist could hope to be president, and for this very reason Federalist support
was eagerly sought by all Republican candidates
for the presidency.   The favor of Mr. Webster as
the head of an independent and necessarily disinterested faction was, of course, strongly desired in
many quarters.   His political position and his
high reputation as a lawyer, orator, and statesman
made him, therefore, a character of the first importance in Washington, a fact to which Mr. Clay
at once gave public recognition by placing his future rival at the head of the Judiciary Committee
of the House.

The six years of congressional life which now
ensued were among the most useful if not the most
brilliant in Mr. Webster's whole public career.
He was free from the annoyance of opposition at
home, and was twice returned by a practically
unanimous popular vote.   He held a commanding
and influential and at the same time a thoroughly
independent position in Washington, where he was
regarded as the first man on the floor of the House
in point of ability and reputation.   He was not
only able to show his great capacity for practical
legislation, but he was at liberty to advance his
own views on public questions in his own way,
unburdened by the outside influences of party and
of association which had affected him so much in

his previous term of service and were soon to re-
assert their sway in all his subsequent career.

His return to Congress was at once signalized
by a great speech, which, although of no practical
or immediate moment, deserves careful attention
from the light which it throws on the workings of
his mind and the development of his opinions in
regard to his country. The House had been in
session but a few days when Mr. Webster offered
a resolution in favor of providing by law for the
expenses incident to the appointment of a commissioner to Greece, should the President deem such
an appointment expedient. The Greeks were then
in the throes of revolution, and the sympathy for
the heirs of so much glory in their struggle for
freedom was strong among the American people.
When Mr. Webster rose on January 19, 1824, to
move the adoption of the resolution which he had
laid upon the table of the House, the chamber was
crowded and the galleries were filled by a large
and fashionable audience attracted by the reputation of the orator and the interest felt in his
subject. His hearers were disappointed if they
expected a great rhetorical display, for which the
nature of the subject and the classic memories
clustering about it offered such strong temptations.
Mr. Webster did not rise for that purpose, nor to
make capital by an appeal to a temporary popular
interest. His speech was for a wholly different
purpose. It was the first expression of that grand
conception of the American Union which had

vaguely excited his youthful enthusiasm. This
conception had now come to be part of his intellectual being, and then and always stirred his imagination and his affections to their inmost depths.
It embodied the principle from which he never
swerved, and led to all that he represents and to
all that his influence means in our history.

As the first expression of his conception of the
destiny of the United States as a great and united
nation, Mr. Webster was, naturally, "more fond
of this child" than of any other of his intellectual
family. The speech itself was a noble one, but it
was an eloquent essay rather than a great example
of the oratory of debate. This description can in
no other case be applied to Mr. Webster's parliamentary efforts, but in this instance it is correct,
because the occasion justified such a form. Mr.
Webster's purpose was to show that, though the
true policy of the United States absolutely de-
barred them from taking any part in the affairs of
Europe, yet they had an important duty to perform in exercising their proper influence on the
public opinion of the world. Europe was then
struggling with the monstrous principles of the
"Holy Alliance." Those principles Mr. Webster
reviewed historically. He showed their pernicious
tendency, their hostility to all modern theories of
government, and their especial opposition to the
principles of American liberty. If the doctrines
of the Congress of Laybach were right and could
be made to prevail, then those of America were

wrong and the systems of popular government adopted in the United States were doomed. Against such infamous principles it behooved the people of the United States to raise their voice. Mr. Webster sketched the history of Greece, and made a fine appeal to Americans to give an expression of their sympathy to a people struggling for freedom. He proclaimed, so that all men might hear, the true duty of the United States toward the oppressed of any land, and the responsibility which they held to exert their influence upon the opinions of mankind. The national destiny of his country in regard to other nations was his theme; to give to the glittering declaration of Canning, that he would "call in the new world to redress the balance of the old," a deep and real significance was his object.

The speech touched Mr. Clay to the quick. He supported Mr. Webster's resolution with all the ardor of his generous nature, and supplemented it by another against the interference of Spain in South America. A stormy debate followed, vivified by the flings and taunts of John Randolph, but the unwillingness to take action was so great that Mr. Webster did not press his resolution to a vote. He had at the outset looked for a practical result from his resolution, and had desired the appointment of Mr. Everett as commissioner, a plan in which he had been encouraged by Mr. Calhoun, who had given him to understand that the executive regarded the Greek mission with favor. Before he delivered his speech he became aware that Calhoun had misled him, that Mr. Adams, the secretary of state, considered Everett too much of a partisan, and that the administration was wholly averse to any action in the premises. This destroyed all hope of a practical result, and made an adverse vote certain. The only course was to avoid a decision and trust to what he said for an effect on public opinion. The real purpose of the speech, however, was achieved. Mr. Webster had exposed and denounced the Holy Alliance as hostile to the liberties of mankind, and had declared the unalterable enmity of the United States to its reactionary doctrines. The speech was widely read, not only wherever English was spoken, but it was translated into all the languages of Europe, and was circulated throughout South America. It increased Mr. Webster's fame at home and laid the foundation of his reputation abroad. Above all, it stamped him as a statesman of a broad and national cast of mind.

He now settled down to hard and continuous labor at the routine business of the House, and it was not until the end of March that he had occasion to make another elaborate and important speech. At that time Mr. Clay took up the bill for laying certain protective duties and advocated it strenuously as part of a general and steady policy which he then christened with the name of "the American system." Against this bill, known as the tariff of 1824, Mr. Webster made, as Mr.

Adams wrote in his diary at the time, "an able and powerful speech," which can be more properly considered when we come to his change of position on this question a few years later.

As chairman of the Judiciary Committee, the affairs of the national courts were his particular care. Western expansion demanded an increased number of judges for the circuits, but, unfortunately, decisions in certain recent cases had offended the sensibilities of Virginia and Kentucky, and there was a renewal of the old Jeffersonian efforts to limit the authority of the Supreme Court. Instead of being able to improve, he was obliged to defend the court, and this he did successfully, defeating all attempts to curtail its power by alterations of the act of 1789. These duties and that of investigating the charges brought by Ninian Edwards against Mr. Crawford, the secretary of the treasury, made the session an unusually laborious one, and detained Mr. Webster in Washington until midsummer.

The short session of the next winter was of course marked by the excitement attendant upon the settlement of the presidential election which resulted in the choice of Mr. John Quincy Adams by the House of Representatives. The intense agitation in political circles did not, however, prevent Mr. Webster from delivering one very important speech, nor from carrying through successfully one of the most important and practically useful measures of his legislative career. The speech was

delivered in the debate on the bill for continuing
the national Cumberland road.   Mr. Webster had
already, many years before, defined his position
on the constitutional question involved in internal
improvements.   He now, in response to Mr. Mc-
Duffie of South Carolina, who denounced the measure as partial and sectional, not merely defended
the principle of internal improvements, but declared that it was a policy to be pursued only with
the purest national feeling.   It was not the business of Congress, he said, to legislate for this
State or that, or to balance local interests, and
because they helped one region to help another,
but to act for the benefit of all the States united,
and in making improvements to be guided only by
their necessity.   He showed that these roads would
open up the West to settlement, and incidentally
defended the policy of selling the public lands at
a low price as an encouragement to emigration,
telling his Southern friends very plainly that they
could not expect to coerce the course of population
in favor of their own section.   The whole speech
was conceived in the broadest and wisest spirit,
and marks another step in the development of Mr.
Webster as a national statesman.   It increased
his reputation, and brought to him a great accession of popularity in the West.

The measure which he carried through was the
famous "Crimes Act," perhaps the best monument
that there is of his legislative and constructive
ability.   The criminal law of the United States

had scarcely been touched since the days of the
first Congress, and was very defective and unsatisfactory.   Mr. Webster's first task, in which he
received most essential and valuable though unac-
knowledged assistance from Judge Story, was to
codify and digest the whole body of criminal law.
This done, the hardly less difficult undertaking
followed of carrying the measure through Congress.   In the latter, Mr. Webster, by his skill in
debate and familiarity with his subject, and by his
influence in the House, was perfectly successful.
That he and Judge Story did their work well in
perfecting the bill is shown by the admirable
manner in which the Act stood the test of time
and experience.

When the new Congress came together in 1825,
Mr. Webster at once turned his attention to the
improvement of the judiciary, which he had been
obliged to postpone in order to ward off the attacks
upon the court.   After much deliberation and
thought, aided by Judge Story, and having made
some concessions to his committee, he brought in
a bill increasing the Supreme Court judges to ten,
making ten instead of seven circuits, and providing that six judges should constitute a quorum for
the transaction of business.   Although not a party
question, the measure excited much opposition,
and was more than a month in passing through the
House.   Mr. Webster supported it at every stage
with great ability, and his two most important
speeches, which are in their way models for the

treatment of such a subject, are preserved in his works. The bill was carried by his great strength in debate and by weight of forcible argument. But in the Senate, where it was deprived of the guardianship of its author, it hung along in uncertainty, and was finally lost through the apathy or opposition of those very Western members for whose benefit it had been devised. Mr. Webster took its ultimate defeat very coolly. The Eastern States did not require it, and were perfectly contented with the existing arrangements, and he was entirely satisfied with the assurance that the best lawyers and wisest men approved the principles of the bill. The time and thought which he had expended were not wasted so far as he was personally concerned, for they served to enhance his influence and reputation both as a lawyer and statesman.

This session brought with it also occasions for debate other than those which were offered by measures of purely legislative and practical interest. The administration of Mr. Adams marks the close of the "era of good feeling," as it was called, and sowed the germs of those divisions which were soon to result in new and definite party combinations. Mr. Adams and Mr. Clay represented the conservative and General Jackson and his friends the radical or democratic elements in the now all-embracing Republican party. It was inevitable that Mr. Webster should sympathize with the former, and it was equally inevitable that in doing so he should become the leader of the administration forces in the House, where "his great and commanding influence," to quote the words of an opponent, made him a host himself. The desire of Mr. Adams to send representatives to the Panama Congress, a scheme which lay very near his heart and to which Mr. Clay was equally attached, encountered a bitter and factious resistance in the Senate, sufficient to deprive the measure of any real utility by delaying its passage. In the House a resolution was introduced declaring simply that it was expedient to appropriate money to defray the expenses of the proposed mission. The opposition at once undertook by amendments to instruct the ministers, and generally to go beyond the powers of the House. The real ground of the attack was slavery, threatened, as was supposed, by the attitude of the South American republics — a fact which no one understood or cared to recognize. Mr. Webster stood forth as the champion of the executive. In an elaborate speech of great ability he denounced the unconstitutional attempt to interfere with the prerogative of the President, and discussed with much effect the treaty-making power assailed on another famous occasion, many years before, by the South, and defended at that time also by the eloquence of a representative of Massachusetts. Mr. Webster showed the nature of the Panama Congress, defended its objects and the policy of the administration, and made a full and fine exposition of the

intent of the "Monroe doctrine." The speech
was an important and effective one. It exhibited
in an exceptional way Mr. Webster's capacity for
discussing large questions of public and constitutional law and foreign policy, and was of essential
service to the cause which he espoused. It was
imbued, too, with that sentiment of national unity
which occupied a larger space in his thoughts with
each succeeding year, until it finally pervaded his
whole career as a public man.

At the second session of the same Congress,
after a vain effort to confer upon the country the
benefit of a national bankrupt law, Mr. Webster
was again called upon to defend the executive in
a much more heated conflict than that aroused by
the Panama resolution. Georgia was engaged in
oppressing and robbing the Creek Indians, in open
contempt of the treaties and obligations of the
United States. Mr. Adams sent in a message
reciting the facts and hinting pretty plainly that
he intended to carry out the laws by force unless
Georgia desisted. The message was received with
great wrath by the Southern members. They objected to any reference to a committee, and Mr.
Forsyth of Georgia declared the whole business to
be "base and infamous," while a gentleman from
Mississippi announced that Georgia would act as
she pleased. Mr. Webster, having said that she
would do so at her peril, was savagely attacked as
the organ of the administration, daring to menace
and insult a sovereign State. This stirred Mr.

Webster, although slow to anger, to a determination to carry through the reference at all hazards. He said: —

"He would tell the gentleman from Georgia that if there were rights of the Indians which the United States were bound to protect, that there were those in the House and in the country who would take their part. If we have bound ourselves by any treaty to do certain things, we must fulfill such obligation. High words will not terrify us, loud declamation will not deter us from the discharge of that duty. In my own course in this matter I shall not be dictated to by any State or the representative of any State on this floor. I shall not be frightened from my purpose, nor will I suffer harsh language to produce any reaction on my mind. I will examine with great and equal care all the rights of both parties. . . . I have made these few remarks to give the gentleman from Georgia to understand that it was not by bold denunciation nor by bold assumption that the members of this House are to be influenced in the decision of high public concerns."

When Mr. Webster was thoroughly roused and indignant there was a darkness in his face and a gleam of dusky light in his deep-set eyes which were not altogether pleasant to contemplate. How well Mr. Forsyth and his friends bore the words and look of Mr. Webster we have no means of knowing, but the message was referred to a select committee without a division. The interest to us in all this is the spirit in which Mr. Webster spoke. He loved the Union as intensely then as at any period of his life, but he was still far distant from the frame of mind which induced him to think that his devotion to the Union would be best expressed and the cause of the Union best served by mildness toward the South and rebuke to the North. He believed in 1826 that dignified courage and firm language were the surest means of keeping the peace. He was quite right then, and he would have been always right if he had adhered to the plain words and determined manner to which he treated Mr. Forsyth and his followers.

This session was crowded with work of varying importance, but the close of Mr. Webster's career in the lower house was near at hand. The failing health of Mr. E. H. Mills made it certain that Massachusetts would soon have a vacant seat in the Senate, and every one turned to Mr. Webster as the person above all others entitled to this high office. He himself was by no means so quick in determining to accept the position. He would not even think of it until the impossibility of Mr. Mills's return was assured, and then he had to meet the opposition of the administration and all its friends, who regarded with alarm the prospect of losing such a tower of strength in the House. Mr. Webster, indeed, felt that he could render the best service in the lower branch, and urged the senatorship upon Governor Lincoln, who was elected, but declined. After this there seemed to be no escape from a manifest destiny. Despite the opposition of his friends in Washington, and

his own reluctance, he finally accepted the office
of United States senator, which was conferred
upon him by the legislature of Massachusetts in
June, 1827.

In tracing the labors of Mr. Webster during
three years spent in the lower house, no allusion
has been made to the purely political side of his
career at this time, nor to his relations with the
public men of the day. The period was important,
generally speaking, because it showed the first
signs of the development of new parties, and to
Mr. Webster in particular, because it brought him
gradually toward the political and party position
which he was to occupy during the rest of his life.
When he took his seat in Congress, in the autumn
of 1823, the intrigues for the presidential succession were at their height. Mr. Webster was then
strongly inclined to Mr. Calhoun, as was suspected
at the time of that gentleman's visit to Boston.
He soon became convinced, however, that Mr.
Calhoun's chances of success were slight, and his
good opinion of the distinguished South Carolinian
seems also to have declined. It was out of the
question for a man of Mr. Webster's temperament
and habits of thought, to think for a moment of
supporting Jackson, a candidate on the ground of
military glory and unreflecting popular enthusiasm.
Mr. Adams, as the representative of New England, and as a conservative and trained statesman,
was the natural and proper candidate to receive
the aid of Mr. Webster. But here party feelings

and traditions stepped in. The Federalists of New
England had hated Mr. Adams with the peculiar
bitterness which always grows out of domestic
quarrels, whether in public or private life; and
although the old strife had sunk a little out of
sight, it had never been healed. The Federalist
leaders in Massachusetts still disliked and dis-
trusted Mr. Adams with an intensity none the less
real because it was concealed. In the nature of
things Mr. Webster now occupied a position of
political independence; but he had been a steady
party man when his party was in existence, and
he was still a party man so far as the old Federalist feelings retained vitality and force. He had,
moreover, but a slight personal acquaintance with
Mr. Adams and no very cordial feeling toward
him. This disposed of three presidential candidates. The fourth was Mr. Clay, and it is not
very clear why Mr. Webster refused an alliance
in this quarter. Mr. Clay had treated him with
consideration, they were personal friends, their
opinions were not dissimilar and were becoming
constantly more alike. Possibly there was an instinctive feeling of rivalry on this very account.
At all events, Mr. Webster would not support
Clay. Only one candidate remained: Mr. Crawford, the representative of all that was extreme
among the Republicans, and, in a party sense,
most odious to the Federalists. But it was a time
when personal factions flourished rankly in the
absence of broad differences of principle. Mr.

Crawford was bidding furiously for support in every and any quarter, and to Mr. Crawford, accordingly, Mr. Webster began to look as a possible leader for himself and his friends. Just how far Mr. Webster went in this direction cannot be readily or surely determined, although we get some light on the subject from an attack made on Mr. Crawford just at this time. Ninian Edwards, recently senator from Illinois, had a quarrel with Mr. Crawford, and sent in a memorial to Congress containing charges against the secretary of the treasury which were designed to break him down as a candidate for the presidency. Of the merits of this quarrel it is not very easy to judge, even if it were important. The character of Edwards was none of the best, and Mr. Crawford had unquestionably made a highly unscrupulous use, politically, of his position. The members of the administration, although they had no great love for Edwards, who had been appointed minister to Mexico, were distinctly hostile to Mr. Crawford, and refused to attend a dinner from which Edwards had been expressly excluded. Mr. Webster's part in the affair came from his being on the committee charged with the investigation of the Edwards memorial. Mr. Adams, who was of course excited by the presidential contest, disposed to regard his rivals with extreme disfavor, and especially and justly suspicious of Mr. Crawford, speaks of Mr. Webster's conduct in the matter with the utmost bitterness. He refers to it again

and again as an attempt to screen Crawford and
break down Edwards, and denounces Mr. Webster
as false, insidious, and treacherous. Much of this
may be credited to the heated animosities of the
moment, but there can be no doubt that Mr.
Webster took the matter into his own hands in
the committee, and made every effort to protect
Mr. Crawford, in whose favor he also spoke in the
House. It is likewise certain that there was an
attempt to bring about an alliance between Crawford and the Federalists of the North and East.
The effort was abortive, and even before the conclusion of the Edwards business Mr. Webster
avowed that he should take but little part in the
election, and that his only purpose was to secure
the best terms possible for the Federalists, and
obtain recognition for them from the next administration. At that time he wished Mr. Mason to
be attorney-general, and had already turned his
thoughts toward the English mission for himself.

To this waiting policy he adhered, but when
the popular election was over, and the final decision had been thrown into the House of Representatives, more definite action became necessary.
From the questions which he put to his brother
and others as to the course which he ought to pursue in the election by the House, it is obvious that
he was far from anxious to secure the choice of
Mr. Adams, and was weighing carefully other
contingencies. The feeling of New England could
not, however, be mistaken. Public opinion there

demanded that the members of the House should
stand by the New England candidate to the last.
To this sentiment Mr. Webster submitted, and
soon afterwards took occasion to have an interview
with Mr. Adams in order to make the best terms
possible for the Federalists, and obtain for them
suitable recognition. Mr. Adams assured Mr.
Webster that he did not intend to proscribe any
section or any party, and added that although he
could not give the Federalists representation in
the cabinet, he should give them one of the important appointments. Mr. Webster was entirely
satisfied with this promise and with all that was
said by Mr. Adams, who, as everybody knows,
was soon after elected by the House on the first
ballot.

Mr. Adams on his side saw plainly the necessity
of conciliating Mr. Webster, whose great ability
and influence he thoroughly understood.   He told
Mr. Clay that he had a high opinion of Mr. Webster, and wished to win his support; and the savage tone displayed in regard to the Edwards affair
now disappears from the Diary. Mr. Adams,
however, although he knew, as he says, that
"Webster was panting for the English mission,"
and hinted that the wish might be gratified here-
after, was not ready to go so far at the moment,
and at the same time he sought to dissuade Mr.
Webster from being a candidate for the speakership, for which in truth the latter had no inclination.   Their relations, indeed, soon grew very

pleasant. Mr. Webster naturally became the leader of the administration forces in the House, while the President on his side sought Mr. Webster's advice, admired his oration on Adams and Jefferson, dined at his house, and lived on terms of friendship and confidence with him. It is to be feared, however, that all this was merely on the surface. Mr. Adams at the bottom of his heart never, in reality, relaxed in his belief that Mr. Webster was morally unsound. Mr. Webster, on the other hand, whose Federalist opposition to Mr. Adams had only been temporarily allayed, was not long in coming to the conclusion that his services, if appreciated, were not properly recognized by the administration. There was a good deal of justice in this view. The English mission never came, no help was to be obtained for Mr. Mason's election as senator from New Hampshire, the speakership was to be refused in order to promote harmony and strength in the House. To all this Mr. Webster submitted, and fought the battles of the administration in debate as no one else could have done. Nevertheless, all men like recognition, and Mr. Webster would have preferred something more solid than words and confidence or the triumph of a common cause. When the Massachusetts senatorship was in question Mr. Adams urged the election of Governor Lincoln, and objected on the most flattering grounds to Mr. Webster's withdrawal from the House. It is not a too violent conjecture to suppose that Mr.

Webster's final acceptance of a seat in the Senate was due in large measure to a feeling that he had sacrificed enough for the administration. There can be no doubt that coolness grew between the President and the senator, and that the appointment to England, if still desired, never was made, so that when the next election came on Mr. Webster was inactive, and, despite his hostility to Jackson, viewed the overthrow of Mr. Adams with a good deal of indifference and perhaps some satisfaction. It is none the less true, however, that during these years when the first foundations of the future Whig party were laid, Mr. Webster formed the political affiliations which were to last through life. He inevitably found himself associated with Clay and Adams, and opposed to Jackson, Benton, and Van Buren, while at the same time he and Calhoun were fast drifting apart. He had no specially cordial feeling to his new associates; but they were at the head of the conservative elements of the country, they were nationalists in policy, and they favored the views which were most affected in New England. As a conservative and nationalist by nature and education, and as the great New England leader, Mr. Webster could not avoid becoming the parliamentary chief of Mr. Adams's administration, and thus paved the way for leadership in the Whig party of the future.

In narrating the history of these years, I have confined myself to Mr. Webster's public services

and political course. But it was a period in his
career which was crowded with work and achievement, bringing fresh fame and increased reputation, and also with domestic events both of joy
and sorrow. Mr. Webster steadily pursued the
practice of the law, and was constantly engaged in
the Supreme Court. To these years belong many
of his great arguments, and also the prosecution
of the Spanish claims, a task at once laborious and
profitable. In the summer of 1824 Mr. Webster
first saw Marshfield, his future home, and in the
autumn of the same year he visited Monticello,
where he had a long interview with Mr. Jefferson,
of whom he has left a most interesting description.
During the winter he formed the acquaintance
and lived much in the society of some well-known
Englishmen then traveling in this country. This
party consisted of the Earl of Derby, then Mr.
Stanley, Lord Wharncliffe, then Mr. Stuart Wort-
ley; Lord Taunton, then Mr. Labouchere, and
Mr. Denison, afterwards speaker of the House of
Commons. With Mr. Denison this acquaintance
was the foundation of a lasting and intimate friendship maintained by correspondence. In June,
1825, came the splendid oration at Bunker Hill,
and then a visit to Niagara, which, of course, appealed strongly to Mr. Webster. His account of
it, however, although indicative of a deep mental
impression, shows that his power of describing
nature fell far short of his wonderful talent for
picturing human passions and action. The next

vacation brought the eulogy on Adams and Jefferson, when perhaps Mr. Webster may be considered to have been in his highest physical and intellectual perfection. Such at least was the opinion of Mr. Ticknor, who says: —

"He was in the perfection of manly beauty and strength; his form filled out to its finest proportions, and his bearing, as he stood before the vast multitude, that of absolute dignity and power. His manner of speaking was deliberate and commanding. I never heard him when his manner was so grand and appropriate; . . . when he ended the minds of men were wrought up to an uncontrollable excitement, and then followed three tremendous cheers, inappropriate indeed, but as inevitable as any other great movement of nature."

He had held the vast audience mute for over two hours, as John Quincy Adams said in his diary, and finally their excited feelings found vent in cheers. He spoke greatly because he felt greatly. His emotions, his imagination, his entire oratorical temperament were then full of quick sensibility. When he finished writing the imaginary speech of John Adams in the quiet of his library and the silence of the morning hour, his eyes were wet with tears.

A year passed by after this splendid display of eloquence, and then the second congressional period, which had been so full of work and intellectual activity and well-earned distinction, closed, and he entered upon that broader field which opened to him in the Senate of the United States, where his greatest triumphs were still to be achieved.

CHAPTER VI

THE new dignity conferred on Mr. Webster by the people of Massachusetts had hardly been assumed when he was called upon to encounter a trial which must have made all his honors seem poor indeed. He had scarcely taken his seat when he was obliged to return to New York, where failing health had arrested Mrs. Webster's journey to the capital, and where, after much suffering, she died on January 21, 1828. The blow fell with terrible severity upon her husband. He had many sorrows to bear during his life, but this surpassed all others. His wife was the love of his youth, the mother of his children, a charming woman whose strong but gentle influence for good was now lost to him irreparably. In his last days his thoughts reverted to her, and as he followed her body to the grave, on foot in the wet and cold, and leading his children by the hand, it must indeed have seemed as if the wine of life had been drunk and only the lees remained. He was excessively pale, and to those who looked upon him seemed crushed and heart-broken.

The only relief was to return to his work and to

the excitement of public affairs; but the cloud hung over him long after he was once more in his place in the Senate. Death had made a wound in his life which time healed, but of which the scar remained. Whatever were Mr. Webster's faults, his affection for those nearest to him, and especially for the wife of his youth, was deep and strong.

"The very first day of Mr. Webster's arrival and taking his seat in the Senate," Judge Story writes to Mr. Ticknor, "there was a process bill on its third reading, filled, as he thought, with inconvenient and mischievous provisions. He made, in a modest undertone, some inquiries, and, upon an answer being given, he expressed in a few words his doubts and fears. Immediately Mr. Tazewell from Virginia broke out upon him in a speech of two hours. Mr. Webster then moved an adjournment, and on the next day delivered a most masterly speech in reply, expounding the whole operation of the intended act in the clearest manner, so that a recommitment was carried almost without an effort. It was a triumph of the most gratifying nature, and taught his opponents the danger of provoking a trial of his strength, even when he was overwhelmed by calamity. In the labors of the court he has found it difficult to work himself up to high efforts; but occasionally he comes out with all his powers, and when he does, it is sure to attract a brilliant audience."

It would be impossible to give a better picture than that presented by Judge Story of Mr. Webster's appearance and conduct in the month immediately following the death of his wife. We can see how his talents, excited by the conflicts of the Senate and the court, struggled, sometimes successfully, sometimes in vain, with the sense of loss and sorrow which oppressed him.

He did not again come prominently forward in the Senate until the end of April, when he roused himself to prevent injustice. The bill for the relief of the surviving officers of the Revolution seemed on the point of being lost. The object of the measure appealed to Mr. Webster's love for the past, to his imagination, and his patriotism. He entered into the debate, delivered the fine and dignified speech which is preserved in his works, and saved the bill.

A fortnight after this he made his famous speech on the tariff of 1828, a bill making extensive changes in the rates of duties imposed in 1816 and 1824. This speech marks an important change in Mr. Webster's views and in his course as a statesman. He now gave up his position as the ablest opponent in the country of the protective policy, and went over to the support of the tariff and the "American system" of Mr. Clay. This change, in every way of great importance, subjected Mr. Webster to severe criticism both then and subsequently. It is, therefore, necessary to examine briefly his previous utterances on this question in order to reach a correct understanding of his motives in taking this important step and to appreciate his reasons for the adoption of a policy with which, after the year 1828, he was so closely identified.

When Mr. Webster first entered Congress he was a thorough-going Federalist. But the Federalists of New England differed from their great chief, Alexander Hamilton, on the question of a protective policy. Hamilton, in his report on manufactures, advocated with consummate ability the adoption of the principle of protection for nascent industries as an integral and essential part of a true national policy, and urged it on its own merits, without any reference to its being incident to revenue. The New England Federalists, on the other hand, coming from exclusively commercial communities, were in principle free-traders. They regarded with disfavor the doctrine that protection was a good thing in itself, and desired it, if at all, only in the most limited form and purely as an incident to raising revenue. With these opinions Mr. Webster was in full sympathy, and he took occasion when Mr. Calhoun, in 1814, spoke in favor of the existing double duties as a protective measure, and also in favor of manufactures, during the debate on the repeal of the embargo, to define his position on this important question. A few brief extracts will show his views, which were expressed very clearly and with his wonted ability and force.

"I consider," he said, "the imposition of double duties as a mere financial measure. Its great object was to raise revenue, not to foster manufactures. . . . I do not say the double duties ought to be continued. I think they ought not. But what I particularly object to is the holding out of delusive expectations to those concerned in manufactures. . . . In respect to manufactures it is necessary to speak with some precision. I am not, generally speaking, their enemy. I am their friend; but I am not for rearing them or any other interest in hot-beds. I would not legislate precipitately, even in favor of them; above all, I would not profess intentions in relation to them which I did not purpose to execute. I feel no desire to push capital into extensive manufactures faster than the general progress of our wealth and population propels it.

" I am not in haste to see Sheffields and Birminghams in America. Until the population of the country shall be greater in proportion to its extent, such establishments would be impracticable if attempted, and if practicable they would be unwise."

He then pointed out the inferiority and the perils of manufactures as an occupation in comparison with agriculture, and concluded as follows : —

" I am not anxious to accelerate the approach of the period when the great mass of American labor shall not find its employment in the field ; when the young men of the country shall be obliged to shut their eyes upon external nature, upon the heavens and the earth, and immerse themselves in close and unwholesome workshops; when they shall be obliged to shut their ears to the bleatings of their own flocks upon their own hills, and to the voice of the lark that cheers them at the plough, that they may open them in dust and smoke and steam to the perpetual whirl of spools and spindles, and the grating of rasps and saws. I have made these re-

marks, sir, not because I perceive any immediate danger
of carrying our manufactures to an extensive height, but
for the purpose of guarding and limiting my opinions,
and of checking, perhaps, a little the high-wrought
hopes of some who seem to look to our present infant
establishments for 'more than their nature or their state
can bear.'

" *It is the true policy of government to suffer the different pursuits of society to take their own course, and
not to give excessive bounties or encouragements to one
over another.   This, also, is the true spirit of the Constitution.   It has not, in my opinion, conferred on the
government the power of changing the occupations of the
people of different States and sections, and of forcing
them into other employments.*   It cannot prohibit commerce any more than agriculture, nor manufactures any
more than commerce.   It owes protection to all."

The sentences in italics constitute a pretty strong
and explicit statement of the *laissez faire* doctrine,
and it will be observed that the tone of all the
extracts is favorable to free trade and hostile to
protection and even to manufactures in a marked
degree.   We see, also, that Mr. Webster, with
his usual penetration and justice of perception,
saw very clearly that uniformity and steadiness of
policy were more essential than even the policy
itself, and in his opinion were most likely to be
attained by refraining from protection as much as
possible.

When the tariff of 1816 was under discussion
Mr. Webster made no elaborate speech against it,

probably feeling that it was hopeless to attempt to defeat the measure as a whole, but he devoted himself with almost complete success to the task of reducing the proposed duties and to securing modifications of various portions of the bill.

In 1820, when the tariff recommended at the previous session was about to come before Congress, Mr. Webster was not in public life. He attended, however, a meeting of merchants and agriculturists, held in Faneuil Hall in the summer of that year, to protest against the proposed tariff, and he spoke strongly in favor of the free trade resolutions which were then adopted. He began by saying that he was a friend to manufactures, but not to the tariff, which he considered as most injurious to the country.

"He certainly thought it might be doubted whether Congress would not be acting somewhat against the spirit and intention of the Constitution in exercising a power to control essentially the pursuits and occupations of individuals in their private concerns — a power to force great and sudden changes both of occupation and property upon individuals, *not as incidental to the exercise of any other power, but as a substantial and direct power.*"

It will be observed that he objects to the constitutionality of protection as a "direct power," and in the speech of 1814, in the portion quoted in italics, he declared against any general power still more forcibly and broadly. It is an impossible piece of subtlety and refining, therefore, to argue

that Mr. Webster always held consistently to his
views as to the limitations of the revenue power as
a source of protection, and that he put protection
in 1828, and subsequently sustained it after his
change of position, on new and general constitutional grounds. In the speeches of 1814 and 1820
he declared expressly against the doctrine of a
general power of protection, saying, in the latter
instance: —

" It would hardly be contended that Congress possessed that sort of general power by which it might declare that particular occupations should be pursued in
society and that others should not. *If such power belonged to any government in this country, it certainly
did not belong to the general government.*"

Mr. Webster took the New England position
that there was no general power, and having so
declared in this speech of 1820, he then went on
to show that protection could only come as incidental to revenue, and that, even in this way, it
became unconstitutional when the incident was
turned into the principle and when protection and
not revenue was the object of the duties. After
arguing this point, he proceeded to discuss the
general expediency of protection, holding it up as
a thoroughly mistaken policy, a failure in England
which that country would gladly be rid of, and
defending commerce as the truest and best support
of the government and of general prosperity. He
took up next the immediate effects of the proposed

tariff, and, premising that it would confessedly
cause a diminution of the revenue, said: —

" In truth, every man in the community not immediately benefited by the new duties would suffer a double
loss.   In the first place, by shutting out the former com-
modity, the price of the domestic manufacture would be
raised.   The consumer, therefore, must pay more for it,
and insomuch as government will have lost the duty on
the imported article, a tax equal to that duty must be
paid to the government.   The real amount, then, of this
bounty on a given article will be precisely the amount
of the present duty added to the amount of the proposed duty."

He then went on to show the injustice which
would be done to all manufacturers of unprotected
articles, and ridiculed the idea of the connection
between home industries artificially developed and
national independence.   He concluded by assailing manufacturing as an occupation, attacking it
as a means of making the rich richer and the poor
poorer; of injuring business by concentrating capital in the hands of a few who obtained control of
the corporations; of distributing capital less widely
than commerce; of breeding up a dangerous and
undesirable population; and of leading to the hurt-
ful employment of women and children.   The
meeting, the resolutions, and the speech were all
in the interests of unrestricted commerce and free
trade, and Mr. Webster's doctrines were on the
most approved pattern of New England Federalism, which, professing a mild friendship for man-

ufactures and unwillingly conceding the minimum of protection solely as an incident to revenue, was, at bottom, thoroughly hostile to both. In 1820 Mr. Webster stood forth, both politically and constitutionally, as a free-trader, moderate but at the same time decided in his opinions.

When the tariff of 1824 was brought before Congress and advocated with great zeal by Mr. Clay, who upheld it as the "American system," Mr. Webster opposed the policy in the fullest and most elaborate speech he had yet made on the subject. A distinguished American economist, Mr. Edward Atkinson, has described this speech of 1824 briefly and exactly in the following words: —

"It contains a refutation of the exploded theory of the balance of trade, of the fallacy with regard to the exportation of specie, and of the claim that the policy of protection is distinctively the American policy which can never be improved upon, and it indicates how thoroughly his judgment approved and his better nature sympathized with the movement towards enlightened and liberal commercial legislation, then already commenced in Great Britain."

This speech was in truth one of great ability, showing a remarkable capacity for questions of political economy, and opening with an admirable discussion of the currency and of finance, in regard to which Mr. Webster always held and advanced the soundest, most scientific, and most enlightened views. Now, as in 1820, he stood forth as the especial champion of commerce, which, as he said, had thriven without protection, had brought revenue to the government and wealth to the country, and would be grievously injured by the proposed tariff. He made his principal objection to the protection policy on the ground of favoritism to some interests at the expense of others when all were entitled to equal consideration. Of England he said, "Because a thing has been wrongly done, it does not follow that it can be undone; and this is the reason, as I understand it, for which exclusion, prohibition, and monopoly are suffered to remain in any degree in the English system." After examining at length the different varieties of protection, and displaying very thoroughly the state of current English opinion, he defined the position which he, in common with the Federalists of New England, then as always adhered to in the following words: —

" Protection, when carried to the point which is now recommended, that is, to entire prohibition, seems to me destructive of all commercial intercourse between nations. We are urged to adopt the system on general principles; . . . I do not admit the general principle; on the contrary, I think freedom of trade the general principle, and restriction the exception."

He pointed out that the proposed protective policy involved a decline of commerce, and that steadiness and uniformity, the most essential requisites in any policy, were endangered. He then with great power dealt with the various points summarized by Mr. Atkinson, and concluded with a detailed and learned examination of the various clauses of the bill, which finally passed by a small majority and became law.

In 1828 came another tariff bill, so bad and so extreme in many respects that it was called the "bill of abominations." It originated in the agitation of the woolen manufacturers which had started the year before, and for this bill Mr. Webster spoke and voted. He changed his ground on this important question absolutely and entirely, and made no pretense of doing anything else. The speech which he made on this occasion is a celebrated one, but it is so solely on account of the startling change of position which it announced. Mr. Webster has been attacked and defended for his action at this time with great zeal, and all the constitutional and economic arguments for and against protection are continually brought forward in this connection. From the tone of the discussion, it is to be feared that many of those who are interested in the question have not taken the trouble to read what he said. The speech of 1828 is by no means equal in any way to its predecessors in the same field. It is brief and simple to the last degree. It has not a shred of constitutional argument, nor does it enter at all into a discussion of general principles. It makes but one point, and treats that point with great force as the only one to be made under the circumstances, and thereby presents the single and sufficient reason for its author's vote. A few lines from the speech give the marrow of the whole matter. Mr. Webster said: —

"New England, sir, has not been a leader in this policy. On the contrary, she held back herself and tried to hold others back from it, from the adoption of the Constitution to 1824. Up to 1824 she was accused of sinister and selfish designs, *because she discountenanced the progress of this policy.* . . . Under this angry denunciation against her the act of 1824 passed. Now the imputation is of a precisely opposite character. . . . Both charges, sir, are equally without the slightest foundation. The opinion of New England up to 1824 was founded in the conviction that, on the whole, it was wisest and best, both for herself and others, that manufactures should make haste slowly. . . . When, at the commencement of the late war, duties were doubled, we were told that we should find a mitigation of the weight of taxation in the new aid and succor which would be thus afforded to our own manufacturing labor. Like arguments were urged, and prevailed, but not by the aid of New England votes, when the tariff was afterwards arranged at the close of the war in 1816. Finally, after a winter's deliberation, the act of 1824 received the sanction of both Houses of Congress and settled the policy of the country. What, then, was New England to do ? . . . Was she to hold out forever against the course of the government, and see herself losing on one side and yet make no effort to sustain herself on the other ? No, sir. Nothing was left to New England but to conform herself to the will of others. Nothing was left to her but to consider that the government had fixed and determined its own policy; and that policy was *protection*. . . . I believe, sir, almost every man from New England who voted against the law of 1824 declared that if, notwithstanding his opposition to that law, it should still pass, there would be no alternative but to consider the course and policy of the government as then settled and fixed, and to act accordingly. The law did pass ; and a vast increase of investment in manufacturing establishments was the consequence."

Opinion in New England changed for good and sufficient business reasons, and Mr. Webster changed with it. Free trade had commended itself to him as an abstract principle, and he had sustained and defended it as in the interest of commercial New England. But when the weight of interest in New England shifted from free trade to protection Mr. Webster followed it. His constituents were by no means unanimous in support of the tariff in 1828, but the majority favored it, and Mr. Webster went with the majority. At a public dinner given to him in Boston at the close of the session, he explained to the dissentient minority the reasons for his vote, which were very simple. He thought that good predominated over evil in the bill, and that the majority throughout the whole State of which he was the representative favored the tariff, and therefore he had voted in the affirmative.

Much fault has been found, as has been said, both at the time and since, with Mr. Webster's

change of position on this question. It has been
held up as a monument of inconsistency, and as
indicating a total absence of deep conviction.
That Mr. Webster was, in a certain sense, inconsistent is beyond doubt, but consistency is the bug-
bear of small minds, as well as a mark of strong
characters, while its reverse is often the proof of
wisdom. On the other hand, it may be fairly
argued that, holding as he did that the whole thing
was purely a business question to be decided according to circumstances, his course, in view of
the policy adopted by the government, was at bottom perfectly consistent. As to the want of deep
conviction, Mr. Webster's vote on this question
proves nothing. He had believed in free trade as
an abstract general principle, and there is no reason to suppose that he ever abandoned his belief
on this point. But he had too clear a mind ever
to be run away with by the extreme vagaries of
the Manchester school. He knew that there was
no morality, no immutable right and wrong, in an
impost or a free list. It has been the fashion to
refer to Mr. Disraeli's declaration that free trade
was "a mere question of expediency" as a proof
of that gentleman's cynical indifference to moral
principles. That the late Earl of Beaconsfield had
no deep convictions on any subject may be readily
admitted, but in this instance he uttered a very
plain and simple truth, which all the talk in the
world about free trade as the harbinger and foundation of universal peace on earth cannot disguise.

Mr. Webster never at any time treated the question of free trade or protection as anything but one of expediency. Under the lead of Mr. Calhoun, in 1816, the South and West initiated a protective policy, and after twelve years it had become firmly established and New England had adapted herself to it. Mr. Webster, as a New England representative, resisted the protective policy at the outset as against her interests, but when she had conformed to the new conditions, he came over to its support simply on the ground of expediency. He rested the defense of his new position upon the doctrine which he had always consistently preached, that uniformity and permanency were the essential and sound conditions of any policy, whether of free trade or protection. In 1828, neither at the dinner in Boston nor in the Senate, did he enter into any discussion of general principles or constitutional theories. He merely said, in substance, You have chosen to make protection necessary to New England, and therefore I am now forced to vote for it. This was the position which he continued to hold to the end of his life. As he was called upon, year after year, to defend protection, and as New England became more and more wedded to the tariff, he elaborated his arguments on many points, but the essence of all he said afterwards is to be found in the speech of 1828. On the constitutional point he was obliged to make a more violent change. He held, of course, to his opinion that, under the revenue power, protection could be incidental only, because from that doctrine there was no escape. But he dropped the condemnation expressed in 1814 and the doubts uttered in 1820 as to the theory that it was within the direct power of Congress to enact a protective tariff, and assumed that they had this right as one of the general powers in the Constitution, or that at all events they had exercised it, and that therefore the question was henceforward to be considered as *res adjudicata*. The speech of 1828 marks the separation of Mr. Webster from the opinions of the old school of New England Federalism. Thereafter he stood forth as the champion of the tariff and of the "American system" of Henry Clay. Regarding protection in its true light, as a mere question of expediency, he followed the interests of New England and of the great industrial communities of the North. That he shifted his ground at the proper moment, bad as the "bill of abominations" was, and that, as a Northern statesman, he was perfectly justified in doing so, cannot be fairly questioned or criticised. It is true that his course was in one sense a sectional one, but everybody else's on this question was the same, and it could not be, it never has been, and never will be otherwise.

The tariff of 1828 was destined indirectly to have far more important results to Mr. Webster than the brief speech in which he signalized his change of position on the question of protection. Soon after the passage of the act, in May, 1828, the South Carolina delegation held a meeting to take steps to resist the operation of the tariff, but nothing definite was then accomplished. Popular meetings in South Carolina, characterized by much violent talk, followed, however, during the summer, and in the autumn the legislature of the State put forth the famous "exposition and protest" which emanated from Mr. Calhoun, and embodied in the fullest and strongest terms the principles of "nullification." These movements were viewed with regret and with some alarm throughout the country, but they were rather lost sight of in the intense excitement of the presidential election. The accession of Jackson then came to absorb the public attention, and brought with it the sweeping removals from office which Mr. Webster strongly denounced. At the same time he was not led into the partisan absurdity of denying the President's power of removal, and held to the impregnable position of steady resistance to the evils of patronage, which could be cured only by the operation of an enlightened public sentiment. It is obvious now that, in the midst of all this agitation about other matters, Mr. Calhoun and the South Carolinians never lost sight of the conflict for which they were preparing, and that they were on the alert to bring nullification to the front in a more menacing and pronounced fashion than had yet been attempted.

The grand assault was finally made in the Senate, under the eye of the great nullifier, who then

occupied the chair of the Vice-President, and came
in an unexpected way.   In December, 1829, Mr.
Foote of Connecticut introduced a harmless resolution of inquiry respecting the sales and surveys
of the Western lands.   In the long-drawn debate
which ensued, General Hayne of South Carolina,
on January 19, 1830, made an elaborate attack on
the New England States.   He accused them of a
desire to check the growth of the West in the interests of the protective policy, and tried to show
the sympathy which should exist between the West
and South, and lead them to make common cause
against the tariff.   Mr. Webster felt that this attack could not be left unanswered, and the next
day he replied to it.   This first speech on Foote's
resolution has been so obscured by the greatness
of the second that it is seldom referred to and but
little read.   Yet it is one of the most effective
retorts, one of the strongest pieces of destructive
criticism, ever uttered in the Senate, although its
purpose was simply to repel the charge of hostility
to the West on the part of New England.   The
accusation was in fact absurd, and but few years
had elapsed since Mr. Webster and New England
had been assailed by Mr. McDuffie for desiring
to build up the West at the expense of the South
by the policy of internal improvements.   It was
not difficult, therefore, to show the groundlessness
of this new attack, but Mr. Webster did it with
consummate art and great force, shattering Hayne's
elaborate argument to pieces and treading it under

foot.   Mr. Webster only alluded incidentally to the tariff agitation in South Carolina, but the crushing nature of the reply inflamed and mortified Mr. Hayne, who, on the following day, insisted on Mr. Webster's presence, and spoke for the second time at great length.   He made again a bitter attack upon New England, upon Mr. Webster personally, and upon the character and patriotism of Massachusetts.   He then made a full exposition of the doctrine of nullification, giving free expression of the views and principles entertained by his master and leader, who presided over the discussion.   The debate had now drifted far from the original resolution, but its real object had been reached at last.   The war upon the tariff had been begun, and the standard of nullification and of resistance to the Union and to the laws of Congress had been planted boldly in the Senate of the United States.   The debate was adjourned and Mr. Hayne did not conclude till January 25. The next day Mr. Webster replied in the second speech on Foote's resolution, which is popularly known as the "Reply to Hayne."

This great speech marks the highest point attained by Mr. Webster as a public man.   He never surpassed it, he never equaled it afterwards. It was his zenith intellectually, politically, and as an orator.   His fame grew and extended in the years which followed, he won ample distinction in other fields, he made many other splendid speeches, but he never went beyond the reply which he made to the Senator from South Carolina on January 26, 1830.

The doctrine of nullification, which was the main point both with Hayne and Webster, was no new thing. The word was borrowed from the Kentucky resolutions of 1799, and the principle was contained in the more cautious phrases of the contemporary Virginia resolutions and of the Hartford Convention in 1814. The South Carolinian reproduction in 1830 was fuller and more elaborate than its predecessors and supported by more acute reasoning, but the principle was unchanged. Mr. Webster's argument was simple but overwhelming. He admitted fully the right of revolution. He accepted the proposition that no one was bound to obey an unconstitutional law; but the essential question was who was to say whether a law was unconstitutional or not. Each State has that authority, was the reply of the nullifiers, and if the decision is against the validity of the law it cannot be executed within the limits of the dissenting State. The vigorous sarcasm with which Mr. Webster depicted a practical nullification, and showed that it was nothing more nor less than revolution when actually carried out, was really the conclusive answer to the nullifying doctrine. But Mr. Calhoun and his school eagerly denied that nullification rested on the right to revolt against oppression. They argued that it was a constitutional right; that they could live within the Constitution and beyond it, — inside the house and outside it

at one and the same time.   They contended that,
the Constitution being a compact between the
States, the Federal government was the creation
of the States; yet, in the same breath, they declared that the general government was a party to
the contract from which it had itself emanated, in
order to get rid of the difficulty of proving that,
while the single dissenting State could decide
against the validity of a law, the twenty or more
other States, also parties to the contract, had no
right to deliver an opposite judgment which should
be binding as the opinion of the majority of the
court.   There was nothing very ingenious or very
profound in the argument by which Mr. Webster
demonstrated the absurdity of the doctrine which
attempted to make nullification a peaceable constitutional privilege, when it could be in practice
nothing else than revolution.   But the manner in
which he put the argument was magnificent and
final.   As he himself said, in this very speech, of
Samuel Dexter, "his statement was argument, his
inference demonstration."

The weak places in his armor were historical in
their nature.   It was probably necessary, at all
events Mr. Webster felt it to be so, to argue that
the Constitution at the outset was not a compact
between the States, but a national instrument, and
to distinguish the cases of Virginia and Kentucky
in 1799 and of New England in 1814, from that
of South Carolina in 1830.   The former point he
touched upon lightly, the latter he discussed ably,

eloquently, ingeniously, and at length.   Unfortunately the facts were against him in both instances.
When the Constitution was adopted by the votes
of States at Philadelphia, and accepted by the
votes of States in popular conventions, it is safe
to say that there was not a man in the country
from Washington and Hamilton on the one side,
to George Clinton and George Mason on the
other, who regarded the new system as anything
but an experiment entered upon by the States and
from which each and every State had the right
peaceably to withdraw, a right which was very
likely to be exercised.   When the Virginia and
Kentucky resolutions appeared they were not opposed on constitutional grounds, but on those of
expediency and of hostility to the revolution which
they were considered to embody.   Hamilton, and
no one knew the Constitution better than he,
treated them as the beginnings of an attempt to
change the government, as the germs of a conspir-
acy to destroy the Union.   As Dr. Von Holst
tersely and accurately states it, "there was no
time as yet to attempt to strangle the healthy
human mind in a net of logical deductions."   That
was the work reserved for John C. Calhoun.

What is true of 1799 is true of the New England leaders at Washington when they discussed
the feasibility of secession in 1804; of the declaration in favor of secession made by Josiah Quincy
in Congress a few years later; of the resistance of
New England during the war of 1812, and of the

right of "interposition" set forth by the Hartford
Convention. In all these instances no one troubled himself about the constitutional aspect; it
was a question of expediency, of moral and political right or wrong. In every case the right was
simply stated, and the uniform answer was, such
a step means the overthrow of the present system.

When South Carolina began her resistance to
the tariff in 1830, times had changed, and with
them the popular conception of the government
established by the Constitution. It was now a
much more serious thing to threaten the existence
of the Federal government than it had been in
1799, or even in 1814. The great fabric which
had been gradually built up made an overthrow of
the government look very terrible; it made peaceable secession a mockery, and a withdrawal from
the Union equivalent to civil war. The boldest
hesitated to espouse any principle which was
avowedly revolutionary, and on both sides men
wished to have a constitutional defense for every
doctrine which they promulgated. This was the
feeling which led Mr. Calhoun to elaborate and
perfect with all the ingenuity of his acute and
logical mind the arguments in favor of nullification
as a constitutional principle. At the same time
the theory of nullification, however much elaborated, had not altered in its essence from the bald
and brief statement of the Kentucky resolutions.
The vast change had come on the other side of the
question, in the popular idea of the Constitution.

It was no longer regarded as an experiment from
which the contracting parties had a right to withdraw, but as the charter of a national government
which the greatest men among its framers hoped
it would come to be. "It is a critical moment,"
said Mr. Bell of New Hampshire to Mr. Webster,
on the morning of January 26, "and it is time, it
is high time that the people of this country should
know what this Constitution *is*." "Then," answered Mr. Webster, "by the blessing of heaven
they shall learn, this day, before the sun goes
down, what I understand it to be." With these
words on his lips he entered the senate chamber,
and when he replied to Hayne he stated what the
Union and the government had come to be at that
moment. He defined the character of the Union
as it existed in 1830, and that definition so magnificently stated, and with such grand eloquence,
went home to the hearts of the people, and put
into noble words the sentiment which they felt but
had not expressed. This was the significance of
the reply to Hayne. It mattered not what men
thought of the Constitution in 1789. The government which was then established might have degenerated into a confederation little stronger than its
predecessor. But the Constitution did its work
better, and converted a confederacy into a nation.
Mr. Webster set forth the national conception of
the Union. He expressed what many men were
vaguely thinking and believing, and the principles
which he made clear and definite went on broaden-

ing and deepening until, thirty years afterwards, they had a force sufficient to sustain the North and enable her to triumph in the terrible struggle which resulted in the preservation of national life.   When Mr. Webster showed that practical nullification was revolution, he had answered completely the South Carolinian doctrine, for revolution is not susceptible of constitutional argument.   But in the state of public opinion at that time it was necessary to discuss nullification on constitutional grounds also, and Mr. Webster did this as eloquently and ably as the nature of the case admitted. Whatever the historical defects of his position, he put weapons into the hands of every friend of the Union, and gave reasons and arguments to the doubting and timid.   Yet after all is said, the meaning of Mr. Webster's speech in our history and its significance to us are, that it set forth with every attribute of eloquence the nature of the Union as it had developed under the Constitution. He took the vague popular conception and gave it life and form and character.   He said, as he alone could say, the people of the United States are a nation, they are the masters of an empire, their union is indivisible, and the words which then rang out in the senate chamber have come down through long years of political conflict and of civil war, until at last they are part of the political creed of every one of his fellow countrymen.

The reply to Hayne cannot, however, be dismissed with a consideration of its historical and

political meaning or of its constitutional significance. It has a personal and literary importance
of hardly less moment. There comes an occasion,
a period perhaps, in the life of every man when he
touches his highest point, when he does his best,
or even, under a sudden inspiration and excitement, something better than his best, and to which
he can never again attain. At the moment it is
often impossible to detect this point, but when the
man and his career have passed into history, and
we can survey it all spread out before us like a
map, the pinnacle of success can easily be discovered. The reply to Hayne was the zenith of Mr.
Webster's life, and it is the place of all others
where it is fit to pause and study him as a parliamentary orator and as a master of eloquence.

Before attempting, however, to analyze what he
said, let us strive to recall for a moment the scene
of his great triumph. On the morning of the
memorable day, the senate chamber was packed
by an eager and excited crowd. Every seat on
the floor and in the galleries was occupied, and all
the available standing-room was filled. The protracted debate, conducted with so much ability on
both sides, had excited the attention of the whole
country, and had given time for the arrival of
hundreds of interested spectators from all parts
of the Union, and especially from New England.
The fierce attacks of the Southern leaders had
angered and alarmed the people of the North.
They longed with an intense longing to have these

assaults met and repelled, and yet they could not believe that this apparently desperate feat could be successfully accomplished. Men of the North and of New England could be known in Washington, in those days, by their indignant but dejected looks and downcast eyes. They gathered in the senate chamber on the appointed day, quivering with anticipation, and with hope and fear struggling for the mastery in their breasts. With them were mingled those who were there from mere curiosity, and those who had come rejoicing in the confident expectation that the Northern champion would suffer failure and defeat.

In the midst of the hush of expectation, in that dead silence which is so peculiarly oppressive because it is possible only when many human beings are gathered together, Mr. Webster rose. He had sat impassive and immovable during all the preceding days, while the storm of argument and invective had beaten about his head. At last his time had come; and as he rose and stood forth, drawing himself up to his full height, his personal grandeur and his majestic calm thrilled all who looked upon him. With perfect quietness, unaffected apparently by the atmosphere of intense feeling about him, he said, in a low, even tone: "Mr. President: When the mariner has been tossed for many days in thick weather and on an unknown sea, he naturally avails himself of the first pause in the storm, the earliest glance of the sun, to take his latitude and ascertain how far the elements have driven him from his true course. Let us imitate this prudence; and, before we float farther on the waves of this debate, refer to the point from which we departed, that we may, at least, be able to conjecture where we now are. I ask for the reading of the resolution before the Senate." This opening sentence was a piece of consummate art. The simple and appropriate image, the low voice, the calm manner, relieved the strained excitement of the audience, which might have ended by disconcerting the speaker if it had been maintained. Every one was now at his ease; and when the monotonous reading of the resolution ceased Mr. Webster was master of the situation, and had his listeners in complete control. With breathless attention they followed him as he proceeded. The strong masculine sentences, the sarcasm, the pathos, the reasoning, the burning appeals to love of State and country, flowed on unbroken. As his feelings warmed the fire came into his eyes; there was a glow on his swarthy cheek; his strong right arm seemed to sweep away resistlessly the whole phalanx of his opponents, and the deep and melodious cadences of his voice sounded like harmonious organ-tones as they filled the chamber with their music. As the last words died away into silence, those who had listened looked wonderingly at each other, dimly conscious that they had heard one of the grand speeches which are landmarks in the history of eloquence; and the men of the North and of New England went forth full of the pride of victory, for their champion had triumphed, and no assurance was needed to prove to the world that this time no answer could be made.

As every one knows, this speech contains much more than the argument against nullification, which has just been discussed, and exhibits all its author's intellectual gifts in the highest perfection.   Mr. Hayne had touched on every conceivable subject of political importance, including slavery, which, however covered up, was really at the bottom of every Southern movement, and was certain sooner or later to come to the surface.   All these various topics Mr. Webster took up, one after another, displaying a most remarkable strength of grasp and ease of treatment.   He dealt with them all effectively and yet in just proportion.   Throughout there are bursts of eloquence skillfully mingled with statement and argument, so that the listeners were never wearied by a strained and continuous rhetorical display; and yet, while the attention was closely held by the even flow of lucid reasoning, the emotions and passions were from time to time deeply aroused and strongly excited.   In many passages of direct retort Mr. Webster used an irony which he employed always in a perfectly characteristic way.   He had a strong natural sense of humor, but he never made fun or descended to trivial efforts to excite laughter against his opponent.   He was not a witty man or a maker of epigrams.   But he was a master in the use of a cold, dignified sarcasm, which at times, and in this instance particularly, he used freely and mercilessly. Beneath the measured sentences there is a lurking smile which saves them from being merely savage and cutting attacks, and yet brings home a keen sense of the absurdity of the opponent's position. The weapon resembled more the sword of Richard than the scimetar of Saladin, but it was none the less a keen and trenchant blade. There is probably no better instance of Mr. Webster's power of sarcasm than the famous passage in which he replied to Hayne's taunt about the "murdered coalition," which was said to have existed between Adams and Calhoun. In a totally different vein is the passage about Massachusetts, perhaps in its way as good an example as we have of Webster's power of appealing to the higher and more tender feelings of human nature. The thought is simple and even obvious, and the expression unadorned, and yet what he said had that subtle quality which stirred and still stirs the heart of every man born on the soil of the old Puritan Commonwealth.

The speech as a whole has all the qualities which made Mr. Webster a great orator, and the same traits run through his other speeches. An analysis of the reply to Hayne, therefore, gives us all the conditions necessary to forming a correct idea of Mr. Webster's eloquence, of its characteristics and its value. The Attic school of oratory subordinated form to thought to avoid the misuse of

ornament, and triumphed over the more florid
practice of the so-called "Asiatics." Rome gave
the palm to Atticism, and modern oratory has gone
still farther in the same direction, until its predominant quality has become that of making sustained appeals to the understanding. Logical vigi-
lance and long chains of reasoning, avoided by
the ancients, are the essentials of our modern oratory. Many able men have achieved success under
these conditions as forcible and convincing speakers. But the grand eloquence of modern times is
distinguished by the bursts of feeling, of imagery
or of invective, joined with convincing argument.
This combination is rare, and whenever we find
a man who possesses it we may be sure that, in
greater or less degree, he is one of the great masters of eloquence as we understand it. The names
of those who in debate or to a jury have been in
every-day practice strong and effective speakers,
and also have thrilled and shaken large masses of
men, readily occur to us. To this class belong
Chatham and Burke, Fox, Sheridan and Erskine,
Mirabeau and Vergniaud, Patrick Henry and Daniel Webster.

Mr. Webster was of course essentially modern
in his oratory. He relied chiefly on the sustained
appeal to the understanding, and he was a conspicuous example of the prophetic character which
Christianity, and Protestantism especially, has
given to modern eloquence. At the same time
Mr. Webster was in some respects more classical,

and resembled more closely the models of antiquity, than any of those who have been mentioned
as belonging to the same high class. He was wont
to pour forth the copious stream of plain, intelligible observations, and indulge in the varied appeals to feeling, memory, and interest, which Lord
Brougham sets down as characteristic of ancient
oratory. It has been said that while Demosthenes
was a sculptor, Burke was a painter. Mr. Webster
was distinctly more of the former than the latter.
He rarely amplified or developed an image or a description, and in this he followed the Greek rather
than the Englishman.   Dr. Francis Lieber wrote:
"To test Webster's oratory, which has ever been
very attractive to me, I read a portion of my favorite speeches of Demosthenes, and then read,
always aloud, parts of Webster; then returned to
the Athenian; and Webster stood the test." Apart
from the great compliment which this conveys,
such a comparison is very interesting as showing
the similarity between Mr. Webster and the Greek
orator. Not only does the test indicate the merit
of Mr. Webster's speeches, but it also proves that
he resembled the Athenian, and that the likeness
was more striking than the inevitable difference
born of race and time. Yet there is no indication
that Webster ever made a study of the ancient
models or tried to form himself upon them.

The cause of the classic self-restraint in Webster
was partly due to the artistic sense which made
him so devoted to simplicity of diction, and partly

to the cast of his mind.   He had a powerful historic imagination, but not in the least the imagination of the poet, which

" Bodies forth the forms of things unknown."

He could describe with great vividness, brevity,
and force what had happened in the past, what
actually existed, or what the future promised.
But his fancy never ran away with him or carried
him captive into the regions of poetry.   Imagination of this sort is readily curbed and controlled,
and, if less brilliant, is safer than that defined by
Shakespeare.   For this reason, Mr. Webster rarely
indulged in long, descriptive passages, and while
he showed the highest power in treating anything
with a touch of humanity about it, he was sparing
of images drawn wholly from nature, and was not
peculiarly successful in depicting in words natural
scenery or phenomena.   The result is that in his
highest flights, while he is often grand and affecting, full of life and power, he never shows the
creative imagination.   But if he falls short on the
poetic side, there is the counterbalancing advantage that there is never a false note nor an over-
wrought description which offends our taste and
jars upon our sensibilities.

Mr. Webster showed his love of direct simplicity in his style even more than in his thought or
the general arrangement and composition of his
speeches.   His sentences are, as a rule, short, and
therefore pointed and intelligible, but they never

become monotonous and harsh, the fault to which brevity is always liable. On the contrary, they are smooth and flowing, and there is always a sufficient variety of form. The choice of language is likewise simple. Mr. Webster was a remorseless critic of his own style, and he had an almost extreme preference for Anglo-Saxon words and a corresponding dislike of Latin derivatives. The only exception he made was in his habit of using "commence" instead of its far superior synonym "begin." His style was vigorous, clear, and direct in the highest degree, and at the same time warm and full of vitality. He displayed that rare union of great strength with perfect simplicity, the qualities which made Swift the almost unrivaled master of pure, simple, and forcible English.

Charles Fox is credited with saying that a good speech never reads well. This opinion, taken in the sense in which it was intended, that a carefully prepared speech, which reads like an essay, lacks the freshness and glow that should characterize the oratory of debate, is undoubtedly correct. But it is equally true that when a speech which we know to have been good in delivery is equally good in print, a higher intellectual plane is reached and a higher level of excellence is attained than is possible to either the mere essay or to the effective retort or argument, which loses its flavor with the occasion which draws it forth. Mr. Webster's speeches on the tariff, on the bank, and on like subjects, able as they are, are necessarily dry, but

his speeches on nobler themes are admirable reading. This is, of course, due to the variety and
ease of treatment, to their power, and to the purity
of the style. At the same time, the immediate
effect of what he said was immense, greater, even,
than the intrinsic merit of the speech itself. There
has been much discussion as to the amount of preparation which Mr. Webster made. His occasional
orations were, of course, carefully written out beforehand, a practice which was entirely proper;
but in his great parliamentary speeches, and often
in legal arguments as well, he made but slight
preparation in the ordinary sense of the term.
The notes for the two speeches on Foote's resolution were jotted down on a few sheets of note-
paper. The delivery of the second one, his masterpiece, was practically extemporaneous, and yet
it fills seventy octavo pages and occupied four
hours. He is reported to have said that his whole
life had been a preparation for the reply to Hayne.
Whether he said it or not, the statement is perfectly true. The thoughts on the Union and on
the grandeur of American nationality had been
garnered up for years, and this in a greater or
less degree was true of all his finest efforts. The
preparation on paper was trifling, but the mental
preparation extending over weeks or days, sometimes, perhaps, over years, was elaborate to the
last point. When the moment came, a night's
work would put all the stored-up thoughts in order,
and on the next day they would pour forth with

all the power of a strong mind thoroughly saturated with its subject, and yet with the vitality of unpremeditated expression, having the fresh glow of morning upon it, and no trace of the lamp.

More than all this, however, in the immediate effect of Mr. Webster's speeches was the physical influence of the man himself. We can but half understand his eloquence and its influence if we do not carefully study his physical attributes, his temperament and disposition. In face, form, and voice, nature did her utmost for Daniel Webster. No envious fairy was present at his birth to mar these gifts by her malign influence. He seemed to every one to be a giant; that, at least, is the word we most commonly find applied to him, and there is no better proof of his enormous physical impressiveness than this well-known fact, for Mr. Webster was not a man of extraordinary stature. He was five feet ten inches in height, and, in health, weighed a little less than two hundred pounds. These are the proportions of a large man, but there is nothing remarkable about them. We must look elsewhere than to mere size to discover why men spoke of Webster as a giant. He had a swarthy complexion and straight black hair. His head was very large, the brain weighing, as is well known, more than any on record, except those of Cuvier and of the celebrated bricklayer. At the same time his head was of noble shape, with a broad and lofty brow, and his features were finely cut and full of massive strength. His eyes

were extraordinary. They were very dark and
deep-set, and, when he began to rouse himself to
action, shone with the deep light of a forge-fire,
getting ever more glowing as excitement rose.
His voice was in harmony with his appearance.
It was low and musical in conversation; in debate
it was high but full, ringing out in moments of
excitement like a clarion, and then sinking to deep
notes with the solemn richness of organ-tones,
while the words were accompanied by a manner in
which grace and dignity mingled in complete ac-
cord. The impression which he produced upon
the eye and ear it is difficult to express. There is
no man in all history who came into the world so
equipped physically for speech. In this direction
nature could do no more. The mere look of the
man and the sound of his voice made all who saw
and heard him feel that he must be the embodiment of wisdom, dignity, and strength, divinely
eloquent, even if he sat in dreamy silence or uttered nothing but heavy commonplaces.

It is commonly said that no one of the many
pictures of Mr. Webster gives a true idea of what
he was. We can readily believe this when we
read the descriptions which have come down to us.
That indefinable quality which we call personal
magnetism, the power of impressing by one's personality every human being who comes near, was
at its height in Mr. Webster. He never, for instance, punished his children, but when they did
wrong he would send for them and look at them

silently. The look, whether of anger or sorrow, was punishment and rebuke enough. It was the same with other children. The little daughter of Mr. Wirt once came into a room where Mr. Webster was sitting with his back toward her, and touched him on the arm. He turned suddenly, and the child started back with an affrighted cry at the sight of the dark, stern, melancholy face. But the cloud passed as swiftly as the shadows on a summer sea, and the next moment the look of affection and humor brought the frightened child into Mr. Webster's arms, and they were friends and playmates in an instant.

The power of a look and of changing expression, so magical with a child, was hardly less so with men. There have been very few instances in history where there is such constant reference to merely physical attributes as in the case of Mr. Webster. His general appearance and his eyes are the first and last things alluded to in every contemporary description. Every one is familiar with the story of the English navvy who pointed at Mr. Webster in the streets of Liverpool and said, "There goes a king." Sidney Smith exclaimed when he saw him, "Good heavens, he is a small cathedral by himself." Carlyle, no lover of America, wrote to Emerson : —

" Not many days ago I saw at breakfast the notablest of all your notabilities, Daniel Webster. He is a magnificent specimen. You might say to all the world, 'This is our Yankee Englishman; such limbs we make

in Yankee land!' As a logic fencer, or parliamentary
Hercules, one would incline to back him at first sight
against all the extant world. The tanned complexion;
that amorphous crag-like face; the dull black eyes under the precipice of brows, like dull anthracite furnaces
needing only to be *blown;* the mastiff mouth accurately
closed; I have not traced so much of *silent Berserkir
rage* that I remember of in any man. 'I guess I should
not like to be your nigger!' Webster is not loquacious,
but he is pertinent, conclusive; a dignified, perfectly
bred man, though not English in breeding; a man worthy of the best reception among us, and meeting such
I understand."

Such was the effect produced by Mr. Webster
when in England, and it was a universal impression. Wherever he went men felt in the depths
of their being the amazing force of his personal
presence. He could control an audience by a
look, and could extort applause from hostile listeners by a mere glance. On one occasion, after
the 7th of March speech, there is a story that a
noted abolitionist leader was present in the crowd
gathered to hear Mr. Webster, and this bitter opponent is reported to have said afterwards, "When
Webster, speaking of secession, asked ' what is to
become of me,' I was thrilled with a sense of some
awful impending calamity." The story may be
apocryphal, but there can be no doubt of its essential truth so far as the effect of Mr. Webster's
personal presence goes. People looked at him,
and that was enough. Mr. Parton in his essay

speaks of seeing Webster at a public dinner, sitting at the head of the table with a bottle of
Madeira under his yellow waistcoat, and looking
like Jove. When he presided at the Cooper memorial meeting in New York he uttered only a
few stately platitudes, and yet every one went
away with the firm conviction that he. had spoken
words of the profoundest wisdom and grandest
eloquence.

The temptation to rely on his marvelous physical gifts grew on him as he became older, which
was to be expected with a man of his temperament.
Even in his early days, when he was not in action,
he had an impassible and slumberous look; and
when he sat listening to the invective of Hayne,
no emotion could be traced on his cold, dark,
melancholy face, or in the cavernous eyes shining
with a dull light. This all vanished when he began to speak, and, as he poured forth his strong,
weighty sentences, there was no lack of expression
or of movement. But Mr. Webster, despite his
capacity for work, and his protracted and often
intense labor, was constitutionally indolent, and
this sluggishness of temperament increased very
much as he grew older. It extended from the
periods of repose to those of action until, in his
later years, a direct stimulus was needed to make
him exert himself. Even to the last the mighty
power was still there in undiminished strength,
but it was not willingly put forth. Sometimes the
outside impulse would not come; sometimes the

most trivial incident would suffice, and like a spark
on the train of gunpowder would bring a sudden
burst of eloquence, electrifying all who listened.
On one occasion he was arguing a case to the jury.
He was talking in his heaviest and most ponderous
fashion, and with half-closed eyes. The court
and the jurymen were nearly asleep as Mr. Webster argued on, stating the law quite wrongly to
his nodding listeners. The counsel on the other
side interrupted him and called the attention of
the court to Mr. Webster's presentation of the
law. The judge, thus awakened, explained to the
jury that the law was not as Mr. Webster stated
it. While this colloquy was in progress Mr. Webster roused up, pushed back his thick hair, shook
himself, and glanced about him with the look of
a caged lion. When the judge paused, he turned
again to the jury, his eyes no longer half shut but
wide open and glowing with excitement. Raising
his voice, he said, in tones which made every one
start: "If my client could recover under the law
as I stated it, how much more is he entitled to
recover under the law as laid down by the court; "
and then, the jury now being thoroughly awake,
he poured forth a flood of eloquent argument and
won his case. In his latter days Mr. Webster
made many careless and dull speeches and carried
them through by the power of his look and manner, but the time never came when, if fairly
aroused, he failed to sway the hearts and under-
standings of men by a grand and splendid elo-

quence. The lion slept very often, but it never became safe to rouse him from his slumber.

It was soon after the reply to Hayne that Mr. Webster made his great argument for the government in the White murder case. One other address to a jury in the Goodridge case, and the defense of Judge Prescott before the Massachusetts Senate, which is of similar character, have been preserved to us. The speech for Prescott is a strong, dignified appeal to the sober, and yet sympathetic, judgment of his hearers, but wholly free from any attempt to confuse or mislead, or to sway the decision by unwholesome pathos. Under the circumstances, which were very adverse to his client, the argument was a model of its kind, and contains some very fine passages full of the solemn force so characteristic of its author. The Goodridge speech is chiefly remarkable for the ease with which Mr. Webster unraveled a complicated set of facts, demonstrated that the accuser was in reality the guilty party, and carried irresistible conviction to the minds of the jurors. It was connected with a remarkable exhibition of his power of cross-examination, which was not only acute and penetrating, but extremely terrifying to a recalcitrant witness. The argument in the White case, as a specimen of eloquence, stands on far higher ground than either of the other two, and, apart from the nature of the subject, ranks with the very best of Mr. Webster's oratorical triumphs. The opening of the speech, comprising the account of the murder and the analysis of the workings of a mind seared with the remembrance of a horrid crime, must be placed among the very finest masterpieces of modern oratory. The description of the feelings of the murderer has a touch of the creative power, but, taken in conjunction with the wonderful picture of the deed itself, the whole exhibits the highest imaginative excellence, and displays the possession of an extraordinary dramatic force such as Mr. Webster rarely exerted. It has the same power of exciting a kind of horror and of making us shudder with a creeping, nameless terror as the scene after the murder of Duncan, when Macbeth rushes out from the chamber of death, crying, "I have done the deed. Didst thou not hear a noise?" I have studied this famous exordium with extreme care, and I have sought diligently in the works of all the great modern orators, and of some of the ancient as well, for similar passages of higher merit. My quest has been in vain. Mr. Webster's description of the White murder, and of the ghastly haunting sense of guilt which pursued the assassin, has never been surpassed in dramatic force by any speaker, whether in debate or before a jury. Perhaps the most celebrated descriptive passage in the literature of modern eloquence is the picture drawn by Burke of the descent of Hyder Ali upon the plains of the Carnatic, but even that certainly falls short of the opening of Webster's speech in simple force as well as in dramatic power. Burke depicted with all the ardor of his nature and with a wealth of color a great invasion which swept thousands to destruction. Webster's theme was a cold-blooded murder in a quiet New England town. Comparison between such topics, when one is so infinitely larger than the other, seems at first sight almost impossible. But Mr. Webster also dealt with the workings of the human heart under the influence of the most terrible passions, and those have furnished sufficient material for the genius of Shakespeare. The test of excellence is in the treatment, and in this instance Mr. Webster has never been excelled. The effect of that exordium, delivered as he alone could have delivered it, must have been appalling. He was accused of having been brought into the case to hurry the jury beyond the law and evidence, and his whole speech was certainly calculated to drive any body of men, terror-stricken by his eloquence, wherever he wished them to go. Mr. Webster did not have that versatility and variety of eloquence which we associate with the speakers who have produced the most startling effect upon that complex thing called a jury. He never showed that rapid alternation of wit, humor, pathos, invective, sublimity, and ingenuity which have been characteristic of the greatest advocates. Before a jury as everywhere else he was direct and simple. He awed and terrified jurymen; he convinced their reason; but he commanded rather than persuaded, and carried them with him by sheer force of eloquence and argument, and by his overpowering personality.

The extravagant admiration which Mr. Webster excited among his followers has undoubtedly exaggerated his greatness in many respects; but, high as the praise bestowed upon him as an orator has been, in that direction at least he has certainly not been overestimated. The reverse rather is true. Mr. Webster was, of course, the greatest orator this country has ever produced. Patrick Henry's fame rests wholly on tradition. The same is true of Hamilton, who, moreover, never had an opportunity adequate to his talents, which were unquestionably of the first order. Fisher Ames's reputation was due to a single speech which is distinctly inferior to many of Webster's. Clay's oratory has not stood the test of time; his speeches, which were so wonderfully effective when he uttered them, seem dead and cold and rather thin as we read them to-day. Calhoun was a great debater, but was too dry and hard for the highest eloquence. John Quincy Adams, despite his physical limitations, carried the eloquence of combat and bitter retort to the highest point in the splendid battles of his congressional career, but his learning, readiness, power of expression, argument, and scathing sarcasm were not rounded into a perfect whole by the more graceful attributes which also form an essential part of oratory.

Mr. Webster need not fear comparison with any of his countrymen, and he has no reason to shun

it with the greatest masters of speech in England.
He had much of the grandeur of Chatham, with
whom it is impossible to compare him or indeed
any one else, for the Great Commoner lives only
in fragments of doubtful accuracy. Sheridan was
universally considered to have made the most splendid speech of his day. Yet the speech on the Be-
gums as given by Moore does not cast Webster's
best work at all into the shade. Webster did not
have Sheridan's brilliant wit, but on the other
hand he was never forced, never involved, never
guilty of ornament, which fastidious judges would
now pronounce tawdry. Webster's best speeches
read much better than anything of Sheridan, and,
so far as we can tell from careful descriptions, his
manner, look, and delivery were far more imposing. The "manly eloquence" of Fox seems to
have resembled Webster's more closely than that
of any other of his English rivals. Fox was more
fertile, more brilliant, more surprising than Webster, and had more quickness and dash, and a
greater ease and charm of manner. But he was
often careless, and sometimes fell into repetitions,
from which, of course, no great speaker can be
wholly free any more than he can keep entirely
clear of commonplaces. Webster gained upon him
by superior finish and by greater weight of argument. Before a jury Webster fell behind Erskine as he did behind Choate, although neither
of them ever produced anything at all comparable
to the speech on the White murder; but in the

Senate, and in the general field of oratory, he rises high above them both. The man with whom Webster is oftenest compared, and the last to be mentioned, is of course Burke. It may be conceded at once that in creative imagination, and in richness of imagery and language, Burke ranks above Webster. But no one would ever have said of Webster as Goldsmith did of Burke:—

"Who, too deep for his hearers, still went on refining,
    And thought of convincing while they thought of dining."

Webster never sinned by over refinement or over ingenuity, for both were utterly foreign to his nature. Still less did he impair his power in the Senate as Burke did in the Commons by talking too often and too much. If he did not have the extreme beauty and grace of which Burke was capable, he was more forcible and struck harder and more weighty blows. He was greatly aided in this by his brief and measured periods, and his strength was never wasted in long and elaborate sentences. Webster, moreover, would never have degenerated into the ranting excitement which led Burke to draw a knife from his bosom and cast it on the floor of the House. This illustrates what was, perhaps, Mr. Webster's very strongest point, — his absolute good taste. He may have been ponderous at times in his later years. We know that he was occasionally heavy, pompous, and even dull, but he never violated the rules of the nicest taste. Other men have been more versatile, possessed of a richer imagination and more gorgeous

style, with a more brilliant wit and a keener sarcasm, but there is not one who is so absolutely
free from faults of taste as Webster, or who is so
uniformly simple and pure in thought and style,
even to the point of severity.[1]

It is easy to compare Mr. Webster with this
and the other great orator, and to select points of
resemblance and of difference, and show where
Mr. Webster was superior and where he fell behind. But the final verdict must be upon all his
qualities taken together. He had the most extraordinary physical gifts of face, form, and voice,
and employed them to the best advantage. Thus
equipped, he delivered a long series of great
speeches which can be read to-day with the deep-
est interest, instruction, and pleasure. He had
dignity, grandeur, and force, a strong historic imagination, and great dramatic power when he chose
to exert it. He possessed an unerring taste, a
capacity for vigorous and telling sarcasm, a glow
and fire none the less intense because they were
subdued, perfect clearness of statement joined to
the highest skill in argument, and he was master
of a style which was as forcible as it was simple
and pure. Take him for all in all, he was not

[1] A volume might be written comparing Mr. Webster with
other great orators. Only the briefest and most rudimentary
treatment of the subject is possible here. A more excellent study
of the comparative excellence of Webster's eloquence has been
made by Judge Chamberlain, librarian of the Boston Public
Library, in a speech at the dinner of the Dartmouth Alumni,
which has since been printed as a pamphlet.

only the greatest orator this country has ever
known, but in the history of eloquence his name
will stand with those of Demosthenes and Cicero,
of Chatham and Burke.

CHAPTER VII

THE STRUGGLE WITH JACKSON AND THE RISE OF
THE WHIG PARTY

In the year preceding the delivery of his great
speech Mr. Webster had lost his brother Ezekiel
by sudden death, and he had married for his second wife Miss Leroy of New York. The former
event was a terrible grief to him, and taken in
conjunction with the latter seemed to make a complete break with the past, and with its struggles
and privations, its joys and successes. The slender girl whom he had married in Salisbury church
and the beloved brother were both gone, and with
them went those years of youth in which, —

> " He had sighed deep, laughed free,
> Starved, feasted, despaired, been happy."

One cannot come to this dividing line in Mr.
Webster's life without regret. There was enough
of brilliant achievement and substantial success in
what had gone before to satisfy any man, and it
had been honest, simple, and unaffected. A wider
fame and a greater name lay before him, but with
them came also ugly scandals, bitter personal attacks, an ambition which warped his nature, and

finally a terrible mistake. One feels inclined to
say of these later years, with the Roman lover: —

> "Shut them in
> With their triumphs and their glories and the rest,
> Love is best."

The home changed first, and then the public
career. The reply which, as John Quincy Adams
said, "utterly demolished the fabric of Hayne's
speech and left scarcely a wreck to be seen," went
straight home to the people of the North. It gave
eloquent expression to the strong but undefined
feeling in the popular mind. It found its way
into every house and was read everywhere; it took
its place in the school books, to be repeated by
shrill boy voices, and became part of the literature
and of the intellectual life of the country. In
those solemn sentences men read the description
of what the United States had come to be under
the Constitution, and what American nationality
meant in 1830. The leaders of the young war
party in 1812 were the first to arouse the national
sentiment, but no one struck the chord with such
a master hand as Mr. Webster, or drew forth such
long and deep vibrations. There is no single utterance in our history which has done so much by
mere force of words to strengthen the love of
nationality and implant it deeply in the popular
heart, as the reply to Hayne.

Before the delivery of that speech Mr. Webster
was a distinguished statesman, but the day after
he awoke to a national fame which made all his

other triumphs pale. Such fame brought with it, of course, as it always does in this country, talk of the presidency. The reply to Hayne made Mr. Webster a presidential candidate, and from that moment he was never free from the gnawing, haunting ambition to win the grand prize of American public life. There was a new force in his career, and in all the years to come the influence of that force must be reckoned and remembered.

Mr. Webster was anxious that the party of opposition to General Jackson, which then passed by the name of National Republicans, should be in some way strengthened, solidified, and placed on a broad platform of distinct principles. He saw with great regret the ruin which was threatened by the anti-masonic schism, and it would seem that he was not indisposed to take advantage of this to stop the nomination of Mr. Clay, who was peculiarly objectionable to the opponents of masonry. He earnestly desired the nomination himself, but even his own friends in the party told him that this was out of the question, and he acquiesced in their decision. Mr. Clay's personal popularity, moreover, among the National Republicans was, in truth, invincible, and he was unanimously nominated by the convention at Baltimore. The action of the anti-masonic element in the country doomed Clay to defeat, which he was likely enough to encounter in any event; but the consolidation of the party so ardently desired by Mr. Webster was brought about by acts of the administration, which completely overcame any intestine divisions among its opponents.

The session of 1831–1832, when the country was preparing for the coming presidential election, marks the beginning of the fierce struggle with Andrew Jackson which was to give birth to a new and powerful organization known in our history as the Whig party, and destined, after years of conflict, to bring overwhelming defeat to the "Jacksonian democracy." There is no occasion here to enter into a history of the famous bank controversy. Established in 1816, the Bank of the United States, after a period of difficulties, had become a powerful and valuable financial organization. In 1832 it applied for a continuance of its charter, which then had three years still to run. Mr. Webster did not enter into the personal contest which had already begun, but in a speech of great ability advocated a renewal of the charter, showing, as he always did on such themes, a knowledge and a grasp of the principles and intricacies of public finance unequaled in our history except by Hamilton. In a second speech he made a most effective and powerful argument against a proposition to give the States authority to tax the bank, defending the doctrines laid down by Chief Justice Marshall in McCullough v. Maryland, and denying the power of Congress to give the States the right of such taxation, because by so doing they violated the Constitution. The amendment was defeated, and the bill for the continu-

ance of the charter passed both houses by large
majorities.

Jackson returned the bill with a veto. He had
the audacity to rest his veto upon the ground that
the bill was unconstitutional, and that it was the
duty of the President to decide upon the constitutionality of every measure without feeling in the
least bound by the opinion of Congress or of the
Supreme Court. His ignorance was so crass that
he failed to perceive the distinction between a new
bill and one to continue an existing law, while his
vanity and his self-assumption were so colossal
that he did not hesitate to assert that he had the
right and the power to declare an existing law,
passed by Congress, approved by Madison, and
held to be constitutional by an express decision
of the Supreme Court, to be invalid, because he
thought fit to say so. To overthrow such doctrines
was not difficult, but Mr. Webster refuted them
with a completeness and force which were irresistible. At the same time he avoided personal attack
in the dignified way which was characteristic of
him, despite the extraordinary temptation to indulge in invective and telling sarcasm to which
Jackson by his ignorance and presumption had so
exposed himself. The bill was lost, the great conflict with the bank was begun, and the Whig party
was founded.

Another event of a different character, which
had occurred not long before, helped to widen the
breach and to embitter the contest between the

parties of the administration and of the opposition. When in 1829 Mr. McLane had received his instructions as minister to England, he had been directed by Mr. Van Buren to reopen negotiations on the subject of the West Indian trade, and in so doing the secretary of state had reflected on the previous administration, and had said that the party in power would not support the pretensions of its predecessors. Such language was, of course, at variance with all traditions, was wholly improper, and was mean and contemptible in dealing with a foreign nation. In 1831 Mr. Van Buren was nominated as minister to England, and came up for confirmation in the Senate some time after he had actually departed on his mission. Mr. Webster opposed the confirmation in an eloquent speech full of just pride in his country and of vigorous indignation against the slight which Mr. Van Buren had put upon her by his instructions to Mr. McLane. He pronounced a splendid "rebuke upon the first instance in which an American minister had been sent abroad as the representative of his party and not as the representative of his country." The opposition was successful, and Mr. Van Buren's nomination was rejected. It is no doubt true that the rejection was a political mistake, and that, as was commonly said at the time, it created sympathy for Mr. Van Buren and insured his succession to the presidency. Yet no one would now think so well of Mr. Webster if, to avoid awakening popular sympathy and party

enthusiasm in behalf of Mr. Van Buren, he had
silently voted for that gentleman's confirmation.
To do so was to approve the despicable tone adopted
in the instructions to McLane.   As a patriotic
American, above all as a man of intense national
feelings, Mr. Webster could not have done otherwise than resist with all the force of his eloquence
the confirmation of a man who had made such an
undignified and unworthy exhibition of partisan-
ship.   Politically he may have been wrong, but
morally he was wholly right, and his rebuke stands
in our history as a reproach which Mr. Van Buren's subsequent success can neither mitigate nor
impair.

There was another measure, however, which
had a far different effect from those which tended
to build up the opposition to Jackson and his followers.   A movement was begun by Mr. Clay
looking to a revision and reduction of the tariff,
which finally resulted in a bill reducing duties on
many articles to a revenue standard, and leaving
those on cotton and woolen goods and iron unchanged.   In the debates which occurred during
the passage of this bill Mr. Webster took but little part, but they caused a furious outbreak on
the part of the South Carolinians led by Hayne,
and ended in the confirmation of the protective
policy.   When Mr. Webster spoke at the New
York dinner in 1831, he gave his hearers to understand very clearly that the nullification agitation was not at an end, and after the passage of

the new tariff bill he saw close at hand the danger
which he had predicted.

In November, 1832, South Carolina in convention passed her famous ordinance nullifying the
revenue laws of the United States, and her legislature, which assembled soon after, enacted laws
to carry out the ordinance, and gave an open defiance to the Federal government. The country
was filled with excitement. It was known that
Mr. Calhoun, having published a letter in defense
of nullification, had resigned the vice-presidency,
accepted the senatorship of South Carolina, and
was coming to the capital to advocate his favorite
doctrine. But the South Carolinians had made
one trifling blunder. They had overlooked the
President. Jackson was a Southerner and a Democrat, but he was also the head of the nation,
and determined to maintain its integrity. On
December 10, before Congress assembled, he issued his famous proclamation in which he took up
vigorously the position adopted by Mr. Webster
in his reply to Hayne, and gave the South Carolinians to understand that he would not endure
treason, but would enforce constitutional laws even
though he should be compelled to use bayonets to
do it. The legislature of the recalcitrant State
replied in an offensive manner which only served
to make Jackson angry. He, too, began to say
some pretty violent things, and, as he generally
meant what he said, the gallant leaders of nullification and other worthy people grew very uneasy.

There can be no doubt that the outlook was very
threatening, and the nullifiers were extremely likely
to be the first to suffer from the effects of the impending storm.

Mr. Webster was in New Jersey, on his way to
Washington, when he first received the proclamation, and at Philadelphia he met Mr. Clay, and
from a friend of that gentleman received a copy of
a bill which was to do away with the tariff by
gradual reductions, prevent the imposition of any
further duties, and which at the same time declared
against protection and in favor of a tariff for revenue only. This headlong plunge into concession
and compromise was not at all to Mr. Webster's
taste. He was opposed to the scheme for economical reasons, but still more on the far higher ground
that there was open resistance to laws of undoubted
constitutionality, and until that resistance was
crushed under foot any talk of compromise was
a blow at the national dignity and the national
existence which ought not to be tolerated for an
instant. His own course was plain. He proposed
to sustain the administration, and when the national honor should be vindicated and all unconstitutional resistance ended, then would come the
time for concessions. Jackson was not slow in
giving Mr. Webster something to support. At
the opening of the session a message was sent to
Congress asking that provision might be made to
enable the President to enforce the laws by means
of the land and naval forces if necessary. The

message was referred to a committee, who at once reported the celebrated "Force Bill," which embodied the principles of the message and had the entire approval of the President.   But Jackson's party broke, despite the attitude of their chief, for many of them were from the South and could not bring themselves to the point of accepting the Force Bill.   The moment was critical, and the administration turned to Mr. Webster and took him into their councils.   On February 8 Mr. Webster rose, and, after explaining in a fashion which no one was likely to forget, that this was wholly an administration measure, he announced his intention, as an independent senator, of giving it his hearty and inflexible support.   The combination thus effected was overwhelming.   Mr. Calhoun was now thoroughly alarmed, and we can well imagine that the threats of hanging, in which it was rumored that the President had indulged, began to have a good deal of practical significance to a gentleman who, as secretary of war, had been familiar with the circumstances attending the deaths of Arbuthnot and Ambrister.   At all events, Mr. Calhoun lost no time in having an interview with Mr. Clay, and the result was that the latter, on February 11, announced that he should, on the following day, introduce a tariff bill, a measure of the same sort having already been started in the House.   The bill as introduced did not involve such a complete surrender as that which Mr. Webster had seen in Philadelphia, but it necessitated

most extensive modifications and gave all that
South Carolina could reasonably demand. Mr.
Clay advocated it in a brilliant speech, resting his
defense on the ground that this was the only way
to preserve the tariff, and that it was founded on
the great constitutional doctrine of compromise.
Mr. Webster opposed the bill briefly, and then
introduced a series of resolutions combating the
proposed measure on economical principles and on
those of justice, and especially assailing the readiness to abandon the rightful powers of Congress
and yield them up to any form of resistance.
Before, however, he could speak in support of his
resolutions, the Force Bill came up, and Mr.
Calhoun made his celebrated argument in support
of nullification. This Mr. Webster was obliged
to answer, and he replied with the great speech
known in his works as "The Constitution not a
compact between sovereign States." In a general
way the same criticism is applicable to this debate
as to that with Hayne, but there were some important differences. Mr. Calhoun's argument was
superior to that of his follower. It was dry and
hard, but it was a splendid specimen of close and
ingenious reasoning, and, as was to be expected,
the originator and master surpassed the imitator
and pupil. Mr. Webster's speech, on the other
hand, in respect to eloquence, was decidedly inferior to the masterpiece of 1830. Mr. Curtis says:
"Perhaps there is no speech ever made by Mr.
Webster that is so close in its reasoning, so com-

pact, and so powerful." To the first two qualities
we can readily assent, but that it was equally powerful may be doubted. So long as Mr. Webster
confined himself to defending the Constitution as
it actually was and as what it had come to mean
in point of fact, he was invincible. Just in proportion as he left this ground and attempted to
argue on historical premises that it was a fundamental law, he weakened his position, for the historical facts were against him. In the reply to
Hayne he touched but slightly on the historical,
legal, and theoretical aspects of the case, and he
was overwhelming. In the reply to Calhoun he
devoted his strength chiefly to these topics, and,
meeting his keen antagonist on the latter's own
chosen ground, he put himself at a disadvantage.
In the actual present and in the steady course of
development, the facts were wholly with Mr. Webster. Whatever the people of the United States
understood the Constitution to mean in 1789, there
can be no question that a majority in 1833 regarded it as a fundamental law, and not as a compact — an opinion which has now become universal.
But it was quite another thing to argue that what
the Constitution had come to mean was what it
meant when it was adopted. The identity of meaning at these two periods was the proposition which
Mr. Webster undertook to maintain, and he upheld it as well and as plausibly as the nature of
the case admitted. His reasoning was close and
vigorous; but he could not destroy the theory of

the Constitution as held by leaders and people in
1789, or reconcile the Virginia and Kentucky resolutions or the Hartford Convention with the fun-
damental-law doctrines. Nevertheless, it would
be an error to suppose that because the facts of
history were against Mr. Webster in these particu-
lars, this able, ingenious, and elaborate argument
was thrown away. It was a fitting supplement
and complement to the reply to Hayne. It reiterated the national principles, and furnished those
whom the statement and demonstration of an existing fact could not satisfy with an immense maga-
zine of lucid reasoning and plausible and effective
arguments. The reply to Hayne gave magnificent
expression to the popular feeling, while that to
Calhoun supplied the arguments which, after years
of discussion, converted that feeling into a fixed
opinion, and made it strong enough to carry the
North through four years of civil war. But in
his final speech in this debate Mr. Webster came
back to his original ground, and said, in conclusion, "Shall we have a general government? Shall
we continue the union of States under a *government*
instead of a league? This vital and all-important
question the people will decide." The vital question went to the great popular jury, and they cast
aside all historical premises and deductions, all
legal subtleties and refinements, and gave their
verdict on the existing facts. The world knows
what that verdict was, and will never forget that
it was largely due to the splendid eloquence of

Daniel Webster when he defended the cause of nationality against the slaveholding separatists of South Carolina.

While this great debate was in progress, and Mr. Webster and the faithful adherents of Jackson were pushing the Force Bill to a vote, Mr. Clay was making every effort to carry the compromise tariff.   In spite of his exertions, the Force Bill passed on February 20, but close behind came the tariff, which Mr. Webster opposed, on its final passage, in a vigorous speech.   There is no need to enter into his economical objections, but he made his strongest stand against the policy of sacrificing great interests to soothe South Carolina.   Mr. Clay replied, but did not then press a vote, for, with that dexterous management which he had exhibited in 1820 and was again to display in 1850, he had succeeded in getting his tariff bill carried rapidly through the House, in order to obviate the objection that all money bills must originate in the lower branch.   The House bill passed the Senate, Mr. Webster voting against it, and became law.   There was no further need of the Force Bill.   Clay, Calhoun, even the daring Jackson ultimately, were very glad to accept the easy escape offered by a compromise.   South Carolina had in reality prevailed, although Mr. Clay had saved protection in a modified form.   Her threats of nullification had brought the United States government to terms, and the doctrines of Calhoun went home to the people of the South with the glory of substantial victory about them, to breed and foster separatism and secession, and prepare the way for armed conflict with the nobler spirit of nationality which Mr. Webster had roused in the North.

Speaking of Mr. Webster at this period, Mr. Benton says : —

" He was the colossal figure on the political stage during that eventful time, and his labors, splendid in their day, survive for the benefit of distant posterity." ... " It was a splendid era in his life, both for his intellect and his patriotism. No longer the advocate of classes or interests, he appeared as the great defender of the Union, of the Constitution, of the country, and of the administration to which he was opposed. Released from the bonds of party and the narrow confines of class and corporation advocacy, his colossal intellect expanded to its full proportions in the field of patriotism, luminous with the fires of genius, and commanding the homage not of party but of country. His magnificent harangues touched Jackson in his deepest-seated and ruling feeling, love of country, and brought forth the response which always came from him when the country was in peril and a defender presented himself. He threw out the right hand of fellowship, treated Mr. Webster with marked distinction, commended him with public praise, and placed him on the roll of patriots. And the public mind took the belief that they were to act together in future, and that a cabinet appointment or a high mission would be the reward of his patriotic service. It was a crisis in the life of Mr. Webster. He stood in public opposition to Mr. Clay and Mr. Calhoun. With

Mr. Clay he had a public outbreak in the Senate. He was cordial with Jackson. The mass of his party stood by him on the proclamation. He was at a point from which a new departure might be taken : one at which he could not stand still; from which there must be either advance or recoil. It was a case in which *will* more than *intellect* was to rule. He was above Mr. Clay and Mr. Calhoun in intellect, below them in will: and he was soon seen coöperating with them (Mr. Clay in the lead) in the great measure condemning President Jackson."

This is of course the view of a Jacksonian leader, but it is none the less full of keen analysis and comprehension of Mr. Webster, and in some respects embodies very well the conditions of the situation. Mr. Benton naturally did not see that an alliance with Jackson was utterly impossible for Mr. Webster, whose proper course was therefore much less simple than it appeared to the senator from Missouri. There was in reality no common ground possible between Webster and Jackson except defense of the national integrity. Mr. Webster was a great orator, a splendid advocate, a trained statesman and economist, a remarkable constitutional lawyer, and a man of immense dignity, not headstrong in temper, and without peculiar force of will. Jackson, on the other hand, was a rude soldier, unlettered, intractable, arbitrary, with a violent temper and a most despotic will. Two men more utterly incompatible it would have been difficult to find, and nothing could have been more wildly fantastic than to suppose an

alliance between them, or to imagine that Mr.
Webster could ever have done anything but oppose
utterly those mad gyrations of personal government which the President called his "policy."

Yet at the same time it is perfectly true that
just after the passage of the tariff bill Mr. Webster was at a great crisis in his life. He could
not act with Jackson. That way was shut to him
by nature, if by nothing else. But he could have
maintained his position as the independent and
unbending defender of nationality and as the foe
of compromise. He might then have brought Mr.
Clay to his side, and remained himself the undis-
puted head of the Whig party. The coalition between Clay and Calhoun was a hollow, ill-omened
thing, certain to go violently to pieces, as, in fact,
it did, within a few years, and then Mr. Clay, if
he had held out so long, would have been helpless
without Mr. Webster. But such a course required
a very strong will and great tenacity of purpose,
and it was on this side that Mr. Webster was
weak, as Mr. Benton points out. Instead of waiting for Mr. Clay to come to him, Mr. Webster
went over to Clay and Calhoun, and formed for
a time the third in that ill-assorted partnership.
There was no reason for his doing so. In fact
every good reason was against it. Mr. Clay had
come to Mr. Webster with his compromise, and
had been met with the reply "that it would be
yielding great principles to faction; and that the
time had come to test the strength of the Consti-

tution and the government." This was a brave,
manly answer, but Mr. Clay, nationalist as he
was, had straightway deserted his friend and ally,
and gone over to the separatist for support. Then
a sharp contest had occurred between Mr. Webster and Mr. Clay in the debate on the tariff;
and when it was all over, the latter wrote with
frank vanity and a slight tinge of contempt: "Mr.
Webster and I came in conflict, and I have the
satisfaction to tell you that he gained nothing.
My friends flatter me with my having completely
triumphed. There is no permanent breach between us. I think he begins already to repent his
course." Mr. Clay was intensely national, but
his theory of preserving the Union was by continual compromise, or, in other words, by constant
yielding to the aggressive South. Mr. Webster's
plan was to maintain a firm attitude, enforce absolute submission to all constitutional laws, and prove
that agitation against the Union could lead only
to defeat. This policy would not have resulted in
rebellion, but, if it had, the hanging of Calhoun
and a few like him, and the military government
of South Carolina, by the hero of New Orleans,
would have taught slaveholders such a lesson that
we should probably have been spared four years
of civil war. Peaceful submission, however, would
have been the sure outcome of Mr. Webster's
policy. But a compromise appealed as it always
does to the timid, balance-of-power party. Mr.
Clay prevailed, and the manufacturers of New

England, as well as elsewhere, finding that he had
secured for them the benefit of time and of the
chapter of accidents, rapidly came over to his support. The pressure was too much for Mr. Webster. Mr. Clay thought that if Mr. Webster "had
to go over the work of the last few weeks he would
have been for the compromise, which commands
the approbation of a great majority." Whether
Mr. Webster repented his opposition to the compromise no one can say, but the change of opinion
in New England, the general assent of the Whig
party, and the dazzling temptations of presidential
candidacy prevailed with him. He fell in behind
Mr. Clay, and remained there in a party sense
and as a party man for the rest of his life.

The terrible prize of the presidency was indeed
again before his eyes. Mr. Clay's overthrow at
the previous election had removed him, for the
time being at least, from the list of candidates,
and thus freed Mr. Webster from his most dangerous rival. In the summer of 1833 Mr. Webster made a tour through the Western States, and
was received everywhere with enthusiasm, and
hailed as the great expounder and defender of the
Constitution. The following winter he stood forward as the preëminent champion of the Bank
against the President. Everything seemed to point
to him as the natural candidate of the opposition.
The legislature of Massachusetts nominated him
for the presidency, and he himself deeply desired
the office, for the fever now burned strongly within

him. But the movement came to nothing. The anti-masonic schism still distracted the opposition. The Kentucky leaders were jealous of Mr. Webster, and thought him "no such man" as their idol Henry Clay. They admitted his greatness and his high traits of character, but they thought his ambition mixed with too much self-love. Governor Letcher wrote to Mr. Crittenden in 1836 that Clay was more elevated, disinterested, and patriotic than Webster, and that the verdict of the country had had a good effect on the latter. Despite the interest and enthusiasm which Mr. Webster aroused in the West, he had no real hold upon that section or upon the masses of the people, and the Western Whigs turned to Harrison. There was no hope in 1836 for Mr. Webster, or, for that matter, for his party either. He received the electoral vote of faithful Massachusetts, and that was all. As it was then, so it had been at the previous election, and so it was to continue to be at the end of every presidential term. There never was a moment when Mr. Webster had any real prospect of attaining to the presidency. Unfortunately he never could realize this. He would have been more than human, perhaps, if he had done so. The tempting bait hung always before his eyes. The prize seemed to be always just coming within his reach and was really never near it. But the longing had entered his soul. He could not rid himself of the idea of this final culmination to his success; and it warped his feelings and actions, injured his career, and embittered his last years.

This notice of the presidential election of 1836 has somewhat anticipated the course of events. Soon after the tariff compromise had been effected, Mr. Webster renewed his relations with Mr. Clay, and, consequently, with Mr. Calhoun, and their redoubtable antagonist in the President's chair soon gave them enough to do. The most immediate obstacle to Mr. Webster's alliance with General Jackson was the latter's attitude in regard to the bank. Mr. Webster had become satisfied that the bank was, on the whole, a useful and even necessary institution. No one was better fitted than he to decide on such a question, and few persons would now be found to differ from his judgment on this point. In a general way he may be said to have adopted the Hamiltonian doctrine in regard to the expediency and constitutionality of a national bank. There were intimations in the spring of 1833 that the President, not content with preventing the re-charter of the bank, was planning to strike it down, and practically deprive it of even the three years of life which still remained to it by law. The scheme was perfected during the summer, and, after changing his secretary of the treasury until he got one who would obey, President Jackson dealt his great blow. On September 26 Mr. Taney signed the order removing the deposits of the government from the Bank of the United States. The result was an immediate contraction of loans, commercial distress, and great confusion.

The President had thrown down the gage, and the leaders of the opposition were not slow to take it up. Mr. Clay opened the battle by introducing two resolutions, — one condemning the action of the President as unconstitutional, the other attacking the policy of removal, and a long and bitter debate ensued. A month later, Mr. Webster came forward with resolutions from Boston against the course of the President. He presented the resolutions in a powerful and effective speech, depicting the deplorable condition of business and the injury caused to the country by the removal of the deposits. He rejected the idea of leaving the currency to the control of the President, or of doing away entirely with paper, and advocated the re-charter of the present bank, or the creation of a new one; and, until the time for that should arrive, the return of the deposits, with its consequent relief to business and a restoration of stability and of confidence for the time being at least. He soon found that the administration had determined that no law should be passed, and that the doctrine that Congress had no power to establish a bank should be upheld. He also discovered that the constitutional pundit in the White House, who was so opposed to a single national bank, had created, by his own fiat, a large number of small national banks in the guise of state banks, to which the public deposits were committed, and the

collection of the public revenues intrusted. Such
an arbitrary policy, at once so ignorant, illogical,
and dangerous, aroused Mr. Webster thoroughly,
and he entered immediately upon an active campaign against the President. Between the presentation of the Boston resolutions and the close of
the session he spoke on the bank, and the subjects
necessarily connected with it, no less than sixty-
four times. He dealt entirely with financial topics, — chiefly those relating to the currency, and
with the constitutional questions raised by the
extension of the executive authority. This long
series of speeches is one of the most remarkable
exhibitions of intellectual power ever made by
Mr. Webster, or indeed by any public man in our
history. In discussing one subject in all its bear-
ings, involving of necessity a certain amount of
repetition, he not only displayed an extraordinary
grasp of complicated financial problems and a wide
knowledge of their scientific meaning and history,
but he showed an astonishing fertility in argument, coupled with great variety and clearness of
statement and cogency of reasoning. With the
exception of Hamilton, Mr. Webster is the only
statesman in our history who was capable of such
a performance on such a subject, when a thorough
knowledge had to be united with all the resources
of debate and all the arts of the highest eloquence.

The most important speech of all was that delivered in answer to Jackson's "Protest," sent in as
a reply to Mr. Clay's resolutions which had been

sustained by Mr. Webster as chairman of the
Committee on Finance. The "Protest" asserted,
in brief, that the Legislature could not order a
subordinate officer to perform certain duties free
from the control of the President; that the President had the right to put his own conception of
the law into execution; and, if the subordinate
officer refused to obey, then to remove such officer;
and that the Senate had therefore no right to censure his removal of the secretary of the treasury,
in order to reach the government deposits. To
this doctrine Mr. Webster replied with great elaboration and ability. The question was a very nice
one. There could be no doubt of the President's
power of removal, and it was necessary to show
that this power did not extend to the point of de-
priving Congress of the right to confer by law
specified and independent powers upon an inferior
officer, or of regulating the tenure of office. To
establish this proposition in such a way as to take
it out of the thick and heated atmosphere of personal controversy, and put it in a shape to carry
conviction to the popular understanding, was a
delicate and difficult task, requiring, in the highest
degree, lucidity and ingenuity of argument. It
is not too high praise to say that Mr. Webster
succeeded entirely. The real contest was for the
possession of that debatable ground which lies between the defined limits of the executive and legislative departments. The struggle consolidated and
gave coherence to the Whig party as representing

the opposition to executive encroachments. At
the time Jackson, by his imperious will and marvelous personal popularity, prevailed and obtained
the acceptance of his doctrines. But the conflict
has gone on, and the balance of advantage now
rests perhaps with the legislature. This tendency
is quite as dangerous as that of which Jackson
was the exponent. The executive department might
be crippled; and the influence and power of Congress, and especially of the Senate, might become
far greater than they should be, under the system
of proportion and balance embodied in the Constitution.

At the next session the principal subject of discussion was the trouble with France. Irritated at
the neglect of the French government to provide
funds for the payment of their debt to us, Jackson
sent in a message severely criticising them, and
recommending the passage of a law authorizing
reprisals on French property. The President and
his immediate followers were eager for war, Calhoun and his faction regarded the whole question
as only matter for "an action of assumpsit," while
Mr. Webster and Mr. Clay desired to avoid hostilities, but wished the country to maintain a firm
and dignified attitude. Under the lead of Mr.
Clay, the recommendation of reprisals was rejected,
and under that of Mr. Webster a clause smuggled
into the Fortification Bill to give the President
three millions to spend as he liked was struck out
and the bill was subsequently lost. This affair,

which brought us to the verge of war with France, soon blew over, however, and caused only a temporary ripple, although Mr. Webster's attack on the Fortification Bill left a sting behind.

In this same session Mr. Webster made an exhaustive speech on the question of executive patronage and the President's power of appointment and removal. He now went much farther than in his answer to the "Protest," asserting not only the right of Congress to fix the tenure of office, but also that the power of removal, like the power of appointment, was in the President and Senate jointly. The speech contained much that was valuable, but in its main doctrine was radically unsound. The construction of 1789, which decided that the power of removal belonged to the President alone, was clearly right, and Mr. Webster failed to overthrow it. His theory, embodied in a bill which provided that the President should state to the Senate, when he appointed to a vacancy caused by removal, his reasons for such removal, was thoroughly mischievous. It was more dangerous than Jackson's doctrine, for it tended to take the power of patronage still more from a single and responsible person and vest it in a large and therefore wholly irresponsible body which has always been too much inclined to degenerate into an office-broking oligarchy, and thus degrade its high and important functions. Mr. Webster argued his proposition with his usual force and perspicuity, but the speech is strongly partisan and exhibits the disposition of an advocate to fit the Constitution to his particular case, instead of dealing with it on general and fundamental principles.

The session closed with a resolution offered by Mr. Benton to expunge the resolutions of censure upon the President, which was overwhelmingly defeated, and was then laid upon the table, on the motion of Mr. Webster. He also took the first step to prevent the impending financial disaster growing out of the President's course toward the bank, by carrying a bill to stop the payment of treasury warrants by the deposit banks in current bank-notes, and to compel their payment in gold and silver. The rejection of Benton's resolutions served to embitter the already intense conflict between the President and his antagonists, and Mr. Webster's bill, while it showed the wisdom of the opposition, was powerless to remedy the mischief which was afoot.

In this same year (1835) the independence of Texas was achieved, and in the session of 1835–36 the slavery agitation began its march, which was only to terminate on the field of battle and in the midst of contending armies. Mr. Webster's action at this time in regard to this great question, which was destined to have such an effect upon his career, can be more fitly narrated when we come to consider his whole course in regard to slavery in connection with the "7th of March" speech. The other matters of this session demand but a brief notice. The President animadverted in his message upon the loss of the Fortification Bill, due to the defeat of the three million clause. Mr. Webster defended himself most conclusively and effectively, and before the session closed the difficulties with France were practically settled. He also gave great attention to the ever-pressing financial question, trying to mitigate the evils which the rapid accumulation of the public funds was threatening to produce. He felt that he was powerless, that nothing indeed could be done to avert the approaching disaster; but he struggled to modify its effects and delay its progress.

Complications increased rapidly during the summer. The famous "Specie Circular," issued by the secretary of the treasury without authority of law, weakened all banks which did not hold the government deposits, forced them to contract their loans, and completed the derangement of domestic exchange. This grave condition of affairs confronted Congress when it assembled in December, 1836. A resolution was introduced to rescind the Specie Circular, and Mr. Webster spoke at length in the debate, defining the constitutional duties of the government toward the regulation of the currency, and discussing in a masterly manner the intricate questions of domestic exchanges and the excessive circulation of bank-notes. On another occasion he reiterated his belief that a national bank was the true remedy for existing ills, but that only hard experience could convince the country of its necessity.

At this session the resolution to expunge the vote of censure of 1833 was again brought forward by Mr. Benton. The Senate had at last come under the sway of the President, and it was clear that the resolution would pass. This precious scheme belongs to the same category of absurdities as the placing Oliver Cromwell's skull on Temple Bar, and throwing Robert Blake's body on a dunghill by Charles Stuart and his friends. It was not such a mean and cowardly performance as that of the heroes of the Restoration, but it was far more "childish-foolish." The miserable and ludicrous nature of such a proceeding disgusted Mr. Webster beyond measure. Before the vote was taken he made a brief speech which is a perfect model of dignified and severe protest against a silly outrage upon the Constitution and upon the rights of senators, which he was totally unable to prevent. The original censure is part of history. No "black lines" can take it out. The expunging resolution, which Mr. Curtis justly calls "fantastic and theatrical," is also part of history, and carries with it the ineffaceable stigma affixed by Mr. Webster's indignant protest.

Before the close of the session Mr. Webster made up his mind to resign his seat in the Senate. He had private interests which demanded his attention, and he wished to travel both in the United States and in Europe. He may well have thought, also, that he could add nothing to his fame by remaining longer in the Senate. But besides the

natural craving for rest, it is quite possible that
he believed that a withdrawal from active and official participation in politics was the best preparation for a successful candidacy for the presidency
in 1840. This certainly was in his mind in the
following year (1838), when the rumor was abroad
that he was again contemplating retirement from
the Senate; and it is highly probable that the same
motive was at bottom the controlling one in 1837.
But whatever the cause of his wish to resign, the
opposition of his friends everywhere, and of the
legislature of Massachusetts, formally and strongly
expressed, led him to forego his purpose. He
consented to hold his seat for the present, at least,
and in the summer of 1837 made an extended tour
through the West, where he was received as before with the greatest admiration and enthusiasm.

The distracted condition of the still inchoate
Whig party in 1836, and the extraordinary popularity of Jackson, resulted in the complete victory
of Mr. Van Buren. But the general's chosen
successor and political heir found the great office to
which he had been called, and which he so eagerly
desired, anything but a bed of roses. The ruin
which Jackson's wild policy had prepared was
close at hand, and three months after the inauguration the storm burst with full fury. The banks
suspended specie payments and universal bankruptcy reigned throughout the country. Our business interests were in the violent throes of the
worst financial panic which had ever been known

in the United States. The history of Mr. Van
Buren's administration, in its main features, is
that of a vain struggle with a hopeless network of
difficulties, and with the misfortune and prostra-
tion which grew out of this widespread disaster.
It is not necessary here to enter into the details of
these events. Mr. Webster devoted himself in
the Senate to making every effort to mitigate the
evils which he had prophesied, and to prevent
their aggravation by further injudicious legislation. His most important speech was delivered
at the special session against the first sub-treasury bill and Mr. Calhoun's amendment. Mr.
Calhoun, who had wept over the defeat of the
bank bill in 1815, was now convinced that all
banks were mistakes, and wished to prevent the
acceptance of the notes of specie-paying banks
for government dues. Mr. Webster's speech was
the fullest and most elaborate he ever made on the
subject of the currency and the relations of the
government to it. His theme was the duty and
right of the general government under the Constitution to regulate and control the currency, and
his masterly argument was the best that has ever
been made, leaving in fact nothing to be desired.

In the spring of 1839 there was talk of sending
Mr. Webster to London as commissioner to settle
the boundary disputes, but it came to nothing,
and in the following summer he went to England
in his private capacity accompanied by his family.
The visit was in every way successful. It brought

rest and change as well as pleasure, and was full of interest. Mr. Webster was very well received, much attention was paid him, and much admiration shown for him. He commanded all this, not only by his appearance, his reputation, and his intellectual force, but still more by the fact that he was thoroughly and genuinely American in thought, feeling, and manner.

He reached New York on his return at the end of December, and was there met by the news of General Harrison's nomination by the Whigs. In the previous year it had seemed as if, with Clay out of the way by the defeat of 1832, and Harrison by that of 1836, the great prize must fall to Mr. Webster. His name was brought forward by the Whigs of Massachusetts, but it met with no response even in New England. It was the old story; Mr. Clay and his friends were cool, and the masses of the party did not desire Mr. Webster. The convention turned from the Massachusetts statesman and again nominated the old Western soldier.

Mr. Webster did not hesitate as to the course he should pursue upon his return. He had been reëlected to the Senate in January, 1839, and after the session closed in July, 1840, he threw himself into the campaign in support of Harrison. The people did not desire Mr. Webster to be their president, but there was no one whom they so much wished to hear. He was besieged from all parts of the country with invitations to speak, and he answered generously to the call thus made upon him.

On his way home from Washington, in March, 1837, more than three years before, he had made a speech at Niblo's Garden in New York, — the greatest purely political speech which he ever delivered. He then reviewed and arraigned with the greatest severity the history of Jackson's administration, abstaining in his characteristic way from all personal attack, but showing, as no one else could show, what had been done, and the results of the policy, which were developing as he had predicted. He also said that the worst was yet to come. The speech produced a profound impression. People were still reading it when the worst really came, and the great panic broke over the country. Mr. Webster had, in fact, struck the keynote of the coming campaign in the Niblo-Garden speech of 1837. In the summer of 1840 he spoke in Massachusetts, New York, Pennsylvania, and Virginia, and was almost continually upon the platform. The great feat of 1833-34, when he made sixty-four speeches in the Senate on the bank question, was now repeated under much more difficult conditions. In the first instance he was addressing a small and select body of trained listeners, all more or less familiar with the subject. In 1840 he was obliged to present these same topics, with all their infinite detail and inherent dryness, to vast popular audiences, but nevertheless he achieved a marvelous success. The chief points which he brought out were the condition of the currency, the need of government regulation, the responsibility of the Democrats, the miserable condition of the country, and the exact fulfillment of the prophecies he had made. The argument and the conclusion were alike irresistible, but Mr. Webster showed, in handling his subject, not only the variety, richness, and force which he had displayed in the Senate, but the capacity of presenting it in a way thoroughly adapted to the popular mind, and yet, at the same time, of preserving the impressive tone of a dignified statesman, without any degeneration into mere stump oratory. This wonderful series of speeches produced the greatest possible effect. They were heard by thousands and read by tens of thousands. They fell, of course, upon willing ears. The people, smarting under bankruptcy, poverty, and business depression, were wild for a change; but nothing did so much to swell the volume of public resentment against the policy of the ruling party as these speeches of Mr. Webster, which gave character and form to the whole movement. Jackson had sown the wind, and his unlucky successor was engaged in the agreeable task of reaping the proverbial crop. There was a political revolution. The Whigs swept the country by an immense majority, the great Democratic party was crushed to the earth, and the ignorant misgovernment of Andrew Jackson found at last its fit reward. General Harrison, as soon as he was elected, turned to the two great chiefs of his party to invite them to become the pillars of his administration. Mr. Clay declined any cabinet office, but Mr. Webster, after some hesitation, accepted the secretaryship of state. He resigned his seat in the Senate February 22, 1841, and on March 4 following took his place in the cabinet, and entered upon a new field of public service.

CHAPTER VIII

SECRETARY OF STATE. — THE ASHBURTON
TREATY

THERE is one feature in the history, or rather
in the historic scenery of this period, which we
are apt to overlook. The political questions, the
debates, the eloquence of that day, give us no idea
of the city in which the history was made, or of
the life led by the men who figured in that history.
Their speeches might have been delivered in any
great centre of civilization, and in the midst of a
brilliant and luxurious society. But the Washington of 1841, when Mr. Webster took the post which,
so far as the administration is concerned, is offi-
cially the first in the society of the capital and of
the country, was a very odd sort of place, and
widely different from what it is to-day. It was
not a village, neither was it a city. It had not
grown, but had been created for a special purpose.
A site had been arbitrarily selected, and a city laid
out on the most magnificent scale. But there was
no independent life, for the city was wholly official
in its purposes and its existence. There were a
few great public buildings, a few large private
houses, a few hotels and boarding houses, and a

large number of negro shanties. The general effect was of attempted splendor, which had resulted in slovenliness and straggling confusion. The streets were unpaved, dusty in summer, and deep with mud in winter, so that the mere difficulty of getting from place to place was a serious obstacle to general society. Cattle fed in the streets, and were milked by their owners on the sidewalk. There was a grotesque contrast between the stately capitol where momentous questions were eloquently discussed and such queerly primitive and rude surroundings. Few persons were able to entertain because few persons had suitable houses. Members of Congress usually clubbed together and took possession of a house, and these "messes," as they were called, — although without doubt very agreeable to their members, — did not offer a mode of life which was easily compatible with the demands of general society. Social enjoyments, therefore, were pursued under difficulties; and the city, although improving, was dreary enough.

Society, too, was in a bad condition. The old forms and ceremonies of the men of 1789 and the manners and breeding of our earliest generation of statesmen had passed away, and the new democracy had not as yet a system of its own. It was a period of transition. The old customs had gone, the new ones had not crystallized. The civilization was crude and raw, and in Washington had no background whatever, — such as was to be found in the old cities and towns of the original thirteen

States. The tone of the men in public life had deteriorated and was growing worse, approaching rapidly its lowest point, which it reached during the Polk administration. This was due partly to the Jacksonian democracy, which had rejected training and education as necessary to statesmanship, and had loudly proclaimed the great truths of rotation in office, and the spoils to the victors, and partly to the slavery agitation which was then beginning to make itself felt. The rise of the irrepressible conflict between freedom and slavery made the South overbearing and truculent; it produced that class of politicians known as "Northern men with Southern principles," or, in the slang of the day, as "dough-faces;" and it had not yet built up a strong, vigorous, and aggressive party in the North. The lack of proper social opportunities, and this deterioration among men in public life, led to an increasing violence and roughness in debate, and to a good deal of coarse dissipation in private. There was undoubtedly a brighter side, but it was limited, and the surroundings of the distinguished men who led our political parties in 1841 at the national capital, do not present a very cheerful or attractive picture.

When the new President appeared upon the scene he was followed by a general rush of hungry office-seekers, who had been starving for places for many years. General Harrison was a brave, honest soldier and pioneer, simple in heart and manners, unspoiled and untaught by politics, of

which he had had a good share. He was not a
great man, but he was honorable and well inten-
tioned. He wished to have about him the best
and ablest men of his party, and to trust to their
guidance for a successful administration. But although he had no desire to invent a policy, or to
draft state papers, he was determined to be the
author of his own inaugural speech, and he came
to Washington with a carefully prepared manuscript in his pocket. When Mr. Webster read
this document he found it full of gratitude to the
people, and abounding in allusions to Roman history. With his strong sense of humor, and of the
unities and proprieties as well, he was a good deal
alarmed at the proposed speech; and after much
labor, and the expenditure of a good deal of tact,
he succeeded in effecting some important changes
and additions. When he came home in the evening, Mrs. Seaton, at whose house he was staying,
remarked that he looked worried and fatigued,
and asked if anything had happened. Mr. Webster replied, "You would think that something
had happened if you knew what I have done. I
have killed seventeen Roman proconsuls." It was
a terrible slaughter for poor Harrison, for the
proconsuls were probably very dear to his heart.
His youth had been passed in the time when the
pseudo classicism of the French Republic and
Empire was rampant, and now that, in his old age,
he had been raised to the presidency, his head was
probably full of the republics of antiquity, and of

Cincinnatus called from the plough to take the helm of state.

M. de Bacourt, the French minister at this period, a rather shallow and illiberal man who disliked Mr. Webster, gives, in his recently published correspondence, the following amusing account of the presentation of the diplomatic corps to President Harrison, — a little bit of contemporary gossip which carries us back to those days better than anything else could possibly do. The diplomatic corps assembled at the house of Mr. Fox, the British minister, who was to read a speech in behalf of the whole body, and thence proceeded to the White House where

"the new secretary of state, Mr. Webster, who is much embarrassed by his new functions, came to make his arrangements with Mr. Fox. This done, we were ranged along the wall in order of seniority, and after too long a delay for a country where the chief magistrate has no right to keep people waiting, the old general came in, followed by all the members of his cabinet, who walked in single file, and so kept behind him. He then advanced toward Mr. Fox, whom Mr. Webster presented to him. Mr. Fox read to him his address. Then the President took out his spectacles and read his reply. Then, after having shaken hands with the English minister, he walked from one end of our line to the other, Mr. Webster presenting each of us by name, and he shaking hands with each one without saying a word. This ceremony finished he returned to the room whence he had come, and reappeared with Mrs. Harrison — the widow of his eldest son — upon his arm, whom he pre-

sented to the diplomatic corps *en masse.* Mr. Webster,
who followed, then presented to us Mrs. Finley, the
mother of this Mrs. Harrison, in the following terms :
' Gentlemen, I introduce to you Mrs. Finley, the lady
who attends Mrs. Harrison ; ' and observe that this good
lady who attends the others — takes care of them — is
blind. Then all at once, a crowd of people rushed into
the room. They were the wives, sisters, daughters,
cousins, and lady friends of the President and of all his
ministers, who were presented to us, and *vice versa,* in
the midst of an inconceivable confusion."

Fond, however, as Mr. Webster was of society,
and punctilious as he was in matters of etiquette
and propriety, M. de Bacourt to the contrary notwithstanding, he had far more important duties to
perform than those of playing host and receiving
foreign ministers. Our relations with England
when he entered the cabinet were such as to make
war seem almost inevitable. The northeastern
boundary, undetermined by the treaty of 1783,
had been the subject of continual and fruitless
negotiation ever since that time, and was still
unsettled and more complicated than ever. It
was agreed that there should be a new survey and
a new arbitration, but no agreement could be
reached as to who should arbitrate or what questions should be submitted to the arbitrators, and
the temporary arrangements for the possession of
the territory in dispute were unsatisfactory and
precarious. Much more exciting and perilous than
this old difficulty was a new one and its conse-

quences growing out of the Canadian rebellion in
1837.   Certain of the rebels fled to the United
States, and there, in conjunction with American
citizens, prepared to make incursions into Canada.
For this purpose they fitted out an American
steamboat, the Caroline.   An expedition from
Canada crossed the Niagara River to the American shore, set fire to the Caroline, and let her
drift over the Falls.   In the fray which occurred,
an American named Durfree was killed.   The
British government avowed this invasion to be a
public act and a necessary measure of self-defense;
but it was a question when Mr. Van Buren went
out of office whether this avowal had been made in
an authentic manner.   There was another incident, however, also growing out of this affair, even
more irritating and threatening than the invasion
itself.   In November, 1840, one Alexander Mc-
Leod came from Canada to New York, where he
boasted that he was the slayer of Durfree, and
thereupon was at once arrested on a charge of
murder and thrown into prison.   This aroused
great anger in England, and the conviction of
McLeod was all that was needed to cause immediate war.   In addition to these complications was
the question of the right of search for the impress-
ment of British seamen and for the suppression of
the slave trade.   Our government was, of course,
greatly hampered in action by the rights of Maine
and Massachusetts on the northeastern boundary,
and by the fact that McLeod was within the juris-

diction and in the power of the New York courts, and wholly out of reach of those of the United States. The character of the national representatives on both sides in London tended, moreover, to aggravate the growing irritation between the two countries. Lord Palmerston was sharp and domineering, and Mr. Stevenson, our minister, was by no means mild or conciliatory. Between them they did what they could to render accommodation impossible.

To evolve a satisfactory and permanent peace from these conditions was the task which confronted Mr. Webster, and he was hardly in office before he received a demand from Mr. Fox for the release of McLeod, in which full avowal was made that the burning of the Caroline was a public act. Mr. Webster determined that the proper method of settling the boundary question, when that subject should be reached, was to agree upon a conventional and arbitrary line, and that in the mean time the only way to dispose of McLeod was to get him out of prison, separate him, diplomatically speaking, from the affair of the Caroline, and then take that up as a distinct matter for negotiation with the British government. The difficulty in regard to McLeod was the most pressing, and so to that he gave his immediate attention. His first step was to instruct the attorney-general to proceed to Lockport, where McLeod was imprisoned, and communicate with the counsel for the defense, furnishing them with authentic infor-

mation that the destruction of the Caroline was a
public act, and that therefore McLeod could not
be held responsible.   He then replied to the British minister that McLeod could, of course, be
released only by judicial process, but he also informed Mr. Fox of the steps which had been taken
by the administration to assure the prisoner a
complete defense based on the avowal of the British government that the attack on the Caroline
was a public act.   This threw the responsibility
for McLeod, and for consequent peace or war,
where it belonged, on the New York authorities,
who seemed, however, but little inclined to assist
the general government.   McLeod came before
the Supreme Court of New York in July, on a
writ of habeas corpus, but they refused to release
him on the grounds set forth in Mr. Webster's
instructions to the attorney-general, and he was
remanded for trial in October, which was highly
embarrassing to our government, as it kept this
dangerous affair open.

But this and all other embarrassments to the
secretary of state sank into insignificance beside
those caused him by the troubles in his own political party.   Between the time of the instructions
to the attorney-general and that of the letter to
Mr. Fox, President Harrison died, after only a
month of office.   Mr. Tyler, of whose views but
little was known, at once succeeded, and made no
change in the cabinet of his predecessor.   On the
last day of May, Congress, called in extra session

by President Harrison, convened. A bill establishing a bank was passed, and Mr. Tyler vetoed it on account of constitutional objections to some of its features. The triumphant Whigs were filled with wrath at this unlooked-for check. Mr. Clay reflected on the President with great severity in the Senate, the members of the party in the House were very violent in their expressions of disapproval, and another measure, known as the "Fiscal Corporation Act," was at once prepared. Mr. Webster regarded this state of affairs with great anxiety and alarm. He said that such a contest, if persisted in, would ruin the party and deprive them of the fruits of their victory, besides imperiling the important foreign policy then just initiated. He strove to allay the excitement, and resisted the passage of any new bank measure, much as he wished the establishment of such an institution, advising postponement and delay for the sake of procuring harmony if possible. But the party in Congress would not be quieted. They were determined to force Mr. Tyler's hand at all hazards, and while the new bill was pending, Mr. Clay, stung by the taunts of Mr. Buchanan, made a savage attack upon the President. As a natural consequence, the "Fiscal Corporation" scheme shared the fate of its predecessor. The breach between the President and his party was opened irreparably, and four members of the cabinet at once resigned. Mr. Webster was averse to becoming a party to an obvious combination between the Senate and the cabinet to harass the President, and he was determined not to sacrifice the success of his foreign negotiations to a political quarrel. He therefore resolved to remain in the cabinet for the present, at least, and, after consulting the Massachusetts delegation in Congress, who fully approved his course, he announced his decision to the public in a letter to the "National Intelligencer." His action soon became the subject of much adverse criticism from the Whigs, but at this day no one would question that he was entirely right. It was not such an easy thing to do, however, as it now appears, for the excitement was running high among the Whigs, and there was great bitterness of feeling toward the President. Mr. Webster behaved in an independent and patriotic manner, showing a liberality of spirit, a breadth of view, and a courage of opinion which entitle him to the greatest credit.

Events, which had seemed thus far to go steadily against him in his negotiations, and which had been supplemented by the attacks of the opposition in Congress for his alleged interference with the course of justice in New York, now began to turn in his favor. The news of the refusal of the New York court to release McLeod on a habeas corpus had hardly reached England when the Melbourne ministry was beaten in the House of Commons, and Sir Robert Peel came in, bringing with him Lord Aberdeen as the successor of Lord Palmerston in the department of foreign affairs. The new ministry was disposed to be much more peaceful than their predecessors had been, and the negotiations at once began to move more smoothly. Great care was still necessary to prevent outbreaks on the border, but in October McLeod proved an alibi and was acquitted, and thus the most dangerous element in our relations with England was removed. Matters were still further improved by the retirement of Mr. Stevenson, whose successor in London was Mr. Everett, eminently conciliatory in disposition and in full sympathy with the secretary of state.

Mr. Webster was now able to turn his undivided attention to the long-standing boundary question. His proposition to agree upon a conventional line had been made known by Mr. Fox to his government, and soon afterwards Mr. Everett was informed that Lord Ashburton would be sent to Washington on a special mission. The selection of an envoy well known for his friendly feeling toward the United States, which was also traditional with the great banking-house of his family, was in itself a pledge of conciliation and good-will. Lord Ashburton reached Washington in April, 1842, and the negotiation at once began.

It is impossible and needless to give here a detailed account of that negotiation. We can only glance briefly at the steps taken by Mr. Webster and at the results achieved by him. There were many difficulties to be overcome, and in the winter of 1841–42 the case of the Creole added a fresh and dangerous complication. The Creole was a slave ship, on which the negroes had risen, and, taking possession, had carried her into an English port in the West Indies, where assistance was refused to the crew, and where the slaves were allowed to go free. This was an act of very doubtful legality, it touched both England and the Southern States in a very sensitive point, and it required all Mr. Webster's tact and judgment to keep it out of the negotiation until the main issue had been settled.

The principal obstacle in the arrangement of the boundary dispute arose from the interests and the attitude of Massachusetts and Maine. Mr. Webster obtained with sufficient ease the appointment of commissioners from the former State, and, through the agency of Mr. Sparks, who was sent to Augusta for the purpose, commissioners were also appointed in Maine; but these last were instructed to adhere to the line of 1783 as claimed by the United States. Lord Ashburton and Mr. Webster readily agreed that a treaty must come from mutual conciliation and compromise; but, after a good deal of correspondence, it became apparent that the Maine commissioners and the English envoy could not be brought to an agreement. A deadlock and consequent loss of the treaty were imminent. Mr. Webster then had a long interview with Lord Ashburton. By a process of give and take they agreed on a conventional line and on the concession of certain rights, which made a fair bargain, but unluckily the loss was suffered by Maine and Massachusetts, while the benefits received by the United States accrued to New York, Vermont, and New Hampshire. This brought the negotiators to the point at which they had already been forced to halt so many times before. Mr. Webster now cut the knot by proposing that the United States should indemnify Maine and Massachusetts in money for the loss they were to suffer in territory, and by his dexterous management the commissioners of the two States were persuaded to assent to this arrangement, while Lord Ashburton was induced to admit the agreement into a clause of the treaty. This disposed of the chief question in dispute, but two other subjects were included in the treaty besides the boundary. The first related to the right of search claimed by England for the suppression of the slave trade. This was met by what was called the "cruising convention," a clause which stipulated that each nation should keep its own squadron on the coast of Africa, to enforce separately its own laws against the slave trade, but in mutual coöperation. The other subject of agreement grew out of the Creole case. England supposed that we sought the return of the negroes because they were slaves, but Mr. Webster argued that they were demanded as mutineers and murderers. The result was an article which, while it carefully avoided even the appearance of an attempt to bind England to return fugitive slaves, provided amply

for the extradition of criminals. The case of the
Caroline was disposed of by a formal admission of
the inviolability of national territory and by an
apology for the burning of the steamboat. As to
the action in regard to the slaves on the Creole,
Mr. Webster could only obtain the assurance that
there should be "no officious interference with
American vessels driven by accident or violence
into British ports," and with this he was content
to let the matter drop. On the subject of impress-
ment, the old *casus belli* of 1812, Mr. Webster
wrote a forcible letter to Lord Ashburton. In it
he said that, in future, "in every regularly docu-
mented American merchant vessel, the crew who
navigate it will find their protection in the flag
which is over them." In other words, if you take
sailors out of our vessels, we shall fight; and this
simple statement of fact ended the whole matter,
and was quite as binding on England as any treaty
could have been.

Thus the negotiation closed. The only serious
objection to its results was that the interests of
Maine were sacrificed perhaps unduly, — as a recent discussion of that point seems to show. But
such a sacrifice was fully justified by what was
achieved. A war was averted, a long-standing
and menacing dispute was settled, and a treaty
was concluded which was creditable and honorable
to all concerned. By his successful introduction
of the extradition clause, Mr. Webster rendered
a great service to civilization and to the suppres-

sion and punishment of crime. Mr. Webster was greatly aided throughout — both in his arguments and in the construction of the treaty itself — by the learned and valuable assistance freely given by Judge Story. But he conducted the whole negotiation with great ability and in the spirit of a liberal and enlightened statesman. He displayed the highest tact and dexterity in reconciling so many clashing interests, and avoiding so many perilous side issues, until he had brought the main problem to a solution. In all that he did and said he showed a dignity and an entire sufficiency, which make this negotiation one of the most creditable — so far as its conduct was concerned — in which the United States ever engaged.

While the negotiation was in progress there was a constant murmur among the Whigs about Mr. Webster's remaining in the cabinet, and as soon as the treaty was actually signed a loud clamor began — both among the politicians and in the newspapers — for his resignation. In the midst of this outcry the Senate met and ratified the treaty by a vote of thirty-nine to nine, — a great triumph for its author. But the debate disclosed a vigorous opposition, Benton and Buchanan both assailing Mr. Webster for neglecting and sacrificing American, and particularly Southern, interests. At the same time the controversy which Mr. Webster called "the battle of the maps," and which was made a great deal of in England, began to show itself. A map of 1783, which Mr. Webster obtained, had been discovered in Paris, sustaining the English view, while another was afterwards found in London, supporting the American claim. Neither was of the least consequence, as the new line was conventional and arbitrary; but the discoveries caused a great deal of unreasonable excitement. Mr. Webster saw very plainly that the treaty was not yet secure. It was exposed to attacks both at home and abroad, and had still to pass Parliament. Until it was entirely safe, Mr. Webster determined to remain at his post. The clamor continued about his resignation, and rose round him at his home in Marshfield, whither he had gone for rest. At the same time the Whig convention of Massachusetts declared formally a complete separation from the President. In the language of to-day, they "read Mr. Tyler out of the party." There was a variety of motives for this action. One was to force Mr. Webster out of the cabinet, another to advance the fortunes of Mr. Clay, in favor of whose presidential candidacy movements had begun in Massachusetts, even among Mr. Webster's personal friends, as well as elsewhere. Mr. Webster had just declined a public dinner, but he now decided to meet his friends in Faneuil Hall. An immense audience gathered to hear him, many of them strongly disapproving his course, but after he had spoken a few moments, he had them completely under control. He reviewed the negotiation; he discussed fully the differences in the party; he deplored, and he did not hesitate strongly to condemn these quarrels, because by them the fruits of victory were lost, and Whig policy abandoned. With boldness and dignity he denied the right of the convention to declare a separation from the President, and the implied attempt to coerce himself and others. "I am, gentlemen, a little hard to coax," he said, "but as to being driven, that is out of the question. If I choose to remain in the President's councils, do these gentlemen mean to say that I cease to be a Massachusetts Whig? I am quite ready to put that question to the people of Massachusetts." He was well aware that he was losing party strength by his action; he knew that behind all these resolutions was the intention to raise his great rival to the presidency; but he did not shrink from avowing his independence and his intention of doing what he believed to be right, and what posterity admits to have been so. Mr. Webster never appeared to better advantage, and he never made a more manly speech than on this occasion, when, without any bravado, he quietly set the influence and the threats of his party at defiance.

He was not mistaken in thinking that the treaty was not yet in smooth water. It was again attacked in the Senate, and it had a still more severe ordeal to go through in Parliament. The opposition, headed by Lord Palmerston, assailed the treaty and Lord Ashburton himself, with the greatest virulence, denouncing the one as a capitulation, and the other as a grossly unfit appointment.

Moreover, the language of the President's message led England to believe that we claimed that the right of search had been abandoned. After much correspondence, this misunderstanding drew forth an able letter from Mr. Webster, stating that the right of search had not been included in the treaty, but that the "cruising convention" had rendered the question unimportant. Finally, all complications were dispersed, and the treaty ratified; and then came an attack from an unexpected quarter. General Cass — our minister at Paris — undertook to protest against the treaty, denounce it, and leave his post on account of it. This wholly gratuitous assault led to a public correspondence, in which General Cass, on his own confession, was completely overthrown and broken down by the secretary of state. This was the last difficulty, and the work was finally accepted and complete.

During this important and absorbing negotiation, other matters of less moment, but still of considerable consequence, had been met by Mr. Webster, and successfully disposed of. He made a treaty with Portugal, respecting duties on wines; he carried on a long correspondence with our minister to Mexico in relation to certain American prisoners; he vindicated the course of the United States in regard to the independence of Texas, teaching M. de Bocanegra, the Mexican secretary of state, a lesson as to the duties of neutrality, and administering a severe reproof to that gentleman for imputing bad faith to the United States;

he conducted the correspondence, and directed the policy of the government in regard to the troubles in Rhode Island; he made an effort to settle the Oregon boundary; and, finally, he set on foot the Chinese mission, which, after being offered to Mr. Everett, was accepted by Mr. Cushing with the best results. But his real work came to an end with the correspondence with General Cass at the close of 1842, and in May of the following year he resigned the secretaryship. In the two years during which he had been at the head of the cabinet he had done much. His work added to his fame by the ability which it exhibited in a new field, and has stood the test of time. In a period of difficulty, and even danger, he proved himself singularly well adapted for the conduct of foreign affairs, — a department which is most peculiarly and traditionally the employment and test of a highly trained statesman. It may be fairly said that no one, with the exception of John Quincy Adams, has ever shown higher qualities, or attained greater success in the administration of the State Department, than Mr. Webster did while in Mr. Tyler's cabinet.

On his resignation, he returned at once to private life, and passed the next summer on his farm at Marshfield, — now grown into a large estate, — which was a source of constant interest and delight, and where he was able to have beneath his eyes his beloved sea. His private affairs were in disorder, and required his immediate attention.

He threw himself into his profession, and his practice at once became active, lucrative, and absorbing.   To this period of retirement belong the second Bunker Hill oration and the Girard argument,
which made so much noise in its day.   He kept
himself aloof from politics, but could not wholly
withdraw from them.   The feeling against him,
on account of his continuance in the cabinet, had
subsided, and there was a feeble and somewhat
fitful movement to drop Clay, and present Mr.
Webster as a candidate for the presidency.   Mr.
Webster, however, made a speech at Andover,
defending his course and advocating Whig principles, and declared that he was not a candidate for
office.   He also refused to allow New Hampshire
to mar party harmony by bringing his name forward.   When Mr. Clay was nominated, in May,
1844, Mr. Webster, who had beheld with anxiety
the rise of the Liberty party and prophesied the
annexation of Texas, decided, although he was
dissatisfied with the silence of the Whigs on this
subject, to sustain their candidate.   This was undoubtedly the wisest course; and, having once
enlisted, he gave Mr. Clay a hearty and vigorous
support, making a series of powerful speeches,
chiefly on the tariff, and second in variety and
ability only to those which he had delivered in
the Harrison campaign.   Mr. Clay was defeated
largely by the action of the Liberty party, and
the silence of the Whigs about Texas and slavery
cost them the election.   At the beginning of the

year Mr. Webster had declined a reëlection to the
Senate, but it was impossible for him to remain
out of politics, and the pressure to return soon
became too strong to be resisted. Mr. Choate's
term expired on March 4, 1845, and Mr. Webster
was reëlected senator from Massachusetts to succeed him. On the first of March the intrigue, to
perfect which Mr. Calhoun had accepted the State
Department, culminated, and the resolutions for
the annexation of Texas passed both branches of
Congress. Four days later Mr. Polk's administration, pledged to the support and continuance
of the annexation policy, was in power, and Mr.
Webster had taken his seat in the Senate for his
last term.

CHAPTER IX

RETURN TO THE SENATE. — THE SEVENTH OF MARCH SPEECH

The principal events of Mr. Polk's administration belong to or grow out of the slavery agitation, then beginning to assume most terrible proportions. So far as Mr. Webster is concerned, they form part of the history of his course on the slavery question, which culminated in the famous speech of March 7, 1850. Before approaching that subject, however, it will be necessary to touch very briefly on one or two points of importance in Mr. Webster's career, which have no immediate bearing on the question of slavery, and no relation to the final and decisive stand which Mr. Webster took in regard to it.

The Ashburton treaty was open to one just criticism. It did not go far enough. It did not settle the northwestern as it did the northeastern boundary. Mr. Webster, as has been said, made an effort to deal with the former as well as the latter, but he met with no encouragement, and as he was then preparing to retire from office, the matter dropped. In regard to the northwestern boundary, Mr. Webster agreed with the opinion

of Mr. Monroe's cabinet, that the forty-ninth
parallel was a fair and proper line; but the British
undertook to claim the line of the Columbia River,
and this excited corresponding claims on our side.
The Democracy for political purposes became especially warlike and patriotic. They declared in
their platform that we must have the whole of
Oregon and reoccupy it at once. Mr. Polk embodied this view in his message, together with the
assertion that our rights extended to the line of
54° 40' north, and a shout of "fifty-four-forty or
fight" went through the land from the enthusiastic
Democracy. If this attitude meant anything it
meant war, inasmuch as our proposal for the forty-
ninth parallel, and the free navigation of the Columbia River, made in the autumn of 1845, had
been rejected by England, and then withdrawn by
us. Under these circumstances Mr. Webster felt
it his duty to come forward and exert all his influence to maintain peace, and to promote a clear
comprehension, both in the United States and in
Europe, of the points at issue. His speech on this
subject and with this aim was delivered in Faneuil
Hall. He spoke of the necessity of peace, of the
fair adjustment offered by an acceptance of the
forty-ninth parallel, and derided the idea of casting two great nations into war for such a question
as this. He closed with a forcible and solemn
denunciation of the president or minister who
should dare to take the responsibility for kindling
the flames of war on such a pretext. The speech

was widely read. It was translated into nearly
all the languages of Europe, and on the Continent
had a great effect. About a month later he wrote
to Mr. MacGregor of Glasgow, suggesting that
the British government should offer to accept the
forty-ninth parallel, and his letter was shown to
Lord Aberdeen, who at once acted upon the advice
it contained. While this letter, however, was on
its way, certain resolutions were introduced in the
Senate relating to the national defenses, and to
give notice of the termination of the convention
for the joint occupation of Oregon, which would
of course have been nearly equivalent to a declaration of war. Mr. Webster opposed the resolutions, and insisted that, while the executive, as he
believed, had no real wish for war, this talk was
kept up about "all or none," which left nothing to
negotiate about. The notice finally passed, but
before it could be delivered by our minister in
London, Lord Aberdeen's proposition of the forty-
ninth parallel, as suggested by Mr. Webster, had
been received at Washington, where it was accepted by the truculent administration, agreed to
by the Senate, and finally embodied in a treaty.
Mr. Webster's opposition had served its purpose
in delaying action and saving bluster from being
converted into actual war, — a practical conclusion
by no means desired by the dominant party, who
had talked so loud that they came very near blun-
dering into hostilities merely as a matter of self-
justification. The declarations of the Democratic

convention and of the Democratic President in
regard to England were really only sound and
fury, although they went so far that the final retreat was noticeable and not very graceful. The
Democratic leaders had had no intention of fighting with England when all they could hope to gain
would be glory and hard knocks, but they had a
very definite idea of attacking without bluster and
in good earnest another nation where there was
territory to be obtained for slavery.

The Oregon question led, however, to an attack
upon Mr. Webster which cannot be wholly passed
over. He had, of course, his personal enemies in
both parties, and his effective opposition to war
with England greatly angered some of the most
warlike of the Democrats, and especially Mr. C.
J. Ingersoll of Pennsylvania, a bitter Anglopho-
bist. Mr. Ingersoll, in February, made a savage
attack upon the Ashburton negotiation, the treaty
of Washington, and upon Mr. Webster personally, alleging that as secretary of state he had been
guilty of a variety of grave misdemeanors, including a corrupt use of the public money. Some of
these charges, those relating to the payment of
McLeod's counsel by our government, to instructions to the attorney-general to take charge of
McLeod's defense, and to a threat by Mr. Webster that if McLeod were not released New York
would be laid in ashes, were repeated in the Senate
by Mr. Dickinson of New York. Mr. Webster
peremptorily called for all the papers relating to

the negotiation of 1842, and on the sixth and seventh of April (1846), he made the elaborate speech in defense of the Ashburton treaty, which is included in his collected works. It is one of the strongest and most virile speeches he ever delivered. He was profoundly indignant, and he had the completest mastery of his subject. In fact, he was so deeply angered by the charges made against him, that he departed from his almost invariable practice, and indulged in a severe personal denunciation of Ingersoll and Dickinson. Although he did not employ personal invective in his oratory, it was a weapon which he was capable of using with most terrible effect, and his blows fell with crushing force upon Ingersoll, who writhed under the strokes. Through some inferior officers of the State Department Ingersoll got what he considered proofs, and then introduced resolutions calling for an account of all payments from the secret service fund; for communications made by Mr. Webster to Messrs. Adams and Cushing of the Committee on Foreign Affairs; for all papers relating to McLeod, and for the minutes of the Committee on Foreign Affairs, to show that Mr. Webster had expressed an opinion adverse to our claim in the Oregon dispute. Mr. Ingersoll closed his speech by a threat of impeachment as the result and reward of all this evil-doing, and an angry debate followed, in which Mr. Webster was attacked and defended with equal violence. President Polk replied to the call of the House by saying that he could not feel justified, either morally or legally, in revealing the uses of the secret service fund. Meantime a similar resolution was defeated in the Senate by a vote of forty-four to one, Mr. Webster remarking that he was glad that the President had refused the request of the House; that he should have been sorry to have seen an important principle violated, and that he was not in the least concerned at being thus left without an explanation; he needed no defense, he said, against such attacks.

Mr. Ingersoll, rebuffed by the President, then made a personal explanation, alleging specifically that Mr. Webster had made an unlawful use of the secret service money, that he had employed it to corrupt the press, and that he was a defaulter. Mr. Ashmun of Massachusetts replied with great bitterness, and the charges were referred to a committee. It appeared, on investigation, that Mr. Webster had been extremely careless in his accounts, and had delayed in making them up and in rendering vouchers, faults to which he was naturally prone; but it also appeared that the money had been properly spent, that the accounts had ultimately been made up, and that there was no evidence of improper use. The committee's report was laid upon the table, the charges came to nothing, and Mr. Ingersoll was left in a very unpleasant position with regard to the manner in which he had obtained his information from the State Department. The affair is of interest now merely as showing how deeply rooted was Mr. Webster's habitual carelessness in money matters, even when it was liable to expose him to very grave imputations, and what a very dangerous man he was to arouse and put on the defensive.

Mr. Webster was absent when the intrigue and scheming of Mr. Polk culminated in war with Mexico, and so his vote was not given either for or against it. He opposed the volunteer system as a mongrel contrivance, and resisted it as he had the conscription bill in the war of 1812, as unconstitutional. He also opposed the continued prosecution of the war, and, when it drew toward a close, was most earnest against the acquisition of new territory. In the summer of 1847 he made an extended tour through the Southern States, and was received there, as he had been in the West, with every expression of interest and admiration.

The Mexican war, however, cost Mr. Webster far more than the anxiety and disappointment which it brought to him as a public man. His second son, Major Edward Webster, died near the city of Mexico, from disease contracted by exposure on the march. This melancholy news reached Mr. Webster when important matters which demanded his attention were pending in Congress. Measures to continue the war were before the Senate even after they had ratified the peace. These measures Mr. Webster strongly resisted, and he also opposed, in a speech of great power, the acquisition of new territories by conquest, as threatening the very existence of the nation, the principles of the Constitution, and the Constitution itself. The increase of senators, which was, of course, the object of the South in annexing Texas and in the proposed additions from Mexico, he regarded as destroying the balance of the government, and therefore he denounced the plan of acquisition by conquest in the strongest terms. The course about to be adopted, he said, will turn the Constitution into a deformity, into a curse rather than a blessing; it will make a frame of government founded on the grossest inequality, and will imperil the existence of the Union. With this solemn warning he closed his speech, and immediately left Washington for Boston, where his daughter, Mrs. Appleton, was sinking in consumption. She died on April 28 and was buried on May 1. Three days later, Mr. Webster followed to the grave the body of his son Edward, which had been brought from Mexico. Two such terrible blows, coming so near together, need no comment. They tell their own sad story. One child only remained to him of all who had gathered about his knees in the happy days at Portsmouth and Boston, and his mind turned to thoughts of death as he prepared at Marshfield a final resting-place for himself and those he had loved. Whatever successes or defeats were still in store for him, the heavy cloud of domestic sorrow could never be dispersed in the years that remained, nor could the gaps which had been made be filled or forgotten.

But the sting of personal disappointment and of frustrated ambition, trivial enough in comparison with such griefs as these, was now added to this heavy burden of domestic affliction. The success of General Taylor in Mexico rendered him a most tempting candidate for the Whigs to nominate. His military services and his personal popularity promised victory, and the fact that no one knew Taylor's political principles, or even whether he was a Whig or a Democrat, seemed rather to increase than diminish his attractions in the eyes of the politicians. A movement was set on foot to bring about this nomination, and its managers planned to make Mr. Webster vice-president on the ticket with the victorious soldier. Such an offer was a melancholy commentary on his ambitious hopes. He spurned the proposition as a personal indignity, and, disapproving always of the selection of military men for the presidency, openly refused to give his assent to Taylor's nomination. Other trials, however, were still in store for him. Mr. Clay was a candidate for the nomination, and many Whigs, feeling that his success meant another party defeat, turned to Taylor as the only instrument to prevent this danger. In February, 1848, a call was issued in New York for a public meeting to advance General Taylor's candidacy, which was signed by many of Mr. Webster's personal and political friends. Mr. Webster was surprised and grieved, and bitterly resented this action. His biographer, Mr. Curtis, speaks of it as a blunder which rendered Mr. Webster's nomination hopeless. The truth is, that it was a most significant illustration of the utter futility of Mr. Webster's presidential aspirations. These friends in New York, who no doubt honestly desired his nomination, were so well satisfied that it was perfectly impracticable, that they turned to General Taylor to avoid the disaster threatened, as they believed, by Mr. Clay's success. Mr. Webster predicted truly that Clay and Taylor would be the leading candidates before the convention, but he was wholly mistaken in supposing that the movement in New York would bring about the nomination of the former. His friends had judged rightly. Taylor was the only man who could defeat Clay, and he was nominated on the fourth ballot. Massachusetts voted steadily for Webster, but he never approached a nomination. Even Scott had twice as many votes. The result of the convention led Mr. Webster to take a very gloomy view of the prospects of the Whigs, and he was strongly inclined to retire to his tent and let them go to deserved ruin. In private conversation he spoke most disparagingly of the nomination, the Whig party, and the Whig candidate. His strictures were well deserved, but, as the election drew on, he found or believed it to be impossible to live up to them. He was not ready to go over to the Free-Soil party, he could not remain silent, yet he could not give Taylor a full support. In September, 1848, he made his famous speech at Marsh-

field, in which, after declaring that the "sagacious, wise, far-seeing doctrine of *availability* lay at the root of the whole matter," and that "the nomination was one not fit to be made," he said that General Taylor was personally a brave and honorable man, and that, as the choice lay between him and the Democratic candidate, General Cass, he should vote for the former and advised his friends to do the same. He afterwards made another speech, in a similar but milder strain, in Faneuil Hall. Mr. Webster's attitude was not unlike that of Hamilton when he published his celebrated attack on Adams, which ended by advising all men to vote for that objectionable man. The conclusion was a little impotent in both instances, but in Mr. Webster's case the results were better. The politicians and lovers of availability had judged wisely, and Taylor was triumphantly elected.

Before the new President was inaugurated, in the winter of 1848–49, the struggle began in Congress which led to the delivery of the 7th of March speech by Mr. Webster in the following year. At this point, therefore, it becomes necessary to turn back and review briefly and rapidly Mr. Webster's course in regard to the question of slavery.

His first important utterance on this momentous question was in 1819, when the land was distracted with the conflict which had suddenly arisen over the admission of Missouri. Massachusetts was strongly in favor of the exclusion of slavery from the new States, and utterly averse to any compro-

mise. A meeting was held in the state-house at
Boston, and a committee was appointed to draft a
memorial to Congress, on the subject of the prohibition of slavery in the territories. This memorial, — which was afterwards adopted, — was drawn
by Mr. Webster, as chairman of the committee.
It set forth, first, the belief of its signers that
Congress had the constitutional power "to make
such a prohibition a condition on the admission of
a new State into the Union, and that it is just
and proper that they should exercise that power."
Then came an argument on the constitutional
question, and then the reasons for the exercise of
the power as a general policy. The first point was
that it would prevent further inequality of representation, such as existed under the Constitution
in the old States, but which could not be increased
without danger. The next argument went straight
to the merits of the question, as involved in slavery
as a system. After pointing out the value of the
ordinance of 1787 to the Northwest, the memorial
continued : —

"We appeal to the justice and the wisdom of the
national councils to prevent the further progress of a
great and serious evil. We appeal to those who look
forward to the remote consequences of their measures,
and who cannot balance a temporary or trifling con-
venience, if there were such, against a permanent growing and desolating evil.

" . . . The Missouri territory is a new country. If its
extensive and fertile fields shall be opened as a market

for slaves, the government will seem to become a party to a traffic, which in so many acts, through so many years, it has denounced as impolitic, unchristian, and inhuman. . . . The laws of the United States have denounced heavy penalties against the traffic in slaves, because such traffic is deemed unjust and inhuman. We appeal to the spirit of these laws; we appeal to this justice and humanity; we ask whether they ought not to operate, on the present occasion, with all their force? We have a strong feeling of the injustice of any toleration of slavery. Circumstances have entailed it on a portion of our community, which cannot be immediately relieved from it without consequences more injurious than the suffering of the evil. But to permit it in a new country, where yet no habits are formed which render it indispensable, what is it but to encourage that rapacity and fraud and violence against which we have so long pointed the denunciation of our penal code? What is it but to tarnish the proud fame of the country? What is it but to render questionable all its professions of regard for the rights of humanity and the liberties of mankind."

A year later Mr. Webster again spoke on one portion of this subject, and in the same tone of deep hostility and reproach. This second instance was that famous and much quoted passage of his Plymouth oration in which he denounced the African slave trade. Every one remembers the ringing words: —

" I hear the sound of the hammer, I see the smoke of the furnaces where manacles and fetters are still forged for human limbs. I see the visages of those who, by

stealth and at midnight, labor in this work of hell, —
foul and dark as may become the artificers of such in-
struments of misery and torture.   Let that spot be purified, or let it cease to be of New England.   Let it be
purified, or let it be set aside from the Christian world ;
let it be put out of the circle of human sympathies and
human regards, and let civilized man henceforth have
no communion with it."

This is directed against the African slave trade,
the most hideous feature, perhaps, in the system.
But there was no real distinction between slavers
plying from one American port to another and
those which crossed the ocean for the same purpose.   There was no essential difference between
slaves raised for the market in Virginia — whence
they were exported and sold — and those kidnapped
for the same object on the Guinea coast.   The
physical suffering of a land journey might be less
than that of a long sea-voyage, but the anguish of
separation between mother and child was the same
in all cases.   The chains which clanked on the
limbs of the wretched creatures, driven from the
auction block along the road which passed beneath
the national capitol, and the fetters of the captured
fugitive were no softer or lighter than those forged
for the cargo of the slave ships.   Yet the man
who so magnificently denounced the one in 1820,
found no cause to repeat the denunciation in 1850,
when only domestic traffic was in question.   The
memorial of 1819 and the oration of 1820 place
the African slave trade and the domestic branch

of the business on precisely the same ground of
infamy and cruelty. In 1850 Mr. Webster seems
to have discovered that there was a wide gulf fixed
between them, for the latter wholly failed to excite
the stern condemnation poured forth by the memo-
rialist of 1819 and the orator of 1820. The Fugitive Slave Law, more inhuman than either of the
forms of traffic, was defended in 1850 on good
constitutional grounds; but the eloquent invective
of the early days against an evil which constitutions might necessitate but could not alter or justify, does not go hand in hand with the legal
argument.

The next occasion after the Missouri Compromise, on which slavery made its influence strongly
felt at Washington, was when Mr. Adams's scheme
of the Panama mission aroused such bitter and
unexpected resistance in Congress. Mr. Webster
defended the policy of the President with great
ability, but he confined himself to the international
and constitutional questions which it involved, and
did not discuss the underlying motive and true
source of the opposition. The debate on Foote's
resolution in 1830, in the wide range which it
took, of course included slavery, and Mr. Hayne
had a good deal to say on that subject, which lay
at the bottom of the tariff agitation, as it did at
that of every Southern movement of any real importance. In his reply, Mr. Webster said that
he had made no attack upon this sensitive institution, that he had simply stated that the Northwest

had been greatly benefited by the exclusion of
slavery, and that it would have been better for
Kentucky if she had come within the scope of the
ordinance of 1787. The weight of his remarks
was directed to showing that the complaint of
Northern attacks on slavery as existing in the
Southern States, or of Northern schemes to compel
the abolition of slavery, was utterly groundless
and fallacious. At the same time he pointed out
the way in which slavery was continually used to
unite the South against the North.

" This feeling," he said, " always carefully kept alive,
and maintained at too intense a heat to admit discrimination or reflection, is a lever of great power in our
political machine. There is not and never has been a
disposition in the North to interfere with these interests
of the South. Such interference has never been supposed to be within the power of government ; nor has it
been in any way attempted. The slavery of the South
has always been regarded as a matter of domestic policy
left with the States themselves, and with which the Federal government had nothing to do. Certainly, sir, I
am and ever have been of that opinion. The gentleman, indeed, argues that slavery, in the abstract, is no
evil. Most assuredly, I need not say I differ with him
altogether and most widely on that point. I regard domestic slavery as one of the greatest evils, both moral
and political."

His position is here clearly defined. He admits
fully that slavery within the States cannot be interfered with by the general government, under

the Constitution.   But he also insists that it is a great evil, and the obvious conclusion is that its extension, over which the government does have control, must and should be checked.   This is the attitude of the memorial and the oration.   Nothing has yet changed.   There is less fervor in the denunciation of slavery, but that may be fairly attributed to circumstances which made the maintenance of the general government and the enforcement of the revenue laws the main points in issue.

In 1836 the anti-slavery movement, destined to grow to such vast proportions, began to show itself in the Senate.   The first contest came on the reception of petitions for the abolition of slavery in the District of Columbia.   Mr. Calhoun moved that these petitions should not be received, but his motion was rejected by a large majority.   The question then came on the petitions themselves, and, by a vote of thirty-four to six, their prayer was rejected, Mr. Webster voting with the minority because he disapproved this method of disposing of the matter.   Soon after, Mr. Webster presented three similar petitions, two from Massachusetts and one from Michigan, and moved their reference to a committee of inquiry.   He stated that, while the government had no power whatever over slavery in the States, it had complete control over slavery in the District, which was a totally distinct affair.   He urged a respectful treatment of the petitions, and defended the right of petition and the motives and characters of the petitioners.

He spoke briefly, and, except when he was charged with placing himself at the head of the petitioners, coldly, and did not touch on the merits of the question, either as to the abolition of slavery in the District or as to slavery itself.

The Southerners, especially the extremists and the nullifiers, were always more ready than any one else to strain the powers of the central government to the last point, and use them most tyrannically and illegally in their own interest and in that of their pet institution. The session of 1836 furnished a striking example of this characteristic quality. Mr. Calhoun at that time introduced his monstrous bill to control the United States mails in the interests of slavery, by authorizing postmasters to seize and suppress all anti-slavery documents. Against this measure Mr. Webster spoke and voted, resting his opposition on general grounds, and sustaining it by a strong and effective argument. In the following year, on his way to the North, after the inauguration of Mr. Van Buren, a great public reception was given to him in New York, and on that occasion he made the speech in Niblo's Garden, where he defined the Whig principles, arraigned so powerfully the policy of Jackson, and laid the foundation for the triumphs of the Harrison campaign. In the course of that speech he referred to Texas, and strongly expressed his belief that it should remain independent and should not be annexed. This led him to touch upon slavery. He said: —

" I frankly avow my entire unwillingness to do anything that shall extend the slavery of the African race on this continent, or add other slaveholding States to the Union. When I say that I regard slavery in itself as a great moral, social, and political evil, I only use the language which has been adopted by distinguished men, themselves citizens of slaveholding States. I shall do nothing, therefore, to favor or encourage its further extension. We have slavery already amongst us. The Constitution found it in the Union, it recognized it, and gave it solemn guaranties. To the full extent of the guaranties we are all bound in honor, in justice, and by the Constitution. . . . But when we come to speak of admitting new States, the subject assumes an entirely different aspect. . . . In my opinion, the people of the United States will not consent to bring into the Union a new, vastly extensive, and slaveholding country, large enough for half a dozen or a dozen States. In my opinion, they ought not to consent to it. . . . On the general question of slavery a great portion of the community is already strongly excited. The subject has not only attracted attention as a question of politics, but it has struck a far deeper-toned chord. It has arrested the religious feeling of the country; it has taken strong hold on the consciences of men. He is a rash man, indeed, and little conversant with human nature, and especially has he a very erroneous estimate of the character of the people of this country, who supposes that a feeling of this kind is to be trifled with or despised. It will assuredly cause itself to be respected. It may be reasoned with, it may be made willing — I believe it is entirely willing — to fulfill all existing engagements and all existing duties, to uphold and defend the Constitution as it is established, with whatever regrets about some provisions which it does actually contain. But to coerce it into silence, to endeavor to restrain its free expression, to seek to compress and confine it, warm as it is and more heated as such endeavors would inevitably render it, — should this be attempted, I know nothing, even in the Constitution or in the Union itself, which would not be endangered by the explosion which might follow."

Thus Mr. Webster spoke on slavery and upon the agitation against it, in 1837. The tone was the same as in 1820, and there was the same ring of dignified courage and unyielding opposition to the extension and perpetuation of a crying evil.

In the session of Congress preceding the speech at Niblo's Garden, numerous petitions for the abolition of slavery in the District had been offered. Mr. Webster reiterated his views as to the proper disposition to be made of them; but announced that he had no intention of expressing an opinion as to the merits of the question. Objections were made to the reception of the petitions, the question was stated on the reception, and the whole matter was laid on the table. The Senate, under the lead of Calhoun, was trying to shut the door against the petitioners, and stifle the right of petition; and there was no John Quincy Adams among them to do desperate battle against this infamous scheme.

In the following year came more petitions, and Mr. Calhoun now attempted to stop the agitation

in another fashion. He introduced a resolution
to the effect that these petitions were a direct and
dangerous attack on the "institution" of the slaveholding States. This Mr. Clay improved in a
substitute, which stated that any act or measure
of Congress looking to the abolition of slavery in
the District would be a violation of the faith implied in the cession by Virginia and Maryland, —
a just cause of alarm to the South, and having
a direct tendency to disturb and endanger the
Union. Mr. Webster wrote to a friend that this
was an attempt to make a new Constitution, and
that the proceedings of the Senate, when they
passed the resolutions, drew a line which could
never be obliterated. Mr. Webster also spoke
briefly against the resolutions, confining himself
strictly to demonstrating the absurdity of Mr.
Clay's doctrine of "plighted faith." He disclaimed
carefully, and even anxiously, any intention of
expressing an opinion on the merits of the question; although he mentioned one or two reasonable
arguments against abolition. The resolutions were
adopted by a large majority, Mr. Webster voting
against them on the grounds set forth in his
speech. Whether the approaching presidential
election had any connection with his careful avoid-
ance of everything except the constitutional point,
which contrasted so strongly with his recent utterances at Niblo's Garden, it is, of course, impossible to determine. John Quincy Adams, who had
no love for Mr. Webster, and who was then in

the midst of his desperate struggle for the right
of petition, says, in his Diary, in March, 1838,
speaking of the delegation from Massachusetts: —

"Their policy is dalliance with the South; and they
care no more for the right of petition than is absolutely
necessary to satisfy the feeling of their constituents.
They are jealous of Cushing, who, they think, is playing
a double game. They are envious of my position as
the supporter of the right of petition; and they truckle
to the South to court their favor for Webster. He is
now himself tampering with the South on the slavery
and the Texas question."

This harsh judgment may or may not be correct,
but it shows very plainly that Mr. Webster's cau-
tion in dealing with these topics was noticed and
criticised at this period. The annexation of Texas,
moreover, which he had so warmly opposed, seemed
to him, at this juncture, and not without reason,
to be less threatening, owing to the course of
events in the young republic. Mr. Adams did
not, however, stand alone in thinking that Mr.
Webster, at this time, was lukewarm on the subject. In 1839 Mr. Giddings says "that it was
impossible for any man, who submitted so quietly
to the dictation of slavery as Mr. Webster, to
command that influence which was necessary to
constitute a successful politician." How much
Mr. Webster's attitude had weakened, just at this
period, is shown better by his own action than by
anything Mr. Giddings could say. The ship En-
terprise, engaged in the domestic slave trade from

Virginia to New Orleans, had been driven into
Port Hamilton, and the slaves had escaped. Great
Britain refused compensation. Thereupon, early
in 1840, Mr. Calhoun introduced resolutions de-
claratory of international law on this point, and
setting forth that England had no right to interfere with, or to permit, the escape of slaves from
vessels driven into her ports. The resolutions
were idle, because they could effect nothing, and
mischievous because they represented that the sentiment of the Senate was in favor of protecting
the slave trade. Upon these resolutions, absurd
in character and barbarous in principle, Mr. Webster did not even vote. There is a strange contrast here between the splendid denunciation of the
Plymouth oration and this utter lack of opinion,
upon resolutions designed to create a sentiment
favorable to the protection of slave ships engaged
in the domestic traffic. Soon afterwards, when
Mr. Webster was secretary of state, he advanced
much the same doctrine in the discussion of the
Creole case, and his letter was approved by Calhoun. There may be merit in the legal argument,
but the character of the cargo, which it was sought
to protect, put it beyond the reach of law. We
have no need to go farther than the Plymouth
oration to find the true character of the trade in
human beings as carried on upon the high seas.

After leaving the cabinet, and resuming his law
practice, Mr. Webster, of course, continued to
watch with attention the progress of events. The

formation of the Liberty party, in the summer of
1843, appeared to him a very grave circumstance.
He had always understood the force of the anti-
slavery movement at the North, and it was with
much anxiety that he now saw it take definite
shape, and assume extreme grounds of opposition.
This feeling of anxiety was heightened when he
discovered, in the following winter, while in at-
tendance upon the Supreme Court at Washington,
the intention of the administration to bring about
the annexation of Texas, and spring the scheme
suddenly upon the country. This policy, with its
consequence of an enormous extension of slave
territory, Mr. Webster had always vigorously and
consistently opposed, and he was now thoroughly
alarmed. He saw what an effect the annexation
would produce upon the anti-slavery movement,
and he dreaded the results. He therefore procured
the introduction of a resolution in Congress against
annexation; wrote some articles in the newspapers
against it himself; stirred up his friends in Washington and New York to do the same, and endeavored to start public meetings in Massachusetts.
His friends in Boston and elsewhere, and the
Whigs generally, were disposed to think his alarm
ill-founded. They were absorbed in the coming
presidential election, and were too ready to do
Mr. Webster the injustice of supposing that his
views upon the probability of annexation sprang
from jealousy of Mr. Clay. The suspicion was
unfounded and unfair. Mr. Webster was wholly

right and perfectly sincere. He did a good deal
in an attempt to rouse the North. The only criticism to be made is that he did not do more. One
public meeting would have been enough, if he had
spoken frankly, declared that he knew, no matter
how, that annexation was contemplated, and had
then denounced it as he did at Niblo's Garden.
"One blast upon his bugle-horn were worth a
thousand men." Such a speech would have been
listened to throughout the length and breadth of
the land; but perhaps it was too much to expect
tnis of him in view of his delicate relations with
Mr. Clay. At a later period, in the course of the
campaign, he denounced annexation and the increase of slave territory, but unfortunately it was
then too late. The Whigs had preserved silence
on the subject at their convention, and it was difficult to deal with it without reflecting on their candidate. Mr. Webster vindicated his own position
and his own wisdom, but the mischief could not
then be averted. The annexation of Texas after
the rejection of the treaty in 1844 was carried
through, nearly a year later, by a mixture of trickery and audacity in the last hours of the Tyler
administration.

Four days after the consummation of this project Mr. Webster took his seat in the Senate, and
on March 11 wrote to his son that, "while we feel
as we ought about the annexation of Texas, we
ought to keep in view the true grounds of objection to that measure. Those grounds are, — want

of constitutional power, — danger of too great an extent of territory, and opposition to the increase of slavery and slave representation. It was properly considered, also, as a measure tending to produce war." He then goes on to argue that Mexico had no good cause for war; but it is evident that he already dreaded just that result. When Congress assembled again, in the following December, the first matter to engage their attention was the admission of Texas as a State of the Union. It was impossible to prevent the passage of the resolution, but Mr. Webster stated his objections to the measure. His speech was brief and very mild in tone, if compared with the language which he had frequently used in regard to the annexation. He expressed his opposition to this method of obtaining new territory by resolution instead of treaty, and to acquisition of territory as foreign to the true spirit of the republic, and as endangering the Constitution and the Union by increasing the already existing inequality of representation, and extending the area of slavery. He dwelt on the inviolability of slavery in the States, and did not touch upon the evils of the system itself.

By the following spring the policy of Mr. Polk had culminated, intrigue had done its perfect work, hostilities had been brought on with Mexico, and in May Congress was invited to declare a war which the administration had taken care should already exist. Mr. Webster was absent at this time, and did not vote on the declaration of war;

and when he returned he confined himself to discussing the war measures, and to urging the cessa-
tion of hostilities, and the renewal of efforts to
obtain peace.

The next session — that of the winter of 1846–
47 — was occupied, of course, almost entirely with
the affairs of the war. In these measures Mr.
Webster took scarcely any part; but toward the
close of the session, when the terms on which the
war should be concluded were brought up, he
again came forward. February 1, 1847, Mr.
Wilmot of Pennsylvania introduced the famous
proviso which bears his name, as an amendment
to the bill appropriating three millions of dollars
for extraordinary expenses. By this proviso slavery was to be excluded from all territory thereafter acquired or annexed by the United States.
A fortnight later Mr. Webster, who was opposed
to the acquisition of more territory on any terms,
introduced two resolutions in the Senate, declaring
that the war ought not to be prosecuted for the
acquisition of territory, and that Mexico should
be informed that we did not aim at seizing her
domain. A similar resolution was offered by Mr.
Berrien of Georgia, and defeated by a party vote.
On this occasion Mr. Webster spoke with great
force and in a tone of solemn warning against the
whole policy of territorial aggrandizement. He
denounced all that had been done in this direction, and attacked with telling force the Northern
democracy, which, while it opposed slavery and

favored the Wilmot Proviso, was yet ready to admit
new territory, even without the proviso. His attitude at this time, in opposition to any further
acquisition of territory on any terms, was strong
and determined, but his policy was a terrible confession of weakness. It amounted to saying that
we must not acquire territory because we had not
sufficient courage to keep slavery out of it. The
Whigs were in a minority, however, and Mr.
Webster could effect nothing. When the Wilmot
Proviso came before the Senate Mr. Webster voted
for it, but it was defeated, and the way was clear
for Mr. Polk and the South to bring in as much
territory as they could get, free of all conditions
which could interfere with the extension of slavery.
In September, 1847, after speaking and voting as
has just been described in the previous session of
Congress, Mr. Webster addressed the Whig convention at Springfield on the subject of the Wilmot
Proviso. What he then said is of great importance in any comparison which may be made between his earlier views and those which he afterwards put forward, in March, 1850, on the same
subject. The passage is as follows: —

"We hear much just now of a panacea for the dangers and evils of slavery and slave annexation, which
they call the 'Wilmot Proviso.' That certainly is a just
sentiment, but it is not a sentiment to found any new
party upon. It is not a sentiment on which Massachusetts Whigs differ. There is not a man in this hall who
holds to it more firmly than I do, nor one who adheres
to it more than another.

"I feel some little interest in this matter, sir. Did I not commit myself in 1837 to the whole doctrine, fully, entirely? And I must be permitted to say that I cannot quite consent that more recent discoverers should claim the merit, and take out a patent.

"I deny the priority of their invention. Allow me to say, sir, it is not their thunder.

"There is no one who can complain of the North for resisting the increase of slave representation, because it gives power to the minority in a manner inconsistent with the principles of our government. What is past must stand; what is established must stand; and with the same firmness with which I shall resist every plan to augment the slave representation, or to bring the Constitution into hazard by attempting to extend our dominions, shall I contend to allow existing rights to remain.

"Sir, I can only say that, in my judgment, we are to use the first, the last, and every occasion which occurs, in maintaining our sentiments against the extension of the slave power."

In the following winter Mr. Webster continued his policy of opposition to all acquisitions of territory. Although the cloud of domestic sorrow was already upon him, he spoke against the legislative powers involved in the "Ten Regiment" Bill, and on the 23d of March, after the ratification of the treaty of peace, which carried with it large cessions of territory, he delivered a long and elaborate speech on the "Objects of the Mexican War." The weight of his speech was directed against the acquisition of territory, on account of its effect on the Constitution, and the increased inequality of representation which it involved. He referred to the plan of cutting up Texas so as to obtain ten senators, as "borough-mongering" on a grand scale, a course which he proposed to resist to the last; and he concluded by denouncing the whole project as one calculated to turn the Constitution into a curse rather than a blessing. "I resist it to-day and always," he said. "Whoever falters or whoever flies, I continue the contest."

In June General Taylor was nominated, and soon after Mr. Webster left Washington, although Congress was still in session. He returned in August, in time to take part in the settlement of the Oregon question. The South, with customary shrewdness, was endeavoring to use the territorial organization of Oregon as a lever to help them in their struggle to gain control of the new conquests. A bill came up from the House with no provision in regard to slavery, and Mr. Douglas carried an amendment to it, declaring the Missouri Compromise to be in full force in Oregon. The House disagreed, and, on the question of receding, Mr. Webster took occasion to speak on the subject of slavery in the territories. He was disgusted with the nomination of Taylor and with the cowardly silence of the Whigs on the question of the extension of slavery. In this frame of mind he made one of the strongest and best speeches he ever delivered on this topic. He denied that slavery was an "institution;" he denied that the local right to

hold slaves implied the right of the owner to carry
them with him and keep them in slavery on free
soil; he stated in the strongest possible manner
the right of Congress to control slavery or to prohibit it in the territories; and he concluded with
a sweeping declaration of his opposition to any
extension of slavery or any increase of slave representation. The Oregon bill finally passed under
the pressure of the "Free-Soil" nominations, with
a clause inserted in the House, embodying substantially the principles of the Wilmot Proviso.

When Congress adjourned, Mr. Webster returned to Marshfield, where he made the speech
on the nomination of General Taylor. It was a
crisis in his life. At that moment he could have
parted with the Whigs and put himself at the head
of the constitutional anti-slavery party. The Free-
Soilers had taken the very ground against the extension of slavery which he had so long occupied.
He could have gone consistently, he could have
separated from the Whigs on a great question of
principle, and such a course would have been no
stronger evidence of personal disappointment than
was afforded by the declaration that the nomination of Taylor was one not fit to be made. Mr.
Webster said that he fully concurred in the main
object of the Buffalo Convention, that he was as
good a Free-Soiler as any of them, but that the
Free-Soil party presented nothing new or valuable, and he did not believe in Mr. Van Buren.
He then said it was not true that General Taylor

was nominated by the South, as charged by the Free-Soilers; but he did not confess, what was equally true, that Taylor was nominated through fear of the South, as was shown by his election by Southern votes. Mr. Webster's conclusion was, that it was safer to trust a slaveholder, a man without known political opinions, and a party which had not the courage of its convictions, than to run the risk of the election of another Democrat. Mr. Webster's place at that moment was at the head of a new party based on the principles which he had himself formulated against the extension of slavery. Such a change might have destroyed his chances for the presidency, if he had any, but it would have given him one of the greatest places in American history and made him the leader in the new period. He lost his opportunity. He did not change his party, but he soon after accepted the other alternative and changed his opinions.

His course once taken, he made the best of it, and delivered a speech in Faneuil Hall, in which it is painful to see the effort to push aside slavery and bring forward the tariff and the sub-treasury. He scoffed at this absorption in "one idea," and strove to thrust it away. It was the cry of "peace, peace," when there was no peace, and when Daniel Webster knew there could be none until the momentous question had been met and settled. Like the great composer who heard in the first notes of his symphony "the hand of Fate knocking at the door," the great New England statesman heard the same warning in the hoarse murmur against slavery, but he shut his ears to the dread sound and passed on.

When Mr. Webster returned to Washington, after the election of General Taylor, the strife had already begun over our Mexican conquests. The South had got the territory, and the next point was to fasten slavery upon it. The North was resolved to prevent the further spread of slavery, but was by no means so determined or so clear in its views as its opponent. President Polk urged in his message that Congress should not legislate on the question of slavery in the territories, but that if they did, the right of slaveholders to carry their slaves with them to the new lands should be recognized, and that the best arrangement was to extend the line of the Missouri Compromise to the Pacific. For the originator and promoter of the Mexican war this was a very natural solution, and was a fit conclusion to one of the worst presidential careers this country has ever seen. The plan had only one defect. It would not work. One scheme after another was brought before the Senate, only to fail. Finally, Mr. Webster introduced his own, which was merely to authorize military government and the maintenance of existing laws in the Mexican cessions, and a consequent postponement of the question. The proposition was reasonable and sensible, but it fared little better than the others. The Southerners found, as they always did sooner or later, that facts were

against them. The people of New Mexico peti-
tioned for a territorial government and for the
exclusion of slavery. Mr. Calhoun pronounced
this action "insolent." Slavery was not only to
be permitted, but the United States government
was to be made to force it upon the people of the
territories. Finally, a resolution was offered "to
extend the Constitution" to the territories, — one
of those utterly vague propositions in which the
South delighted to hide well-defined schemes for
extending, not the Constitution, but slaveholding,
to fresh fields and virgin soil. This gave rise to
a sharp debate between Mr. Webster and Mr.
Calhoun as to whether the Constitution extended
to the territories or not. Mr. Webster upheld the
latter view, and the discussion is chiefly interesting
from the fact that Mr. Webster got the better of
Mr. Calhoun in the argument, and as an example
of the latter's excessive ingenuity in sustaining
and defending a more than doubtful proposition.
The result of the whole business was, that nothing
was done, except to extend the revenue laws of
the United States to New Mexico and California.

Before Congress again assembled, one of the
subjects of their debates had taken its fortunes
into its own hands. California, rapidly peopled
by the discoveries of gold, had held a convention
and adopted a frame of government with a clause
prohibiting slavery. When Congress met, the
senators and representatives of California were in
Washington with their free Constitution in their

hands, demanding the admission of their State into the Union.

New Mexico was involved in a dispute with Texas as to boundaries, and if the claim of Texas was sanctioned, two thirds of the disputed territory would come within the scope of the annexation resolutions, and be slaveholding States. Then there was the further question whether the Wilmot Proviso should be applied to New Mexico on her organization as a territory.

The President, acting under the influence of Mr. Seward, advised that California should be admitted, and the question of slavery in the other territories be decided when they should apply for admission. Feeling was running very high in Washington, and there was a bitter and protracted struggle of three weeks, before the House succeeded in choosing a speaker. The state legislatures on both sides took up the burning question, and debated and resolved one way or the other with great excitement. The Southern members held meetings, and talked about secession and about withdrawing from Congress. The air was full of murmurs of dissolution and intestine strife. The situation was grave and even threatening.

In this state of affairs Mr. Clay, now an old man, and with but a short term of life before him, resolved to try once more to solve the problem and tide over the dangers by a grand compromise. The main features of his plan were: the admission of California with her free Constitution; the organization of territorial governments in the Mexican conquests without any reference to slavery; the adjustment of the Texan boundary; a guaranty of the existence of slavery in the District of Columbia until Maryland should consent to its abolition; the prohibition of the slave trade in the District; provision for the more effectual enforcement of the Fugitive Slave Law, and a declaration that Congress had no power over the slave trade between the slaveholding States. As the admission of California was certain, the proposition to bring about the prohibition of the slave trade in the District was the only concession to the North. Everything else was in the interest of the South; but then that was always the manner in which compromises with slavery were made. They could be effected in no other way.

This outline Mr. Clay submitted to Mr. Webster January 21, 1850, and Mr. Webster gave it his full approval, subject, of course, to further and more careful consideration. February 5 Mr. Clay introduced his plan in the Senate, and supported it in an eloquent speech. On the 13th the President submitted the Constitution of California, and Mr. Foote moved to refer it, together with all matters relating to slavery, to a select committee. It now became noised about that Mr. Webster intended to address the Senate on the pending measures, and on the 7th of March he delivered the memorable speech which has always been known by its date.

It may be premised that in a literary and rhetorical point of view the speech of the 7th of March was a fine one. The greater part of it is taken up with argument and statement, and is very quiet in tone. But the famous passage beginning "peaceable secession," which came straight from the heart, and the peroration also, have the glowing eloquence which shone with so much splendor all through the reply to Hayne. The speech can be readily analyzed. With extreme calmness of language Mr. Webster discussed the whole history of slavery in ancient and modern times, and under the Constitution of the United States. His attitude is so judicial and historical, that if it is clear he disapproved of the system, it is not equally evident that he condemned it. He reviewed the history of the annexation of Texas, defended his own consistency, belittled the Wilmot Proviso, admitted substantially the boundary claims of Texas, and declared that the character of every part of the country, so far as slavery or freedom was concerned, was now settled, either by law or nature, and that he should resist the insertion of the Wilmot Proviso in regard to New Mexico, because it would be merely a wanton taunt and reproach to the South. He then spoke of the change of feeling and opinion both at the North and the South in regard to slavery, and passed next to the question of mutual grievances. He depicted at length the grievances of the South, including the tone of the Northern press, the anti-slavery resolutions of the legislature, the utterances of the abolitionists, and the resistance to the Fugitive Slave Law. The last, which he thought the only substantial and legally remediable complaint, he dwelt on at great length, and severely condemned the refusal of certain States to comply with this provision of the Constitution. Then came the grievances, of the North against the South, which were dealt with very briefly. In fact, the Northern grievances, according to Mr. Webster, consisted of the tone of the Southern press and of Southern speeches which, it must be confessed, were at times a little violent and somewhat offensive. The short paragraph reciting the unconstitutional and high-handed action of the South in regard to free negroes employed as seamen on Northern vessels, and the outrageous treatment of Mr. Hoar at Charleston in connection with this matter, was not delivered, Mr. Giddings says, but was inserted afterwards and before publication, at the suggestion of a friend. After this came the fine burst about secession, and a declaration of faith that the Southern convention called at Nashville would prove patriotic and conciliatory. The speech concluded with a strong appeal in behalf of nationality and union.

Mr. Curtis correctly says that a great majority of Mr. Webster's constituents, if not of the whole North, disapproved this speech. He might have added that that majority has steadily increased. The popular verdict has been given against the

7th of March speech, and that verdict has passed into history. Nothing can now be said or written which will alter the fact that the people of this country who maintained and saved the Union have passed judgment upon Mr. Webster and condemned what he said on the 7th of March, 1850, as wrong in principle and mistaken in policy. This opinion is not universal, — no opinion is, — but it is held by the great body of mankind who know or care anything about the subject, and it cannot be changed or substantially modified, because subsequent events have fixed its place and worth irrevocably. It is only necessary, therefore, to examine very briefly the grounds of this adverse judgment, and the pleas put in against it by Mr. Webster and by his most devoted partisans.

From the sketch which has been given of Mr. Webster's course on the slavery question, we see that in 1819 and 1820 he denounced in the strongest terms slavery and every form of slave trade; that while he fully admitted that Congress had no power to touch slavery in the States, he asserted that it was their right and their paramount duty absolutely to stop any further extension of slave territory. In 1820 he was opposed to any compromise on this question. Ten years later he stood out to the last, unaffected by defeat, against the principle of compromise which sacrificed the rights and the dignity of the general government to the resistance and threatened secession of a State.

After the reply to Hayne in 1830, Mr. Webster

became a standing candidate for the presidency,
or for the Whig nomination to that office. From
that time forth the sharp denunciation of slavery
and traffic in slaves disappears, although there is
no indication that he ever altered his original opinion on these points; but he never ceased, sometimes mildly, sometimes in the most vigorous and
sweeping manner, to attack and oppose the extension of slavery to new regions, and the increase of
slave territory. If, then, in the 7th of March
speech, he was inconsistent with his past, such
inconsistency must appear, if at all, in his general
tone in regard to slavery, in his views as to the
policy of compromise, and in his attitude toward
the extension of slavery, the really crucial question
of the time.

As to the first point, there can be no doubt that
there is a vast difference between the tone of the
Plymouth oration and the Boston memorial toward
slavery and the slave trade, and that of the 7th of
March speech in regard to the same subjects. For
many years Mr. Webster had had but little to say
against slavery as a system, but in the 7th of
March speech, in reviewing the history of slavery,
he treats the matter in such a very calm manner,
that he not only makes the best case possible for
the South, but his tone is almost apologetic when
speaking in their behalf. To the grievances of
the South he devotes more than five pages of his
speech, to those of the North less than two. As
to the infamy of making the national capital a

great slave mart, he has nothing to say — although
it was a matter which figured as one of the elements in Mr. Clay's scheme.

But what most shocked the North in this connection were his utterances in regard to the Fugitive
Slave Law.   There can be no doubt that under
the Constitution the South had a perfect right to
claim the extradition of fugitive slaves.   The legal
argument in support of that right was excellent,
but the Northern people could not feel that it was
necessary for Daniel Webster to make it.   The
Fugitive Slave Law was in absolute conflict with
the awakened conscience and moral sentiment of
the North.   To strengthen that law, and urge its
enforcement, was a sure way to make the resistance
to it still more violent and intolerant.   Constitutions and laws will prevail over much, and alle-
giance to them is a high duty, but when they come
into conflict with a deep-rooted moral sentiment,
and with the principles of liberty and humanity,
they must be modified, or else they will be broken
to pieces.   That this should have been the case
in 1850 was no doubt to be regretted, but it was
none the less a fact.   To insist upon the constitutional duty of returning fugitive slaves, to upbraid
the North with their opposition, and to urge upon
them and upon the country the strict enforcement
of the extradition law, was certain to embitter and
intensify the opposition to it.   The statesmanlike
course was to recognize the ground of Northern
resistance, to show the South that a too violent

insistence upon their constitutional rights would
be fatal, and to endeavor to obtain such concessions as would allay excited feelings.   Mr. Webster's strong argument in favor of the Fugitive
Slave Law pleased the South, of course; but it
irritated and angered the North.   It promoted
the very struggle which it proposed to allay, for
it admitted the existence of only one side to the
question.   The consciences of men cannot be co-
erced; and when Mr. Webster undertook to do it
he dashed himself against the rocks.   People did
not stop to distinguish between a legal argument
and a defense of the merits of catching runaway
slaves.   To refer to the original law of 1793 was
idle.   Public opinion had changed in half a century; and what had seemed reasonable at the close
of the eighteenth century was monstrous in the
middle of the nineteenth.

All this Mr. Webster declined to recognize.
He upheld without diminution or modification the
constitutional duty of sending escaping slaves back
to bondage; and from the legal soundness of this
position there is no escape.   The trouble was that
he had no word to say against the cruelty and
barbarity of the system.   To insist upon the necessity of submitting to the hard and repulsive
duty imposed by the Constitution was one thing.
To urge submission without a word of sorrow or
regret was another.   The North felt, and felt
rightly, that while Mr. Webster could not avoid
admitting the force of the constitutional provisions

about fugitive slaves, and was obliged to bow to their behest, yet to defend them without reservation, to attack those who opposed them, and to urge the rigid enforcement of a Fugitive Slave Law, was not in consonance with his past, his conscience, and his duty to his constituents. The constitutionality of a Fugitive Slave Law may be urged and admitted over and over again, but this could not make the North believe that advocacy of slave catching was a task suited to Daniel Webster. The simple fact was that he did not treat the general question of slavery as he always had treated it. Instead of denouncing and deploring it, and striking at it wherever the Constitution permitted, he apologized for its existence, and urged the enforcement of its most obnoxious laws. This was not his attitude in 1820; this was not what the people of the North expected of him in 1850.

In regard to the policy of compromise there is a much stronger contrast between Mr. Webster's attitude in 1850 and his earlier course than in the case of his views on the general subject of slavery. In 1819, although not in public life, Mr. Webster, as is clear from the tone of the Boston memorial, was opposed to any compromise involving an extension of slavery. In 1832–33 he was the most conspicuous and unyielding enemy of the principle of compromise in the country. He then took the ground that the time had come to test the strength of the Constitution and the Union, and that any

concession would have a fatally weakening effect.
In 1850 he supported a compromise which was so
one-sided that it hardly deserves the name. The
defense offered by his friends on this subject —
and it is the strongest point they have been able
to make — is that these sacrifices, or compromises,
were necessary to save the Union, and that — although they did not prevent ultimate secession —
they caused a delay of ten years, which enabled
the North to gather sufficient strength to carry
the civil war to a successful conclusion. It is not
difficult to show historically that the policy of
compromise between the national principle and
unlawful opposition to that principle was an entire
mistake from the very outset, and that if illegal
and partisan state resistance had always been put
down with a firm hand, civil war might have been
avoided. Nothing strengthened the general government more than the well-judged and well-timed
display of force by which Washington and Hamilton crushed the Whiskey Rebellion, or than the
happy accident of peace in 1814, which brought
the separatist movement in New England to a
sudden end. After that period Mr. Clay's policy
of compromise prevailed, and the result was that
the separatist movement was identified with the
maintenance of slavery, and steadily gathered
strength. In 1819 the South threatened and blus-
tered in order to prevent the complete prohibition
of slavery in the Louisiana purchase. In 1832
South Carolina passed the nullification ordinance

because she suffered by the operation of a protective tariff. In 1850 a great advance had been made in their pretensions. Secession was threatened because the South feared that the Mexican conquests would not be devoted to the service of slavery. Nothing had been done, nothing was proposed even, prejudicial to Southern interests; but the inherent weakness of slavery, and the mild conciliatory attitude of Northern statesmen, incited the South to make imperious demands for favors, and seek for positive gains. They succeeded in 1850, and in 1860 they had reached the point at which they were ready to plunge the country into the horrors of civil war solely because they lost an election. They believed, first, that the North would yield everything for the sake of union, and secondly, that if there was a limit to their capacity for surrender in this direction, yet a people capable of so much submission in the past would never fight to maintain the Union. The South made a terrible mistake, and was severely punished for it; but the compromises of 1820, 1833, and 1850 furnished some excuse for the wild idea that the North would not and could not fight. Whether a strict adherence to the strong, fearless policy of Hamilton, which was adopted by Jackson and advocated by Webster in 1832–33, would have prevented civil war, must, of course, remain matter of conjecture. It is at least certain that in that way alone could war have been avoided, and that the Clay policy of compro-

mise made war inevitable by encouraging slaveholders to believe that they could always obtain
anything they wanted by a sufficient show of violence.

It is urged, however, that the policy of compromise having been adopted, a change in 1850 would
have simply precipitated the sectional conflict. In
judging Mr. Webster, the practical question, of
course, is as to the best method of dealing with
matters as they actually were and not as they
might have been had a different course been pursued in 1820 and 1832. The partisans of Mr.
Webster have always taken the ground that in
1850 the choice was between compromise and secession; that the events of 1861 showed that the
South, in 1850, was not talking for mere effect;
that the maintenance of the Union was the paramount consideration of a patriotic statesman; and
that the only practicable and proper course was to
compromise. Admitting fully that Mr. Webster's
first and highest duty was to preserve the Union,
it is perfectly clear now, when all these events
have passed into history, that he took the surest
way to make civil war inevitable, and that the
position of 1832 should not have been abandoned.
In the first place, the choice was not confined to
compromise or secession. The President, the official head of the Whig party, had recommended
the admission of California, as the only matter
actually requiring immediate settlement, and that
the other questions growing out of the new terri-

tories should be dealt with as they arose. Mr. Curtis, Mr. Webster's biographer, says this was an impracticable plan, because peace could not be kept between New Mexico and Texas, and because there was great excitement about the slavery question throughout the country. These seem very insufficient reasons, and only the first has any practical bearing on the matter. General Taylor said: Admit California, for that is an immediate and pressing duty, and I will see to it that peace is preserved on the Texan boundary. Zachary Taylor may not have been a great statesman, but he was a brave and skillful soldier, and an honest man, resolved to maintain the Union, even if he had to shoot a few Texans to do it. His policy was bold and manly, and the fact that it was said to have been inspired by Mr. Seward, a leader in the only Northern party which had any real principle to fight for, does not seem such a monstrous idea as it did in 1850 or does still to those who sustain Mr. Webster's action. That General Taylor's policy was not so wild and impracticable as Mr. Webster's friends would have us think, is shown by the fact that Mr. Benton, Democrat and Southerner as he was, but imbued with the vigor of the Jackson school, believed that each question should be taken up by itself and settled on its own merits. A policy which seemed wise to three such different men as Taylor, Seward, and Benton, could hardly have been so utterly impracticable and visionary as Mr. Webster's partisans would like the world to believe. It was in fact one of the cases which that extremely practical statesman Nicolo Machiavelli had in mind when he wrote that, "Dangers that are seen afar off are easily prevented; but protracting till they are near at hand, the remedies grow unseasonable and the malady incurable."

It may be readily admitted that there was a great and perilous political crisis in 1850, as Mr. Webster said. In certain quarters, in the excitement of party strife, there was a tendency to deride Mr. Webster as a "Union-saver," and to take the ground that there had been no real danger of secession. This, as we can see now very plainly, was an unfounded idea. When Congress met, the danger of secession was very real, although perhaps not very near. The South, although they intended to secede as a last resort, had no idea that they should be brought to that point. Menaces of disunion, ominous meetings and conventions, they probably calculated, would effect their purpose and obtain for them what they wanted, and subsequent events proved that they were perfectly right in this opinion. On February 14 Mr. Webster wrote to Mr. Harvey: —

"I do not partake in any degree in those apprehensions which you say some of our friends entertain of the dissolution of the Union or the breaking up of the government. I am mortified, it is true, at the violent tone assumed here by many persons, because such violence in debate only leads to irritation, and is, moreover, dis-

creditable to the government and the country. But
there is no serious danger, be assured, and so assure our
friends."

The next day he wrote to Mr. Furness, a leader
of the anti-slavery party, expressing his abhorrence
of slavery as an institution, his unwillingness to
break up the existing political system to secure its
abolition, and his belief that the whole matter
must be left with Divine Providence. It is clear
from this letter that he had dismissed any thought
of assuming an aggressive attitude toward slavery,
but there is nothing to indicate that he thought
the Union could be saved from wreck only by
substantial concessions to the South. Between
the date of the letter to Harvey and March 7, Mr.
Curtis says that the aspect of affairs had mate-
rially changed, and that the Union was in serious
peril. There is nothing to show that Mr. Webster thought so, or that he had altered the opinion
which he had expressed on February 14. In fact,
Mr. Curtis's view is the exact reverse of the true
state of affairs. If there was any real and immediate danger to the Union, it existed on February
14, and ceased immediately afterwards, on February 16, as Dr. Von Holst correctly says, when
the House of Representatives laid on the table the
resolution of Mr. Root of Ohio, prohibiting the
extension of slavery to the territories. By that
vote, the victory was won by the slave power, and
the peril of speedy disunion vanished. Nothing
remained but to determine how much the South

would get from their victory, and how hard a bargain they could drive. The admission of California was no more of a concession than a resolution not to introduce slavery in Massachusetts would have been. All the rest of the compromise plan, with the single exception of the prohibition of the slave trade in the District of Columbia, was made up of concessions to the Southern and slaveholding interest. That Henry Clay should have originated and advocated this scheme was perfectly natural. However wrong or mistaken, this had been his steady and unbroken policy from the outset, as the best method of preserving the Union and advancing the cause of nationality. Mr. Clay was consistent and sincere, and, however much he may have erred in his general theory, he never swerved from it. But with Mr. Webster the case was totally different. He had opposed the principle of compromise from the beginning, and in 1833, when concession was more reasonable than in 1850, he had offered the most strenuous and unbending resistance. Now he advocated a compromise which was in reality little less than a complete surrender on the part of the North. On the general question of compromise he was, of course, grossly inconsistent, and the history of the time, as it appears in the cold light of the present day, shows plainly that, while he was brave and true and wise in 1833, in 1850 he was not only inconsistent, but that he erred deeply in policy and statesmanship. It has also been urged in behalf

of Mr. Webster that he went no farther than the
Republicans in 1860 in the way of concession, and
that as in 1860 so in 1850, anything was permissi-
ble which served to gain time.   In the first place,
the *tu quoque* argument proves nothing and has
no weight.   In the second place, the situations in
1850 and in 1860 were very different.

There were at the former period, in reference
to slavery, four parties in the country — the Democrats, the Free-Soilers, the Abolitionists, and
the Whigs.   The three first had fixed and widely
varying opinions; the last was trying to live without opinions, and soon died.   The pro-slavery
Democrats were logical and practical; the Abolitionists were equally logical but thoroughly impracticable and unconstitutional, avowed nullifiers
and secessionists; the Free-Soilers were illogical,
constitutional, and perfectly practical.   As Republicans, the Free-Soilers proved the correctness
and good sense of their position by bringing the
great majority of the Northern people to their
support.   But at the same time their position was
a difficult one, for while they were an anti-slavery
party and had set on foot constitutional opposition
to the extension of slavery, their fidelity to the
Constitution compelled them to admit the legality
of the Fugitive Slave Law and of slavery in the
States.   They aimed, of course, first to check the
extension of slavery and then to efface it by gradual restriction and full compensation to slaveholders.   When they had carried the country in 1860,

they found themselves face to face with a breaking
Union and an impending war. That many of them
were seriously frightened, and, to avoid war and
dissolution, would have made great concessions,
cannot be questioned; but their controlling motive
was to hold things together by any means, no
matter how desperate, until they could get possession of the government. This was the only possible and the only wise policy, but that it involved
them in some contradictions in that winter of excitement and confusion is beyond doubt. History
will judge the men and events of 1860 according
to the circumstances of the time, but nothing that
happened then has any bearing on Mr. Webster's
conduct. He must be judged according to the
circumstances of 1850, and the first and most obvious fact is, that he was not fighting merely to
gain time and obtain control of the general government. The crisis was grave and serious in the
extreme, but neither war nor secession were imminent or immediate, nor did Mr. Webster ever assert that they were. He thought war and secession
might come, and it was against this possibility and
probability that he sought to provide. He wished
to solve the great problem, to remove the source
of danger, to set the menacing agitation at rest.
He aimed at an enduring and definite settlement,
and that was the purpose of the 7th of March
speech. His reasons — and of course they were
clear and weighty in his own mind — proceeded
from the belief that this wretched compromise

measure offered a wise, judicious, and permanent settlement of questions which, in their constant recurrence, threatened more and more the stability of the Union. History has shown how woefully mistaken he was in this opinion.

The last point to be considered in connection with the 7th of March speech is the ground then taken by Mr. Webster with reference to the extension of slavery. To this question the speech was chiefly directed, and it is the portion which has aroused the most heated discussion. What Mr. Webster's views had always been on the subject of slavery extension every one knew then and knows now. He had been the steady and uncompromising opponent of the Southern policy, and in season and out of season, sometimes vehemently, sometimes gently, but always with firmness and clearness, he had declared against it. The only question is, whether he departed from these often-expressed opinions on the 7th of March. In the speech itself he declared that he had not abated one jot in his views in this respect, and he argued at great length to prove his consistency, which, if it were to be easily seen of men, certainly needed neither defense nor explanation. The crucial point was, whether, in organizing the new territories, the principle of the Wilmot Proviso should be adopted as part of the measure. This famous proviso Mr. Webster had declared in 1847 to represent exactly his own views. He had then denied that the idea was the invention of any one man, and scouted the notion that on this doctrine there could be any difference of opinion among Whigs. On March 7 he announced that he would not have the proviso attached to the territorial bills, and should oppose any effort in that direction. The reasons he gave for this apparent change were, that nature had forbidden slavery in the newly conquered regions, and that the proviso, under such circumstances, would be a useless taunt and wanton insult to the South. The famous sentence in which he said that he "would not take pains uselessly to reaffirm an ordinance of nature, nor to reënact the will of God," was nothing but specious and brilliant rhetoric. It was perfectly easy to employ slaves in California, if the people had not prohibited it, and in New Mexico as well, even if there were no cotton nor sugar nor rice plantations in either, and but little arable land in the latter. There was a classic form of slave labor possible in those countries. Any schoolboy could have reminded Mr. Webster of

> " Seius whose eight hundred slaves
> Sicken in Ilva's mines."

Mining was one of the oldest uses to which slave labor had been applied, and it still flourished in Siberia as the occupation of serfs and criminals. Mr. Webster, of course, was not ignorant of this very obvious fact; and that nature, therefore, instead of forbidding slave labor in the Mexican conquests, opened to it a new and almost unlimited field in a region which is to-day one of the great-

est mining countries in the world.   Still less could
he have failed to know that this form of employment for slaves was eagerly desired by the South;
that the slaveholders fully recognized their opportunity, announced their intention of taking advantage of it, and were particularly indignant at the
action of California because it had closed to them
this inviting field.   Mr. Clingman of North Carolina, on January 22, when engaged in threatening
war in order to bring the North to terms, had said,
in the House of Representatives: "But for the
anti-slavery agitation our Southern slaveholders
would have carried their negroes into the mines of
California in such numbers that I have no doubt
but that the majority there would have made it
a slaveholding State."[1]   At a later period Mr.
Mason of Virginia declared, in the Senate, that
he knew of no law of nature which excluded slavery from California. "On the contrary," he said,
"if California had been organized with a territorial form of government only, the people of the
Southern States would have gone there freely, and
have taken their slaves there in great numbers.
They would have done so because the value of the
labor of that class would have been augmented to
them many hundred fold."[2]   These were the views
of practical men and experienced slave owners who
represented the opinions of their constituents, and
who believed that domestic slavery could be em-

[1] *Congressional Globe*, 31st Congress, 1st Session, p. 203.
[2] *Ibid.*, Appendix, p. 510.

ployed to advantage anywhere. Moreover, the
Southern leaders openly avowed their opposition
to securing any region to free labor exclusively,
no matter what the ordinances of nature might be.
In 1848, it must be remembered in this connection, Mr. Webster not only urged the limitation
of slave area, and sustained the power of Congress
to regulate this matter in the territories, but he
did not resist the final embodiment of the principle of the Wilmot Proviso in the bill for the organization of Oregon, where the introduction of
slavery was infinitely more unlikely than in New
Mexico. Cotton, sugar, and rice were excluded,
perhaps, by nature from the Mexican conquests,
but slavery was not. It was worse than idle to
allege that a law of nature forbade slaves in a
country where mines gaped to receive them. The
facts are all as plain as possible, and there is no
escape from the conclusion that in opposing the
Wilmot Proviso, in 1850, Mr. Webster abandoned
his principles as to the extension of slavery. He
practically stood forth as the champion of the
Southern policy of letting the new territories alone,
which could only result in placing them in the
grasp of slavery. The consistency which he labored so hard to prove in his speech was hopelessly
shattered, and no ingenuity, either then or since,
can restore it.

A dispassionate examination of Mr. Webster's
previous course on slavery, and a careful comparison of it with the ground taken in the 7th of

March speech, shows that he softened his utterances in regard to slavery as a system, and that he changed radically on the policy of compromise and on the question of extending the area of slavery. There is a confused story that in the winter of 1847–48 he had given the anti-slavery leaders to understand that he proposed to come out on their ground in regard to Mexico, and to sustain Corwin in his attack on the Democratic policy, but that he failed to do so. The evidence on this point is entirely insufficient to make it of importance, but there can be no doubt that in the winter of 1850 Mr. Webster talked with Mr. Giddings, and led him, and the other Free-Soil leaders, to believe that he was meditating a strong anti-slavery speech. This fact was clearly shown in the recent newspaper controversy which grew out of the celebration of the centennial anniversary of Webster's birth. It is a little difficult to understand why this incident should have roused such bitter resentment among Mr. Webster's surviving partisans. To suppose that Mr. Webster made the 7th of March speech after long deliberation, without having a moment's hesitation in the matter, is to credit him with a shameless disregard of principle and consistency, of which it is impossible to believe him guilty. He undoubtedly hesitated, and considered deeply whether he should assume the attitude of 1833, and stand out unrelentingly against the encroachments of slavery. He talked with Mr. Clay on one side. He talked with Mr.

Giddings, and other Free-Soilers, on the other. With the latter the wish was no doubt father to the thought, and they may well have imagined that Mr. Webster had determined to go with them, when he was still in doubt and merely trying the various positions. There is no need, however, to linger over matters of this sort. The change made by Mr. Webster can be learned best by careful study of his own utterances, and of his whole career. Yet, at the same time, the greatest trouble lies not in the shifting and inconsistency revealed by an examination of the specific points which have just been discussed, but in the speech as a whole. In that speech Mr. Webster failed quite as much by omissions as by the opinions which he actually announced. He was silent when he should have spoken, and he spoke when he should have held his peace. The speech, if exactly defined, is, in reality, a powerful effort, not for compromise or for the Fugitive Slave Law, or any other one thing, but to arrest the whole anti-slavery movement, and in that way put an end to the dangers which threatened the Union and restore lasting harmony between the jarring sections. It was a mad project. Mr. Webster might as well have attempted to stay the incoming tide at Marshfield with a rampart of sand as to seek to check the anti-slavery movement by a speech. Nevertheless, he produced a great effect. His mind once made up, he spared nothing to win the cast. He gathered all his forces; his great intellect, his splendid eloquence, his fame which had become one of the treasured possessions of his country, — all were given to the work. The blow fell with terrible force, and here, at last, we come to the real mischief which was wrought. The 7th of March speech demoralized New England and the whole North. The abolitionists showed by bitter anger the pain, disappointment, and dismay which this speech brought. The Free-Soil party quivered and sank for the moment beneath the shock. The whole anti-slavery movement recoiled. The conservative reaction which Mr. Webster endeavored to produce came and triumphed. Chiefly by his exertions the compromise policy was accepted and sustained by the country. The conservative elements everywhere rallied to his support, and by his ability and eloquence it seemed as if he had prevailed and brought the people over to his opinions. It was a wonderful tribute to his power and influence, but the triumph was hollow and short-lived. He had attempted to compass an impossibility. Nothing could kill the principles of human liberty, not even a speech by Daniel Webster, backed by all his intellect and knowledge, his eloquence and his renown. The anti-slavery movement was checked for the time, and pro-slavery democracy, the only other positive political force, reigned supreme. But amid the falling ruins of the Whig party, and the evanescent success of the Native Americans, the party of human rights revived; and when it rose again, taught by the trials and misfortunes of 1850, it rose with a strength of which Mr. Webster had never dreamed, and, in 1856, polled nearly a million and a half of votes for Fremont. The rise and final triumph of the Republican party was the condemnation of the 7th of March speech and of the policy which put the government of the country in the hands of Franklin Pierce and James Buchanan. When the war came, inspiration was not found in the 7th of March speech. In that dark hour, men remembered the Daniel Webster who replied to Hayne, and turned away from the man who had sought for peace by advocating the great compromise of Henry Clay.

The disapprobation and disappointment which were manifested in the North after the 7th of March speech could not be overlooked. Men thought and said that Mr. Webster had spoken in behalf of the South and of slavery. Whatever his intentions may have been, this was what the speech seemed to mean and this was its effect, and the North saw it more and more clearly as time went on. Mr. Webster never indulged in personal attacks, but at the same time he was too haughty a man ever to engage in an exchange of compliments in debate. He never was in the habit of saying pleasant things to his opponents in the Senate merely as a matter of agreeable courtesy. In this direction, as in its opposite, he usually maintained a cold silence. But on the 7th of March he elaborately complimented Calhoun, and went out of his way to flatter Virginia and Mr. Mason personally. This struck close observers with surprise, but it was the real purpose of the speech which went home to the people of the North. He had advocated measures which with slight exceptions were altogether what the South wanted, and the South so understood it. On the 30th of March Mr. Morehead wrote to Mr. Crittenden that Mr. Webster's appointment as secretary of state would now be very acceptable to the South. No more bitter commentary could have been made. The people were blinded and dazzled at first, but they gradually awoke and perceived the error that had been committed.

Mr. Webster, however, needed nothing from outside to inform him as to his conduct and its results. At the bottom of his heart and in the depths of his conscience he knew that he had made a dreadful mistake. He did not flinch. He went on in his new path without apparent faltering. His speech on the compromise measures went farther than that of the 7th of March. But if we study his speeches and letters between 1850 and the day of his death, we can detect changes in them which show plainly enough that the writer was not at ease, that he was not master of that quiet conscience of which he boasted.

His friends, after the first shock of surprise, rallied to his support, and he spoke frequently at union meetings, and undertook, by making immense efforts, to convince the country that the compromise measures were right and necessary, and that the doctrines of the 7th of March speech ought to be sustained. In pursuance of this object, during the winter of 1850 and the summer of the following year, he wrote several public letters on the compromise measures, and he addressed great meetings on various occasions, in New England, New York, and as far south as Virginia. We are at once struck by a marked change in the character and tone of these speeches, which produced a great effect in establishing the compromise policy. It had never been Mr. Webster's habit to misrepresent or abuse his opponents. Now he confounded the extreme separatism of the abolitionists and the constitutional opposition of the Free-Soil party, and involved all opponents of slavery in a common condemnation. It was willful misrepresentation to talk of the Free-Soilers as if they were identical with the abolitionists, and no one knew better than Mr. Webster the distinction between the two, one being ready to secede to get rid of slavery, the other offering only a constitutional resistance to its extension. His tone toward his opponents was correspondingly bitter. When he first arrived in Boston, after his speech, and spoke to the great crowd in front of the Revere House, he said, "I shall support no agitations having their foundations in unreal, ghostly abstractions." Slavery had now become "an unreal, ghostly abstraction," although it must still have appeared to the negroes something very like a hard fact. There were men in that crowd, too, who had not forgotten the noble words with which Mr. Webster in 1837 had defended the character of the opponents of slavery, and the sound of this new gospel from his lips fell strangely on their ears. So he goes on from one union meeting to another, and in speech after speech there is the same bitter tone which had been so foreign to him in all his previous utterances. The supporters of the anti-slavery movement he denounces as insane. He reiterates his opposition to slave extension, and in the same breath argues that the Union must be preserved by giving way to the South. The feeling is upon him that the old parties are breaking down under the pressure of this "ghostly abstraction," this agitation which he tries to prove to the young men of the country and to his fellow citizens everywhere is "wholly factitious." The Fugitive Slave Law is not in the form which he wants, but still he defends it and supports it. The first fruits of his policy of peace are seen in riots in Boston, and he personally advises with a Boston lawyer who has undertaken the cases against the fugitive slaves. It was undoubtedly his duty, as Mr. Curtis says, to enforce and support the law as the President's adviser, but his personal attention and interest were not required in slave cases, nor would they have been given a year before. The Wilmot Proviso, that doctrine which he claimed as his own in 1847, when it was a sentiment on which Whigs could not differ, he now calls "a mere abstraction." He struggles to put slavery aside for the tariff, but it will not down at his bidding, and he himself cannot leave it alone. Finally he concludes this compromise campaign with a great speech on laying the foundation of the capitol extension, and makes a pathetic appeal to the South to maintain the Union. They are not pleasant to read, these speeches in the Senate and before the people in behalf of the compromise policy. They are harsh and bitter; they do not ring true. Daniel Webster knew when he was delivering them that that was not the way to save the Union, or that, at all events, it was not the right way for him to do it.

The same peculiarity can be discerned in his letters. The fun and humor which had hitherto run through his correspondence seem now to fade away as if blighted. On September 10, 1850, he writes to Mr. Harvey that since March 7 there has not been an hour in which he has not felt a "crushing sense of anxiety and responsibility." He couples this with the declaration that his own part is acted and he is satisfied; but if his anxiety was solely of a public nature, why did it date from March 7, when, prior to that time, there was much greater cause for alarm than afterwards. In everything he said or wrote he continually recurs to the slavery question, and always in a defensive tone, usually with a sneer or a fling at the abolitionists and anti-slavery party. The spirit of unrest had seized him. He was disturbed and ill at ease.

He never admitted it, even to himself, but his mind was not at peace, and he could not conceal the fact. Posterity can see the evidences of it plainly enough, and a man of his intellect and fame knew that with posterity the final reckoning must be made. No man can say that Mr. Webster anticipated the unfavorable judgment which his countrymen have passed upon his conduct, but that in his heart he feared such a judgment cannot be doubted.

It is impossible to determine with perfect accuracy any man's motives in what he says or does. They are so complex, they are so often undefined, even in the mind of the man himself, that no one can pretend to make an absolutely correct analysis. There have been many theories as to the motives which led Mr. Webster to make the 7th of March speech. In the heat of contemporary strife his enemies set it down as a mere bid to secure Southern support for the presidency, but this is a harsh and narrow view. The longing for the presidency weakened Mr. Webster as a public man from the time when it first took possession of him after the reply to Hayne. It undoubtedly had a weakening effect upon him in the winter of 1850, and had some influence upon the speech of the 7th of March. But it is unjust to say that it did more. It certainly was far removed from being a controlling motive. His friends, on the other hand, declared that he was governed solely by the highest and most disinterested patriotism, by the truest

wisdom. This explanation, like that of his foes,
fails by going too far and being too simple. His
motives were mixed. His chief desire was to
preserve and maintain the Union. He wished to
stand forth as the great savior and pacificator.
On the one side was the South, compact, aggressive, bound together by slavery, the greatest political force in the country. On the other was a
weak Free-Soil party, and a widely diffused and
earnest moral sentiment without organization or
tangible political power. Mr. Webster concluded
that the way to save the Union and the Constitution, and to achieve the success which he desired,
was to go with the heaviest battalions. He therefore espoused the Southern side, for the compromise was in the Southern interest, and smote the
anti-slavery movement with all his strength. He
reasoned correctly that peace could come only by
administering a severe check to one of the two
contending parties. He erred in attempting to
arrest the one which all modern history showed
was irresistible. It is no doubt true, as appears
by his cabinet opinion recently printed, that he
stood ready to meet the first overt act on the part
of the South with force. Mr. Webster would not
have hesitated to strike hard at any body of men
or any State which ventured to assail the Union.
But he also believed that the true way to prevent
any overt act on the part of the South was by
concession, and that was precisely the object which
the Southern leaders sought to obtain. We may

grant all the patriotism and all the sincere devotion to the cause of the Constitution which is claimed for him, but nothing can acquit Mr. Webster of error in the methods which he chose to adopt for the maintenance of peace and the preservation of the Union.   If the 7th of March speech was right, then all that had gone before was false and wrong.   In that speech he broke from his past, from his own principles and from the principles of New England, and closed his splendid public career with a terrible mistake.

CHAPTER X

THE LAST YEARS

THE story of the remainder of Mr. Webster's public life, outside of and apart from the slavery question, can be quickly told. General Taylor died suddenly on July 9, 1850, and this event led to an immediate and complete reorganization of the cabinet. Mr. Fillmore at once offered the post of secretary of state to Mr. Webster, who accepted it, resigned his seat in the Senate, and, on July 23, assumed his new position. No great negotiation like that with Lord Ashburton marked this second term of office in the Department of State, but there were a number of important and some very complicated affairs, which Mr. Webster managed with the wisdom, tact, and dignity which made him so admirably fit for this high position.

The best-known incident of this period was that which gave rise to the famous "Hülsemann letter." President Taylor had sent an agent to Hungary to report upon the condition of the revolutionary government, with the intention of recognizing it if there were sufficient grounds for doing so. When the agent arrived, the revolution was crushed, and he reported to the President against recognition.

These papers were transmitted to the Senate in
March, 1850. Mr. Hülsemann, the Austrian
chargé, thereupon complained of the action of our
administration, and Mr. Clayton, then secretary
of state, replied that the mission of the agent had
been simply to gather information. On receiving
further instructions from his government, Mr.
Hülsemann rejoined to Mr. Clayton, and it fell
to Mr. Webster to reply, which he did on December 21, 1850. The note of the Austrian *chargé*
was in a hectoring and highly offensive tone, and
Mr. Webster felt the necessity of administering
a sharp rebuke. "The Hülsemann letter," as it
was called, was accordingly dispatched. It set
forth strongly the right of the United States and
their intention to recognize any *de facto* revolutionary government, and to seek information in
all proper ways in order to guide their action.
The argument on this point was admirably and
forcibly stated, and it was accompanied by a bold
vindication of the American policy, and by some
severe and wholesome reproof. Mr. Webster had
two objects. One was to awaken the people of
Europe to a sense of the greatness of this country,
the other to touch the national pride at home.
He did both. The foreign representatives learned
a lesson which they never forgot, and which opened
their eyes to the fact that we were no longer colo-
nies, and the national pride was also aroused.
Mr. Webster admitted that the letter was, in
some respects, boastful and rough. This was a

fair criticism, and it may be justly said that such
a tone was hardly worthy of the author.   But, on
the other hand, Hülsemann's impertinence fully
justified such a reply, and a little rough domineering was, perhaps, the very thing needed.   It is
certain that the letter fully answered Mr. Webster's purpose, and excited a great deal of popular
enthusiasm.   The affair did not, however, end
here.   Mr. Hülsemann became very mild, but he
soon lost his temper again.   Kossuth and the refu-
gees in Turkey were brought to this country in a
United States frigate.   The Hungarian hero was
received with a burst of enthusiasm that induced
him to hope for substantial aid, which was, of
course, wholly visionary.   The popular excitement
made it difficult for Mr. Webster to steer a proper
course, but he succeeded, by great tact, in showing
his own sympathy, and, so far as possible, that of
the government, for the cause of Hungarian independence and for its leader, without going too far
or committing any indiscretion which could justify
a breach of international relations with Austria.
Mr. Webster's course, including a speech at a
dinner in Boston, in which he made an eloquent
allusion to Hungary and Kossuth, although carefully guarded, aroused the ire of Mr. Hülsemann,
who left the country, after writing a letter of indignant farewell to the secretary of state.   Mr.
Webster replied, through Mr. Hunter, with extreme coolness, confining himself to an approval
of the gentleman selected by Mr. Hülsemann to
represent Austria after the latter's departure.

The other affairs which occupied Mr. Webster's
official attention at this time made less noise than
that with Austria, but they were more complicated
and some of them far more perilous to the peace
of the country. The most important was that
growing out of the Clayton-Bulwer treaty in regard to the neutrality of the contemplated canal in
Nicaragua. This led to a prolonged correspondence about the protectorate of Great Britain in
Nicaragua, and to a withdrawal of her claim to
exact port-charges. It is interesting to observe
the influence which Mr. Webster at once obtained
with Sir Henry Bulwer and the respect in which
he was held by that experienced diplomatist. Besides this discussion with England, there was a
sharp dispute with Mexico about the right of way
over the Isthmus of Tehuantepec, and the troubles
on the Texan boundary before Congress had acted
upon the subject. Then came the Lopez invasion
of Cuba, supported by bodies of volunteers enlisted
in the United States, which, by its failure and its
results, involved our government in a number of
difficult questions. The most serious was the riot
at New Orleans, where the Spanish consulate was
sacked by a mob. To render due reparation for
this outrage without wounding the national pride
by apparent humiliation was no easy task. Mr.
Webster settled everything, however, with a judgment, tact, and dignity which prevented war with
Spain and yet excited no resentment at home. At
a later period, when the Kossuth affair was draw-

ing to an end, the perennial difficulty about the
fisheries revived and was added to our Central
American troubles with Great Britain, and this,
together with the affair of the Lobos Islands, occupied Mr. Webster's attention, and drew forth some
able and important dispatches during the summer
of 1852, in the last months of his life.

While the struggle was in progress to convince
the country of the value and justice of the compromise measures and to compel their acceptance,
another presidential election drew on.   It was the
signal for the last desperate attempt to obtain the
Whig nomination for Mr. Webster, and it seemed
at first sight as if the party must finally take up
the New England leader.   Mr. Clay was wholly
out of the race, and his last hour was near.   There
was absolutely no one who, in fame, ability, public services, and experience could be compared for
one moment with Mr. Webster.   The opportunity
was obvious enough; it awakened all Mr. Webster's hopes, and excited the ardor of his friends.
A formal and organized movement, such as had
never before been made, was set on foot to promote his candidacy, and a vigorous and earnest
address to the people was issued by his friends in
Massachusetts.   The result demonstrated, if demonstration were needed, that Mr. Webster had
not, even under the most favorable circumstances,
the remotest chance for the presidency.   His friends
saw this plainly enough before the convention met,
but he himself regarded the great prize as at last

surely within his grasp. Mr. Choate, who was to
lead the Webster delegates, went to Washington
the day before the convention assembled. He
called on Mr. Webster and found him so filled
with the belief that he should be nominated that
it seemed cruel to undeceive him. Mr. Choate,
at all events, had not the heart for the task, and
went back to Baltimore to lead the forlorn hope
with gallant fidelity and with an eloquence as brilliant if not so grand as that of Mr. Webster himself. A majority [1] of the convention divided their
votes very unequally between Mr. Fillmore and
Mr. Webster, the former receiving 133, the latter 29, on the first ballot, while General Scott had
131. Forty-five ballots were taken, without any
substantial change, and then General Scott began
to increase his strength, and was nominated on the
fifty-third ballot, receiving 159 votes. Most of
General Scott's supporters were opposed to resolutions sustaining the compromise measures, while
those who voted for Mr. Fillmore and Mr. Webster favored that policy. General Scott owed his
nomination to a compromise, which consisted in
inserting in the platform a clause strongly approv-
ing Mr. Clay's measures. Mr. Webster expected
the Fillmore delegates to come to him, an unlikely

[1] Mr. Curtis says a "great majority continued to divide their
votes between Mr. Fillmore and Mr. Webster." The highest
number reached by the combined Webster and Fillmore votes, on
any one ballot, was 162, three more than was received on the last
ballot by General Scott, who, Mr. Curtis correctly says, obtained
only a "few votes more than the necessary majority."

event when they were so much more numerous than his friends, and, moreover, they never showed the slightest inclination to do so. They were chiefly from the South, and as they chose to consider Mr. Fillmore and not his secretary the representative of compromise, they reasonably enough expected the latter to give way. The desperate stubbornness of Mr. Webster's adherents resulted in the nomination of Scott. It seemed hard that the Southern Whigs should have done so little for Mr. Webster after he had done and sacrificed so much to advance and defend their interests. But the South was practical. In the 7th of March speech they had got from Mr. Webster all they could expect or desire. It was quite possible, in fact it was highly probable, that, once in the presidency, he could not be controlled or guided by the slave power or by any other sectional influence. Mr. Fillmore, inferior in every way to Mr. Webster in intellect, in force, in reputation, would give them a mild, safe administration and be easily influenced by the South. Mr. Webster had served his turn, and the men whose cause he had advocated and whose interests he had protected cast him aside.

The loss of the nomination was a bitter disappointment to Mr. Webster. It was the fashion in certain quarters to declare that it killed him, but this was manifestly absurd. The most that can be said in this respect was, that the excitement and depression caused by his defeat preyed upon his mind and thereby facilitated the inroads of disease, while it added to the clouds which darkened round him in those last days. But his course of action after the convention cannot be passed over without comment. He refused to give his adhesion to General Scott's nomination, and he advised his friends to vote for Mr. Pierce, because the Whigs were divided, while the Democrats were unanimously determined to resist all attempts to renew the slavery agitation. This course was absolutely indefensible. If the Whig party was so divided on the slavery question that Mr. Webster could not support their nominee, then he had no business to seek a nomination at their hands, for they were as much divided before the convention as afterwards. He chose to come before that convention, knowing perfectly well the divisions of the party, and that the nomination might fall to General Scott. He saw fit to play the game, and was in honor bound to abide by the rules. He had no right to say "it is heads I win, and tails you lose." If he had been nominated he would have indignantly and justly denounced a refusal on the part of General Scott and his friends to support him. It is the merest sophistry to say that Mr. Webster was too great a man to be bound by party usages, and that he owed it to himself to rise above them, and refuse his support to a poor nomination and to a wrangling party. If Mr. Webster could no longer act with the Whigs, then his name had no business in that convention at

Baltimore, for the conditions were the same before its meeting as afterward. Great man as he was, he was not too great to behave honorably; and his refusal to support Scott, after having been his rival for a nomination at the hands of their common party, was neither honorable nor just. If Mr. Webster had decided to leave the Whigs and act independently, he was in honor bound to do so before the Baltimore convention assembled, or to have warned the delegates that such was his intention in the event of General Scott's nomination. He had no right to stand the hazard of the die, and then refuse to abide by the result. The Whig party, in its best estate, was not calculated to excite a very warm enthusiasm in the breast of a dispassionate posterity, and it is perfectly true that it was on the eve of ruin in 1852. But it appeared better then, in the point of self-respect, than four years before. In 1848 the Whigs nominated a successful soldier conspicuous only for his availability and without knowing to what party he belonged. They maintained absolute silence on the great question of the extension of slavery, and carried on their campaign on the personal popularity of their candidate. Mr. Webster was righteously disgusted at their candidate and their negative attitude. He could justly and properly have left them on a question of principle; but he swallowed the nomination, "not fit to be made," and gave to his party a decided and public support. In 1852 the Whigs nominated another successful

soldier, who was known to be a Whig, and who
had been a candidate for their nomination before.
In their platform they formally adopted the essential principle demanded by Mr. Webster, and declared their adhesion to the compromise measures.
If there was disaffection in regard to this declaration of 1852, there was disaffection also about the
silence of 1848. In the former case, Mr. Webster
adhered to the nomination; in the latter, he rejected it. In 1848 he might still hope to be president through a Whig nomination. In 1852 he
knew that, even if he lived, there would never be
another chance. He gave vent to his disappointment, put no constraint upon himself, prophesied
the downfall of his party, and advised his friends
to vote for Franklin Pierce. It was perfectly logical, after advocating the compromise measures, to
advise giving the government into the hands of
a party controlled by the South. Mr. Webster
would have been entirely reasonable in taking
such a course before the Baltimore convention.
He had no right to do so after he had sought a
nomination from the Whigs, and it was a breach
of faith to act as he did, to advise his friends to
desert a falling party and vote for the Democratic
candidate.

After the acceptance of the Department of
State, Mr. Webster's health became seriously impaired. His exertions in advocating the compromise measures, his official labors, and the increased
severity of his annual hay-fever, — all contributed

to debilitate him.   His iron constitution weakened
in various ways, and especially by frequent periods
of intense mental exertion, to which were super-
added the excitement and nervous strain insepara-
ble from his career, was beginning to give way.
Slowly but surely he lost ground.   His spirits
began to lose their elasticity, and he rarely spoke
without a tinge of deep sadness being apparent in
all he said.   In May, 1852, while driving near
Marshfield, he was thrown from his carriage with
much violence, injuring his wrists, and receiving
other severe contusions.   The shock was very great,
and undoubtedly accelerated the progress of the
fatal organic disease which was sapping his life.
This physical injury was followed by the keen disappointment of his defeat at Baltimore, which
preyed upon his heart and mind.   During the
summer of 1852 his health gave way more rapidly.
He longed to resign, but Mr. Fillmore insisted on
his retaining his office.   In July he came to Boston, where he was welcomed by a great public
meeting, and hailed with enthusiastic acclamations,
which did much to soothe his wounded feelings.
He still continued to transact the business of his
department, and in August went to Washington,
where he remained until the 8th of September,
when he returned to Marshfield.   On the 20th he
went to Boston, for the last time, to consult his
physician.   He appeared at a friend's house, one
evening, for a few moments, and all who then saw
him were shocked at the look of illness and suffer-

ing in his face. It was his last visit. He went
back to Marshfield the next day, never to return.
He now failed rapidly. His nights were sleepless,
and there were scarcely any intervals of ease or
improvement. The decline was steady and sure,
and as October wore away the end drew near.
Mr. Webster faced it with courage, cheerfulness,
and dignity, in a religious and trusting spirit,
with a touch of the personal pride which was part
of his nature. He remained perfectly conscious
and clear in his mind almost to the very last moment, bearing his sufferings with perfect fortitude,
and exhibiting the tenderest affection toward the
wife and son and friends who watched over him.
On the evening of October 23 it became apparent
that he was sinking, but his one wish seemed to
be that he might be conscious when he was actually
dying. After midnight he roused from an uneasy
sleep, struggled for consciousness, and ejaculated,
"I still live." These were his last words. Shortly
after three o'clock the labored breathing ceased,
and all was over.

A hush fell upon the country as the news of his
death sped over the land. A great gap seemed to
have been made in the existence of every one.
Men remembered the grandeur of his form and
the splendor of his intellect, and felt as if one of
the pillars of the state had fallen. The profound
grief and deep sense of loss produced by his death
were the highest tributes and the most convincing
proofs of his greatness.

In accordance with his wishes, all public forms and ceremonies were dispensed with. The funeral took place at his home on Friday, October 29. Thousands flocked to Marshfield to do honor to his memory, and to look for the last time at that noble form. It was one of those beautiful days of the New England autumn, when the sun is slightly veiled, and a delicate haze hangs over the sea, shining with a tender silvery light. There is a sense of infinite rest and peace on such a day which seems to shut out the noise of the busy world and breathe the spirit of unbroken calm. As the crowds poured in through the gates of the farm, they saw before them on the lawn, resting upon a low mound of flowers, the majestic form, as impressive in the repose of death as it had been in the fullness of life and strength. There was a wonderful fitness in it all. The vault of heaven and the spacious earth seemed in their large simplicity the true place for such a man to lie in state. There was a brief and simple service at the house, and then the body was borne on the shoulders of Marshfield farmers, and laid in the little graveyard which already held the wife and children who had gone before, and where could be heard the eternal murmur of the sea.

In May, 1852, Mr. Webster said to Professor Silliman: "I have given my life to law and politics. Law is uncertain and politics are utterly vain." It is a sad commentary for such a man to

have made on such a career, but it fitly represents
Mr. Webster's feelings as the end of life approached. His last years were not his most fortunate, and still less his best years. Domestic sorrows had been the prelude to a change of policy,
which had aroused a bitter opposition, and to the
pangs of disappointed ambition. A sense of mistake and failure hung heavily upon his spirits, and
the cry of "vanity, vanity, all is vanity," came
readily to his lips. There is an infinite pathos in
those melancholy words which have just been
quoted. The sun of life, which had shone so
splendidly at its meridian, was setting amid clouds.
The darkness which overspread him came from
the action of the 7th of March, and the conflict
which it had caused. If there were failure and
mistake they were there. The presidency could
add nothing, its loss could take away nothing from
the fame of Daniel Webster. He longed for it
eagerly; he had sacrificed much to his desire for
it; his disappointment was keen and bitter at not
receiving what seemed to him the fit crown of his
great public career. But this grief was purely
personal, and will not be shared by posterity, who
feel only the errors of those last years coming after
so much glory, and who care very little for the
defeated ambition which went with them.

Those last two years awakened such fierce disputes, and had such an absorbing interest, that
they have tended to overshadow the half century
of distinction and achievement which preceded

them.   Failure and disappointment on the part of
such a man as Webster seem so great, that they
too easily dwarf everything else, and hide from us
a just and well proportioned view of the whole
career.   Mr. Webster's success had, in truth,
been brilliant, hardly equaled in measure or duration by that of any other eminent·man in our history.   For thirty years he had stood at the head
of the bar and of the Senate, the first lawyer and
the first statesman of the United States.   This is
a long tenure of power for one man in two distinct
departments.   It would be remarkable anywhere.
It is especially so in a democracy.   This great
success Mr. Webster owed solely to his intellectual
power supplemented by great physical gifts.   No
man ever was born into the world better formed
by nature for the career of an orator and statesman.   He had everything to compel the admiration and submission of his fellow men: —

> " The front of Jove himself ;
> An eye like Mars to threaten and command ;
> A station like the herald Mercury
> New-lighted on a heaven-kissing hill ;
> A combination and a form indeed,
> Where every god did seem to set his seal,
> To give the world assurance of a man."

Hamlet's words are a perfect picture of Mr. Webster's outer man, and we have but to add to the
description a voice of singular beauty and power
with the tone and compass of an organ.   The look
of his face and the sound of his voice were in themselves as eloquent as anything Mr. Webster ever
uttered.

But the imposing presence was only the outward sign of the man. Within was a massive and powerful intellect, not creative or ingenious, but with a wonderful vigor of grasp, capacious, penetrating, far-reaching. Mr. Webster's strongest and most characteristic mental qualities were weight and force. He was peculiarly fitted to deal with large subjects in a large way. He was by temperament extremely conservative. There was nothing of the reformer or the zealot about him. He could maintain or construct where other men had built; he could not lay new foundations or invent. We see this curiously exemplified in his feeling toward Hamilton and Madison. He admired them both, and to the former he paid a compliment which has become a familiar quotation. But Hamilton's bold, aggressive genius, his audacity, fertility, and resource, did not appeal to Mr. Webster as did the prudence, the constructive wisdom, and the safe conservatism of the gentle Madison, whom he never wearied of praising. The same description may be given of his imagination, which was warm, vigorous, and keen, but not poetic. He used it well, it never led him astray, and was the secret of his most conspicuous oratorical triumphs.

He had great natural pride and a strong sense of personal dignity, which made him always impressive, but apparently cold, and sometimes solemn in public. In his later years this solemnity degenerated occasionally into pomposity, to which it is always perilously near. At no time in his

life was he quick or excitable. He was indolent
and dreamy, working always under pressure, and
then at a high rate of speed. This indolence increased as he grew older; he would then postpone
longer and labor more intensely to make up the
lost time than in his earlier days. When he was
quiescent, he seemed stern, cold, and latterly
rather heavy, and some outer incentive was needed
to rouse his intellect or touch his heart. Once
stirred, he blazed forth, and, when fairly engaged,
with his intellect in full play, he was as grand and
effective in his eloquence as it is given to human
nature to be. In the less exciting occupations of
public life, as, for instance, in foreign negotiations,
he showed the same grip upon his subject, the
same capacity and judgment as in his speeches,
and a mingling of tact and dignity which proved
the greatest fitness for the conduct of the gravest
public affairs. As a statesman Mr. Webster was
not an "opportunist," as it is the fashion to call
those who live politically from day to day, dealing
with each question as it arises, and exhibiting
often the greatest skill and talent. Still less was
he a statesman of the type of Charles Fox, who
preached to the deaf ears of one generation great
principles which became accepted truisms in the
next. Mr. Webster stands between the two classes.
He viewed the present with a strong perception of
the future, and shaped his policy not merely for
the daily exigency, but with a keen eye to subsequent effects. At the same time he never put

forward and defended single-handed a great principle or idea which, neglected then, was gradually
to win its way and reign supreme among a succeeding generation.

His speeches have a heat and glow which we
can still feel, and a depth and reality of thought
which have secured them a place in literature.
He had not a fiery nature, although there is often
so much warmth in what he said. He was neither
high tempered nor quick to anger, but he could be
fierce, and, when adulation had warped him in
those later years, he was capable of striking ugly
blows which sometimes wounded friends as well as
enemies.

There remains one marked quality to be noticed
in Mr. Webster, which was of immense negative
service to him. This was his sense of humor.
Mr. Nichol, in his recent history of American literature, speaks of Mr. Webster as deficient in
this respect. Either the critic himself is deficient
in humor or he has studied only Webster's collected works, which give no indication of the real
humor in the man. That Mr. Webster was not
a humorist is unquestionably true, and although
he used a sarcasm which made his opponents seem
absurd and even ridiculous at times, and in his
more unstudied efforts would provoke mirth by
some happy and playful allusion, some felicitous
quotation or ingenious antithesis, he was too stately
in every essential respect ever to seek to make
mere fun or to excite the laughter of his hearers

by deliberate exertions and with malice afore-
thought. He had, nevertheless, a real and genuine sense of humor. We can see it in his letters,
and it comes out in a thousand ways in the details
and incidents of his private life. When he had
thrown aside the cares of professional or public
business, he reveled in hearty, boisterous fun,
and he had that sanest of qualities, an honest,
boyish love of pure nonsense. He delighted in a
good story and dearly loved a joke, although no
jester himself. This sense of humor and appreciation of the ridiculous, although they give no color
to his published works, where, indeed, they would
have been out of place, improved his judgment,
smoothed his path through the world, and saved
him from those blunders in taste and those follies
in action which are ever the pitfalls for men with
the fervid, oratorical temperament.

This sense of humor gave, also, a great charm
to his conversation and to all social intercourse
with him. He was a good, but never, so far as
can be judged from tradition, an overbearing
talker. He never appears to have crushed opposition in conversation, nor to have indulged in mono-
logue, which is so apt to be the foible of famous
and successful men who have a solemn sense of
their own dignity and importance. What Lord
Melbourne said of the great Whig historian, "that
he wished he was as sure of anything as Tom
Macaulay was of everything," could not be applied
to Mr. Webster. He owed his freedom from such

a weakness partly, no doubt, to his natural indolence, but still more to the fact that he was not only no pedant, but not even a very learned man. He knew no Greek, although he was familiar with Latin. His quotations and allusions were chiefly drawn from Shakespeare, Milton, Homer, and the Bible, where he found what most appealed to him — simplicity and grandeur of thought and diction. At the same time, he was a great reader, and possessed wide information on a vast variety of subjects, which a clear and retentive memory put always at his command. The result of all this was that he was a most charming and entertaining companion.

These attractions were heightened by his large nature and strong animal spirits. He loved outdoor life. He was a keen sportsman and skillful fisherman. In all these ways he was healthy and manly, without any tinge of the mere student or public official. He loved everything that was large. His soul expanded in the free air and beneath the blue sky. All natural scenery appealed to him, — Niagara, the mountains, the rolling prairie, the great rivers, — but he found most contentment beside the limitless sea, amid brown marshes and sand-dunes, where the sense of infinite space is strongest. It was the same in regard to animals. He cared but little for horses or dogs, but he rejoiced in great herds of cattle, and especially in fine oxen, the embodiment of slow and massive strength. In England the things which chiefly appealed to him were the Tower of London, Westminster Abbey, Smithfield cattle market, and English agriculture. So it was always and everywhere. He loved mountains and great trees, wide horizons, the ocean, the western plains, and the giant monuments of literature and art. He rejoiced in his strength and the overflowing animal vigor that was in him. He was so big and so strong, so large in every way, that people sank into repose in his presence, and felt rest and confidence in the mere fact of his existence. He came to be regarded as an institution, and when he died men paused with a sense of helplessness, and wondered how the country would get on without him. To have filled so large a space in a country so vast, and in a great, hurrying, and pushing democracy, implies a personality of a most uncommon kind.

He was, too, something more than a charming companion in private life. He was generous, liberal, hospitable, and deeply affectionate. He was adored in his home, and deeply loved his children, who were torn from him, one after another. His sorrow, like his joy, was intense and full of force. He had many devoted friends, and a still greater body of unhesitating followers. To the former he showed, through nearly all his life, the warm affection which was natural to him. It was not until adulation and flattery had deeply injured him, and the frustrated ambition for the presidency had poisoned both heart and mind, that he became

dictatorial and overbearing. Not till then did he
quarrel with those who had served and followed
him, as when he slighted Mr. Lawrence for expressing independent opinions, and refused to do
justice to the memory of Story because it might
impair his own glories. They do not present a
pleasant picture, these quarrels with friends, but
they were part of the deterioration of the last
years, and they furnish in a certain way the key
to his failure to attain the presidency. The
country was proud of Mr. Webster; proud of his
intellect, his eloquence, his fame. He was the
idol of the capitalists, the merchants, the lawyers,
the clergy, the educated men of all classes in the
East. The politicians dreaded and feared him
because he was so great, and so little in sympathy
with them, but his real weakness was with the
masses of the people. He was not popular in the
true sense of the word. For years the Whig party
and Henry Clay were almost synonymous terms,
but this could never be said of Mr. Webster. His
following was strong in quality, but weak numeri-
cally. Clay touched the popular heart. Webster
never did. The people were proud of him, wondered at him, were awed by him, but they did not
love him, and that was the reason he was never
president, for he was too great to succeed to the
high office, as many men have, by happy or un-
happy accident. There was also another feeling
which is suggested by the differences with some
of his closest friends. There was a lurking dis-

trust of Mr. Webster's sincerity. We can see it plainly in the correspondence of the Western Whigs, who were not, perhaps, wholly impartial. But it existed, nevertheless. There was a vague, ill-defined feeling of doubt in the public mind; a suspicion that the spirit of the advocate was the ruling spirit in Mr. Webster, and that he did not believe with absolute and fervent faith in one side of any question. There was just enough correctness, just a sufficient grain of truth in this idea, when united with the coldness and dignity of his manner and with his greatness itself, to render impossible that popularity which, to be real and lasting in a democracy, must come from the heart and not from the head of the people, which must be instinctive and emotional, and not the offspring of reason.

There is no occasion to discuss, or hold up to reprobation, Mr. Webster's failings. He was a splendid animal as well as a great man, and he had strong passions and appetites, which he indulged at times to the detriment of his health and reputation. These errors may be mostly fitly consigned to silence. But there was one failing which cannot be passed over in this way. This was in regard to money. His indifference to debt was perceptible in his youth, and for many years showed no sign of growth. But in his later years it increased with terrible rapidity. He earned twenty thousand a year when he first came to Boston, — a very great income for those days. His public

career interfered, of course, with his law practice,
but there never was a period when he could not,
with reasonable economy, have laid up something
at the end of every year, and gradually amassed
a fortune. But he not only never saved, he lived
habitually beyond his means. He did not become
poor by his devotion to the public service, but by
his own extravagance. He loved to spend money
and to live well. He had a fine library and hand-
some plate; he bought fancy cattle; he kept open
house, and indulged in that most expensive of all
luxuries, "gentleman-farming." He never stinted
himself in any way, and he gave away money with
reckless generosity and heedless profusion, often
not stopping to inquire who the recipient of his
bounty might be. The result was debt, then sub-
scriptions among his friends to pay his debts;
then a fresh start and more debts, and more sub-
scriptions and funds for his benefit, and gifts of
money for his table, and checks or notes for several thousand dollars in token of admiration of
the 7th of March speech.[1] This was, of course,

[1] The story of the gift of ten thousand dollars in token of
admiration of the 7th of March speech, referred to by Dr. Von
Holst (*Const. Hist. of the United States*), may be found in a volume entitled, *In Memoriam, B. Ogle Tayloe*, p. 109, and is as
follows: "My opulent and munificent friend and neighbor, Mr.
William W. Corcoran," says Mr. Tayloe, "after the perusal of
Webster's celebrated March speech in defense of the Constitution
and of Southern rights, inclosed to Mrs. Webster her husband's
note for ten thousand dollars given him for a loan to that amount.
Mr. Webster met Mr. Corcoran the same evening, at the President's, and thanked him for the 'princely favor.' Next day he

utterly wrong and demoralizing, but Mr. Webster
came, after a time, to look upon such transactions
as natural and proper. In the Ingersoll debate,
Mr. Yancey accused him of being in the pay of
the New England manufacturers, and his biographer has replied to the charge at length. That
Mr. Webster was in the pay of the manufacturers
in the sense that they hired him, and bade him
do certain things, is absurd. That he was maintained and supported in a large degree by New

addressed to Mr. Corcoran a letter of thanks which I read at Mr.
Corcoran's request." This version is substantially correct. The
morning of March 8 Mr. Corcoran inclosed with a letter of congratulation some notes of Mr. Webster's amounting to some six
thousand dollars. Reflecting that this was not a very solid tribute, he opened his letter and put in a check for a thousand dollars, and sent the notes and the check to Mr. Webster, who wrote
him a letter expressing his gratitude, which Mr. Tayloe doubtless
saw, and which is still in existence. I give the facts in this way
because Mr. George T. Curtis, in a newspaper interview, referring
to an article of mine in the *Atlantic Monthly*, said, " With regard
to the story of the ten thousand dollar check, which story Mr.
Lodge gives us to understand he found in the pages of that very
credulous writer, Dr. Von Holst, although I have not looked into
his volumes to see whether he makes the charge, I have only to
say that I never heard of such an occurrence before, and that it
would require the oath of a very credible witness to the fact to
make me believe it." I may add that I have taken the trouble
not only to look into Dr. Von Holst's volumes but to examine the
whole matter thoroughly. The proof is absolute, my authority
was Mr. Corcoran himself, and indeed it is not necessary to go beyond Mr. Webster's own letter of acknowledgment in search of
evidence, were there the slightest reason to doubt the substantial correctness of Mr. Tayloe's statement. The point is a small
one, but a statement of fact, if questioned, ought always to be
sustained or withdrawn.

England manufacturers and capitalists cannot be
questioned; but his attitude toward them was not
that of servant and dependent.   He seems to have
regarded the merchants and bankers of State Street
very much as a feudal baron regarded his pea-
santry.   It was their privilege and duty to support him, and he repaid them with an occasional
magnificent compliment.   The result was that he
lived in debt and died insolvent, and this was not
the position which such a man as Daniel Webster
should have occupied.

He showed the same indifference to the source
of supplies of money in other ways.   He took a
fee from Wheelock, and then deserted him.   He
came down to Salem to prosecute a murderer, and
the opposing counsel objected that he was brought
there to hurry the jury beyond the law and the
evidence, and it was even murmured audibly in
the court-room that he had a fee from the relatives
of the murdered man in his pocket.   A fee of that
sort he certainly received either then or afterwards.
Every ugly public attack that was made upon him
related to money, and it is painful that the biographer of such a man as Webster should be compelled to give many pages to show that his hero
was not in the pay of manufacturers, and did not
receive a bribe in carrying out the provisions of
the treaty of Guadaloupe-Hidalgo.   The refutation may be perfectly successful, but there ought
to have been no need of it.   The reputation of a
man like Mr. Webster in money matters should

have been so far above suspicion that no one would
have dreamed of attacking it. Debts and sub-
scriptions bred the idea that there might be worse
behind, and although there is no reason to believe
that such was the case, these things are of themselves deplorable enough.

When Mr. Webster failed it was a moral failure. His moral character was not-equal to his intellectual force. All the errors he ever committed,
whether in public or in private life, in political
action or in regard to money obligations, came
from moral weakness. He was deficient in that
intensity of conviction which carries men beyond
and above all triumphs of statesmanship, and
makes them the embodiment of the great moral
forces which move the world. If Mr. Webster's
moral power had equaled his intellectual greatness,
he would have had no rival in our history. But
this combination and balance are so rare that they
are hardly to be found in perfection among the
sons of men. The very fact of his greatness made
his failings all the more dangerous and unfortunate. To be blinded by the splendor of his fame
and the lustre of his achievements and prate about
the sin of belittling a great man is the falsest philosophy and the meanest cant. The only thing
worth having, in history as in life, is truth; and
we do wrong to our past, to ourselves, and to our
posterity if we do not strive to render simple
justice always. We can forgive the errors and
sorrow for the faults of our great ones gone; we

cannot afford to hide or forget their shortcomings. But after all has been said, the question of most interest is, what Mr. Webster represented, what he effected, and what he means in our history. The answer is simple. He stands to-day as the preëminent champion and exponent of nationality. He said once, "There are no Alleghanies in my politics," and he spoke the exact truth. Mr. Webster was thoroughly national. There is no taint of sectionalism or narrow local prejudice about him. He towers up as an American, a citizen of the United States in the fullest sense of the word. He did not invent the Union, or discover the doctrine of nationality. But he found the great fact and the great principle ready to his hand, and he lifted them up, and preached the gospel of nationality throughout the length and breadth of the land. In his fidelity to this cause he never wavered nor faltered. From the first burst of boyish oratory to the sleepless nights at Marshfield, when, waiting for death, he looked through the window at the light which showed him the national flag fluttering from its staff, his first thought was of a united country. To his large nature the Union appealed powerfully by the mere sense of magnitude which it conveyed. The vision of future empire, the dream of the destiny of an unbroken union touched and kindled his imagination. He could hardly speak in public without an allusion to the grandeur of American nationality, and a fervent appeal to keep it sacred and intact. For fifty years, with reiteration ever more frequent, sometimes with rich elaboration, sometimes with brief and simple allusion, he poured this message into the ears of a listening people. His words passed into text-books, and became the first declamations of schoolboys. They were in every one's mouth. They sank into the hearts of the people, and became unconsciously a part of their life and daily thoughts. When the hour came, it was love for the Union and the sentiment of nationality which nerved the arm of the North, and sustained her courage. That love had been fostered, and that sentiment had been strengthened and vivified by the life and words of Webster. No one had done so much, or had so large a share in this momentous task. Here lies the debt which the American people owe to Webster, and here is his meaning and importance in his own time and to us to-day. His career, his intellect, and his achievements are inseparably connected with the maintenance of a great empire and the fortunes of a great people. So long as English oratory is read or studied, so long will his speeches stand high in literature. So long as the Union of these States endures, or holds a place in history, will the name of Daniel Webster be honored and re-membered, and his stately eloquence find an echo in the hearts of his countrymen.

Born of a wealthy Boston family, HENRY CABOT LODGE (1850-1924) earned a law degree and a doctorate in political science at Harvard while serving as an editor on the *North American Review*. He wrote a biography of the prominent Federalist George Cabot, his great-grandfather, helped his cousin John Torrey Morse, Jr., plan the original American Statesmen Series, and contributed the Series volumes on Alexander Hamilton, Daniel Webster, and George Washington. Combining his literary career with an active interest in politics, he was elected to the House of Representatives in 1887 and became a Republican leader in the Senate, where he served from 1893 to 1924.

CHARLES M. WILTSE is Professor of History Emeritus at Dartmouth College. He is the author of *The Jeffersonian Tradition in American Democracy*, a three-volume life of John C. Calhoun, and *The New Nation, 1800-1845*, among other works, and the editor of the fourteen-volume *Papers of Daniel Webster*, currently being published by Dartmouth College.